TOM SA

SOMETIME CHAMPION OF ENGLAND,

HIS LIFE

AND PUGILISTIC CAREER.

CONTAINING

THE WHOLE OF HIS BATTLES, FROM CONTEMPORARY REPORTS;
PERSONAL ANECDOTES; AND THE LITERATURE OF
THE GREAT FIGHT AT FARNBOROUGH

FROM

The 'Times,' 'Punch,' 'All the Year Round,' the 'Saturday Review,' &c.

EDITED BY

THE AUTHOR OF "PUGILISTICA."

1866.

TOM SAYERS
(Champion of England).

From a Photograph published by Geo Newbold.

TOM SAYERS,

CHAMPION OF ENGLAND:

A Fistic Biography.

CHAPTER I.

Birthplace, Parentage, and Youth of Tom Sayers—Works in Sussex as a Bricklayer—Comes to London—His First Ring-battle
with Aby Couch—His Drawn Battle with Collins—His Victory
over Collins—Challenges Jack Grant, and Defeats him—Caunt
brings forward Jack Martin—Sayers' easy Defeat of that Boxer.

HORACE was of opinion that though poets may cele-
brate the great deeds of others, the more heroic part
of performing them lies with the pugilist.

> " Quem tu, Melpomene, semel,
>   Nascentem placido lumine videris,
> Illum non labor Isthmius
> Clarabit pugilem."
>
> Hor., lib. iv., ode iii., l. 1-4.

We will not raise the question between laureate and
champion, Tennyson and Tom Sayers, but maintain that a
due cultivation of the physical and the intellectual powers
—the reader will excuse the transposition in an age too
apt to invert them—is equally advisable and necessary.
Among the ancients, whose wisdom is too apt to be forgotten by modern self-sufficiency, the art so signally practised
by the subject of this Memoir led to even higher honours
than a university degree in these degenerate days; indeed,
the authority already quoted tells us—

> " Hac arte Pollux et vagus Hercules,
>   Innixus arces attigit igneus."—Lib. iii., ode iii.

These same ancients, too, classified athletic sports with

1

judgment. First came *pancratium*, the use of the fist, and
this gave precedence to the boxers; secondly, *palè*, wrestling; and last, the runners. The natural sequence is here
observed, as a man first uses his hands to strike or to ward
off the blow; then comes the close, which involves the
struggle; and lastly, the resource of the vanquished or
the overmatched, who saves himself by swiftness of foot.
But each of these had its gradational merit, and in each
competitors were ranked to contend for prizes and fame,
in the order we have named, which is that in which Homer
himself arranges the gymnic games of the Grecian camp.
These games were not, be it observed, instituted for the
mere purposes of sport or relaxation. They were considered, especially in Greece, as aiding the highest views
of legislative policy, as promoting ardour, emulation, friendship, patriotism, the scorn of ease, the endurance of fatigue,
fortitude under suffering, and forbearance and generosity
to a worthy antagonist. Their philosophers inculcated the
importance of gymnastic contests. Plato, in his "Book of
Laws," after insisting on the high importance of acquiring
bodily force and activity, says:—"A well-governed com-
monwealth, instead of prohibiting the profession of the
boxer, [the term *athlete* was applied to pugilist, wrestler, or
runner, indifferently,] should, on the contrary, propose prizes
for all those exercises which tend to encourage the military
art." For ourselves, a long experience has convinced us
that no better plan can be devised, no surer mode be
adopted, to foster a manly spirit among a people than the
training of youth, and their voluntarily engaging in hardy
and nerve-testing exercises, and the bestowal of rewards
on those who excel in them. It is far, however, from
the intention of the writer of these pages to enter upon
a formal defence of pugilism, or to raise a debate upon
the collateral question of fighting for a prize. The subject has been ably handled by the first writers: the liberal,
the bold, the magnanimous, take up the side of manhood
and courage; the poltroon, the hypocrite, and the stabber,

leaning to the more cruel and deadly resort to lethal weapons; and, lastly, the lily-livered coward, professing horror and disgust at sports and exercises he dares not practise and trembles to witness—denounces and vilifies an art he envies and fears. With an apology for these discursive remarks on the ancient practice of boxing, we will at once proceed to record the pugilistic career of one to whom the shades of Ajax, Entelles, Milo, Dares, Eryx, Gyas, Gerontes, and the deified twins, Castor and Pollux, may well give the fist of friendship for a turn-up on those "yellow fields of asphodel," where poets have feigned departed heroes carry out their sports. To descend, however, to more prosaic times and manners, let us trace the history of our latest Champion in the list of those fistic celebrities who illustrate the annals of British Boxing.

Thomas Sayers was born on the 17th of July 1826, at Brighton, in the humble locality known as "Pimlico," a row of small tenements leading out of Church Street to North Lane. The name, to Londoners, may sound palatial and aristocratic—to the natives of "London by the seaside" it is just the reverse; and the same may be said of Bond Street, Regent Street, Oxford Street, and Cheapside—all of which, in their Brighton reproductions, are of fish, fishy—squalid, and mean, and have nothing in common with their metropolitan prototypes but their names. In Pimlico, then, was Tom born of humble parents. His father, known as "Old Tom Sayers," was a shoemaker, and we have it from his own lips, was born at Storrington, near Steyning, Sussex, and there baptized in 1793; at which place he lived for many years, until he married a Sussex woman. We have been thus particular on account of the "slips" of great sporting authorities on both sides the Atlantic. *Bell's Life* (April 28, 1860) distinctly says, that "the parents of Sayers came from Dingle, in the county of Kerry." Several Yankee journals directly claim him for "Ould Ireland." Accordingly, this Irish extraction of the Champion furnishes subject of allusion in the papers from *All the Year Round,* the *Cornhill Magazine,* the *Saturday Review,* &c., which are preserved in our Appendix. The Anglo-Saxon origin of Sayers is, however, beyond dispute, without an appeal to the Heralds' College.

The pursuits of the youthful Tom appear to have been such as are common to the rising generation of fishy Pimlico, and his youthful fame traditionally survives among the amphibious population of the shingly beach, where he divided his time between helping fishwives with their burdens, pushing off the hog-boats, and in leisure moments polishing off some saucy competitor who might conceit himself able to "take the shine out of young Tom." Many of the Brighton shoremen rather fancy themselves on having at times crossed fists with the man who has since proved so redoubtable a champion. Tom's proclivities were shown when he was not far into his teens, by a frequent attendance at the "academy," where Jack Phelps, the brother of "Brighton Bill," and afterwards the civil and clever Joe Phelps, and his brother Harry, demonstrated with the gloves the art of self-defence.

At the age of sixteen, namely, in 1842, the youthful Tom was among the spectators of the fight between Grady and a novice, at Newmarket Hill, near the Brighton race-course. The first event over, a purse was subscribed, and one Haines, a Brightonian, of some sparring pretensions, offered himself as the claimant. Tom Sayers, the spirit of knightly courage rising within him, accepted the cartel. It is the occasion makes the man :—

> "He who the world subdued had been
> But the first wrestler on the green."

Had Alexander been the son of old Tom Sayers, instead of the purple-born offspring of Philip of Macedon, and, despite prejudice, we doubt if the son of the Sussex shoemaker was not the better man. To return : Tom, though overmatched in age, weight, and experience, tried his " 'prentice han' " to such effect that after a severe uphill fight of seventeen rounds, Haines betook himself to hugging :—

> "Doubtfully it stood,
> As two spent swimmers that do cling together,
> And choke their art."

Haines would not face his man, but relied on his bodily strength and weight; when, at this critical point, Colonel Paine, a local magistrate, settled the question unsatisfactorily to both parties, by putting a stop to the proceedings, and the case was left undecided, each man receiving a half of the stake; Haines did not, however, move for a new trial.

Sayers was in his twenty-third year, and had quitted his native county of Sussex, for the neighbourhood of Camden Town, where he pursued his calling as a bricklayer on the works then in progress for the North-Western Railway. Tom was noted for his cheerful disposition, his readiness for a "spree," and his fearlessness of any biped who might offend him regardless of height, weight, or strength. Among the fistic celebrities of the day and of the neighbourhood was one Abraham Couch, a fellow of goodly proportions, standing 5 feet 11 inches, and weighing 12 stone. The weight of Sayers, at this period, was a pound short of 10 stone; so that this first ring affair of Sayers exhibited in courage and daring some parallel with his last and crowning achievement. His antagonist, too, had the *prestige* of ring victories to boast: for we find in "Fistiana" the following credited to Aby Couch :—"Beat Jack Sullivan; a purse; 14 rounds; 1 hour 38 minutes, January 12, 1848. Beat Harry Coneely; £3 a side; 9 rounds; 28 minutes, Plumstead Marches, June 17, 1848." The challenge, we learn, was consequent upon a gasconade on the part of Couch, that there was no man north of London who dared to meet him, coupled with some disparaging remarks on Sayers, at a sparring exhibition held at Somers' Town. A "tenner" being put down by the friends of both sides, the fight was arranged for the 19th of March 1848, to meet at Greenhithe, whither the friends of both made their way per steamer on the day appointed. Arrived at the spot, Old Tom Oliver quickly arranged the ropes and stakes.

Sayers was seconded by Jack Grady (who fought Norley) and Dan Collins. Croney, of Paddington, and a friend esquired Couch. The details of this *coup d'essai* of the future Champion's ring career are thus reported :—

THE FIGHT.

Round 1. On putting themselves into attitude, the disparity of size was remarkable; Sayers looked rather serious, while Couch had all the confidence of an old stager. Little time was lost in sparring on the part of Couch, who had made up his mind to rush at Sayers and settle him in quick time. However, Tom was not to be got at, and when Couch made his rush, Sayers met him with a severe hit on the right eye, and got away, laughing. "First blood" for Sayers. A sharp rally then took place, which brought them to close quarters, in which Tom fibbed his antagonist cleverly, and in the end both were down—the big one undermost.

2. Couch came up flushed from the in-fighting of the last round; he could not understand it. Sayers was now as cool as a cucumber. Tom feinted him, and drawing Couch on, who let go, but much out of distance. Sayers, with quickness, returned on the nose, heavy counter hits followed, which brought them to a close, and Couch held Tom, who seemed in a tangle how to extricate himself from so strong a grasp; however, by great tact, Tom shifted himself a little, and succeeded in throwing Couch cleverly, and walked to his corner.

3. On time being called Sayers was the first up, and the shouts of the bricklayers were uproarious at their pet's brilliant performance. 2 to 1 was now freely offered on Sayers, who coolly watched his man, feinted him, and tried to plant his favourite right fork; this led to some sharp in-fighting, and Sayers got home on the right eye. Couch now followed him up and missed Tom; they got a little closer, and Sayers knocked Aby down by a heavy right hander on the jaw. "First knock-down blow" for Sayers.

4. Tom made play with his left on the right lamp, which was now fast closing. Couch persevered, and Tom, who was almost without a mark, caught him again on the nose, and sent him all abroad.

5. Couch came up gamely, bleeding from the nose, and his right eye all but blind. He dashed in to make a last struggle, napped a stinger in the ribs, and dropped from exhaustion.

6 and last. Tom came up gaily, dodged his man who came towards him; but it was all over. Couch seemed groggy from the rapid fighting and severe punishment he had received in so short a time. "Take him away," was the cry from all parts of the ring, but the poor fellow would not hear it, he turned round to his seconds and tried in vain to laugh and say it was all right. His head was much disfigured. The game fellow tried to land one, when Tom gave him the finishing touch by a severe hit on the nose. On his seconds taking him up he was dead to the call of time, and Tom was the winner in 12 minutes and 28 seconds.

Remarks.—"There is a tide in the affairs of men, which, if taken at a flood, leads on to fortune," and Sayers dates his success in life from this fight, being comparatively a novice, and never having seen a prize ring before, while his adversary had been twice crowned with victory. Sayers, in this, his maiden effort, proved himself too quick and severe in his delivery for Couch to afford him a chance, therefore remarks are almost unnecessary. Sayers' debut was a credit to him, and the fight was one of the best that had been seen for some time; a gamer chap than Couch never doffed a shirt, while Sayers' gameness could not be spoken of, as he received nothing in the fight to test it. His friends were so satisfied with him, that he received the whole of the stakes, while the loser was not forgotten for his courage and manly conduct.

The spectators of this battle, including the reporter, were convinced that something remarkable in the way of "natural fighting" resided in the young bricklayer, and he quickly found friends willing to back him against Dan Collins, then known as "Tom Spring's waiter." Dan, a civil young fellow—whom we first knew as a " newsboy," a fraternity as full of fun, frolic, and mischief as *les gamins* of Paris—was praised much for his clever glove displays at the " Castle," and the knowledge that his game was unimpeachable. This had been already put to the test by his fight with Ned Donnelly, (of Glasgow,) a formidable boxer, who had won five battles in succession. Collins, then a novice, gave Donnelly immense trouble; 78 rounds, occupying three hours and four minutes, being consumed in Dartford marshes, on a cold December day, before Donnelly could dispose of "Spring's Novice."

On this occasion Sayers went to scale 9 stone 12 pounds, and Collins is stated to have been " within the limit agreed on, namely, 10 stone." Collins was also an inch taller than Tom. The stakes were £50, Spring backing his *protégé*, who was seconded by Jack Grant and Jemmy Welsh; Alec Keene and Jack Macdonald, (afterwards the adviser and second of Heenan,) waiting upon Sayers. A pleasant journey to Edenbridge in Kent, by rail, was enlivened by the presence of a number of gentlemen, officers of the Guards, and sporting Corinthians; the presence and patronage of " mine host of the Castle," and the " Nestor of the Ring," (V. G. Dowling, Esq.,) giving assurance of an orderly affair, and the interest in Collins attracting "the West End division." On setting to the betting stood at 6 to 4 on Collins, who had the suffrages of the *élite;* Tom's following "hailing" from the North and East.

THE FIGHT.

Round 1. As they threw themselves into form, it would have been difficult to find two better models of 9 stone 12 pound men. Sayers was broader framed than his adversary, and rather more set and manly in his points. Collins, though the difference in height was trifling, was longer armed, and freer in the shoulder. Their attitudes were good, their mugs smiling, and an out-and-out good mill was prophesied by all present. Sayers exhibited none of the novice in his style. He broke ground well, as Collins tried to get in on his left, and, after a short spar, sent in his right hand a plunging hit at Collins' ribs; Collins turning at the instant, it caught him far round on the back, where it raised a crimson bump. Collins' left grazed Sayers' ear, the men closed, and in exchanging hits Collins fell.

2. Collins stopped Sayers' right neatly, and Sayers did the same twice with Collins' left. Exchange of sharp hits. Sayers nailed Collins on the left cheek with his right hand heavily; Collins retorted sharply on Sayers' head; Sayers plunged in with his right, Collins stepped back, caught him a smashing upper cut with the right, that knocked him clean down. (Uproarious applause from the Bermondsey division. 2 to 1 on Collins.)

3. Short sparring, the men got to work; good stops on both sides, and a brief pause. Exchanges; Collins was stepping back, when Sayers jumped in, letting go his right, which was short, then, quick as thought, caught his man on the side of the head with his left, and hit him down. (Trick and tie; "Where's your 2 to 1!")

4. A rather scrambling round, in which several sounding body-blows were given and taken; a close—Collins threw Sayers cleverly.

5. Collins stopped his man prettily, with both hands. A short rally and both down.

6. (A cry of "The beaks are coming.") An excellent round. Sharp work for the eyes; hit, stop, counter, and break away; during which his worship made his way to the ropes, and with Act of Parliament in hand demanded a hearing. He was surrounded by a group of remonstrants, who pointed out the inutility of his interference, and offered promises to depart at once and for ever, at the close of the fight. The mar-sport was mild but inexorable, meantime the fun went on.

7. Collins on Sayers' nose; a rally; Sayers under.

8. Sayers made play vigorously, and caught Collins twice heavily with the right. Some confusion among the seconds and the men went to their corners. (His worship had momentarily retired.)

9. Sayers caught Collins on the left cheek bone heavily, and received a rattling return on the jaw. Exchanges; Sayers' right fist coming heavily in contact with the upper and hardest part of

Collins' nob, to the serious damage of that weapon; Collins got down amid some confusion, occasioned by the magistrate's re-appearance in the ring. Time, 27 minutes.

THE ADJOURNMENT.

His worship, still alone, not even accompanied by a constable, drew forth the Act, and called upon all present to be aiding and assisting. He was assured that Her Majesty had not a more loyal set of subjects than those present, as was proved by their conduct at that moment. His worship replied that his duty had brought him there, upon information of the contemplated breach of the peace, and that duty, at whatever personal peril, he would perform. He trusted that some responsible person present would pass his word, that the fight should not continue, and he would retire. If not—as to physical force the threat was idle, but none desired to resist the law; accordingly the ropes were unrove, the stakes drawn from the turf, and with many a longing look at the pretty little spot, the groups moved off. A council of war was now held. The articles provided that in the event of magisterial interference, the referee or stakeholder should name the next place of meeting, "if possible on the same day." The backers of Sayers were reasonable in their views, but his noisy followers, amongst whom the late Tom Paddock, then candidate for the championship, was offensively conspicuous, were for defying law, order, decency, and common sense, and then and there, heedless of the consequence to the more responsible parties, finishing the affair, on the presumption that they had a decided advantage at the time of the interruption. It was now half-past two o'clock, and the word was given to return to the train. Owing, however, to the obstinacy of some, the stupidity of others, and other less excusable motives, the parties who pretended such anxiety "to get the affair off," burnt daylight, every day more valuable at this time of the year, till twenty-five minutes past three, when, all being in their seats, the train returned to Red Hill. A convenient spot chosen, after the needful time for arranging the ring, &c., the men showed, and being once more ready, at a quarter past four o'clock, began the

ADJOURNED FIGHT.

Round 10. Both came to the scratch smiling. Sayers clean about the head, but with a suspicious swelling on the back of the dexter mawley. Collins' eyes were bright, but his nose was swelled, and his left cheek bone ornamented with a "boss" of considerable magnitude and ruby redness. His left ear, too, was puffed. His hands were good, and his activity unimpaired. Sayers began to force the fun, but Collins stopped him cleverly. Collins tried it on with the left, but was equally well stopped. At a second attempt he got home on the breast, staggering Sayers, then delivered the same hand on his eye. A close, and Sayers fell on his face to prevent being thrown. (Offers of 6 to 4 on Collins.)

11. Counters with the left; a pause. Sayers jumped about rather flashily. In close quarters Collins slipped down.

12. Collins nailed Sayers with the left, drawing the claret from

his lips. Sayers threw a piece of string from his right hand on being challenged by Jemmy Welsh. A close, Sayers on his face; a dog fall.

13–25. Sayers no novice. In most of these rounds there was heavy work, the hits being at good distance, the men being alternately down, and the scale of victory trembling, first one way, and then the other. In the 21st round Collins caught Sayers a regular jaw-locker with his right, and followed it up, after a brief struggle, by throwing him a clean cross buttock. In the 24th round, after some close work, the steam getting lower with both men, Collins again threw Sayers heavily.

26. Sayers' right still useful in stopping. He hit short at Collins with his left, who upper-cut him sharply, and slipped down. (Murmurs from the Sayerites, and an appeal. The men were too weak for such an accident to influence the decision of a fight.)

27. A desperate rally. Each fought as if on that round depended the battle. Sayers several times used his damaged hand, though, we suspect, with more pain to himself than soothe to his adversary. Collins paid repeated visits to the eyes, mouth, and ribs of Sayers, who returned the compliments with right good will. The men broke away, turned round from their own hits, or occasional misses, and went at it again and again. Sayers several times cleverly got on by a double hit of the left, the first short and low, in the manner of a feint, the second a stinging chopper over the eye, nose, or mazzard, as luck or good guidance might deliver it. At the close the men got near, embraced, and literally went down together. (It's anybody's fight!" cried the Sayerites, which was met by an offer of £5 to £4, but no takers.)

28–35. Sayers occasionally wild, but as often recovering. Collins made the fighting, and generally finished the rounds by getting down.

36. Collins tried his left, but was stopped. Sayers seemed getting second wind, (perhaps third;) he put in a blow with the sore right hand, and following it up with the left, brought Collins down. (Cheers for Sayers.)

37. Exchanges; Collins grasped Sayers, and after a brief struggle threw him from the hip a catherine-wheeler, his heels flying, and his shoulders and hips striking the ground heavily.

38–43. Sayers fought with considerable judgment, and Collins too much blown to force him. In the last-named round Collins again threw Sayers cleverly.

44. Collins hit Sayers twice on the head, and got down in the return.

45–48. Darkness approaching. Both men struck often and determinedly; but the power of effective hitting was failing. Collins threw Sayers in the forty-seventh round, and was certainly getting the best of the hitting. In the forty-eighth there was an appeal on the score of Sayers dropping deliberately on Collins, who had fallen; but it was frivolous, and overruled.

49. Exchanges; Sayers open-handed. A struggle; Collins under.

50. Collins hit Sayers on the nose heavily with the left; Sayers was short in the return. Collins again nailed his man with the left,

and avoided his attempt to exchange; Sayers returned to his corner, and met Collins slightly as he went in. At this moment the referee entered the ring, and declared it "a drawn battle :" explaining, that he and the umpires had agreed at the time of sunset, more than half an hour previous, that, at forty minutes past five, let what might be the position of the fight, "a draw" should be pronounced. And thus, after an unexampled contest for gallantry and fairness of 1 hour and 52 minutes, the wreath of victory was left to be divided.

Remarks.—These may appear superfluous on a drawn battle ; yet we cannot, in fairness, withhold praise where praise is due. Both did their best to win. We trust the friends of both men will not forget that, though under any circumstances one only can win, each here deserves the success he so bravely struggled for.

It was now arranged that the men should meet for a decisive issue on the 10th of December, in the same ring as Sambo (Welsh) and Jem Cross ; but these two boxers prolonging their battle for two hours and a half, daylight was burnt out, and another adjournment took place, so that it was the 29th of April 1851, before this long-pending affair was ultimately decided. Accordingly, on the day above mentioned, the heroes met within the twenty-four feet square at Chapman's Marsh, Long Reach. "Peter the Great," (our old friend, Crawley,) had now taken up Sayers, who had been a good boy and taken care of himself, in the interval. It is curious that there is really no detailed report extant of this fight. The following "Remarks" appeared on the 4th of May, the Saturday after the battle, in *Bell's Life* :—

"Sayers, on this third occasion, was in first-rate fettle. He is a fine, hardy, powerful young fellow, 5 feet 8 inches in height, and bids fair to prove a 'clipper.' He has, however, much to learn in the *tactique* of the boxing art. His adversary, who was on the former occasion backed from the 'Castle,' through inattention, wanted on the present occasion the countenance he formerly had, and this went so far that, had it not been for the kindness of Jemmy Welsh and some Southwark patrons, who would not see a brave lad deserted in difficulty, Collins would not even have had the fortnight's training he obtained. This, with other depressing circumstances, was not well calculated to improve his

chance against such a formidable adversary. The 'Waterman, No. 8,' having been chartered, at an early hour she
steamed away from Waterloo on a wet, miserable morning,
and after a delay at Blackwall and North Woolwich, reached
her destination off Chapman's Marsh, about two o'clock.
At half-past two, the ring being formed and beaten out,
Collins, followed by Welsh and Jack Grant, and Sayers,
attended by Jem Turner and Sam Martin, entered the enclosure. The coming on of a thunderstorm, with a sweeping
hail-shower, delayed the operations for a brief period, but at
three o'clock the men stood up. The betting, which had
varied from 5 to 4 on Sayers on board the boat, settled
down to about evens at the standing up of the men for 'the
fight.' And here we must, from the unavoidable pressure
on our space, omit the usual detail of the rounds, which
were protracted to the 44th, when Collins, after a courageous struggle, which occupied one hour and twenty-four
minutes, was beaten. We may remark that a more manly
mill has not of late been seen, although the science of the
men is by no means of the very first quality. Collins has
been remarkably unfortunate in his opening career, his trial
battle being with Ned Donnelly, a terrific natural hitter
and a tough customer, although perhaps not A-1 in skill
and stratagems of the ring. His next match was the one
under notice ; and certainly of the ten-stone men, Sayers is
about as formidable and promising a novice as we have
lately seen. At their first meeting, an injury to his adversary's right hand gave Collins a good chance of the battle,
which he improved by his courage and tact. But on this
occasion he was sadly overmatched in strength, weight, and
stamina, while in skill Sayers was nearly his equal. He,
however, did his best, and the best can do no more ; and
we trust his friends and original backers will do a something to make up for what looks very like remissness and
inattention to a brave and deserving, though unlucky, pugilist. Sayers displayed great confidence, hardihood, and
courage, together with unimpaired strength and wind,

throughout the contest. He will prove a tough customer to whoever next has dealings with him in the fistic line."

On this occasion, as there was no stipulation as to weight, Collins weighed 10 stone 2 pounds; Sayers 9 stone 12 pounds.

The great improvement of Sayers on this occasion was evident to every judge of boxing; he took a strong lead, was never headed, and won in a canter. If there was little profit in three trainings, and three fights for one stake, Tom gained confidence and lots of friends. His weight—however, too heavy for the nine-stone men, and underweight for the "middles" and "heavies,"—kept him without a match for nearly a year, during which he was anxiously looking out. At length, to the surprise and delight of the South-warkians, Tom had what they thought the presumptuous hardihood to offer to meet the renowned Jack Grant, for £100 a side. Jack was at the top of his renown. He had beaten James Haggerty, drawn with Mike Madden, (day-light failing,) beaten Alec Keene, and received forfeit from the talented Callaghan of Derby. Winning and nothing else was the idea of the Borough lads. The mill came off at Meldenhall, June 29, 1852, for £100 a side. Grant was attended by Harry Orme and Jemmy Welsh; Sayers, by Ned Adams and Bob Fuller the pedestrian. Betting 6 and 7 to 4 on Grant.

THE FIGHT.

Round 1. On appearing at the scratch, the condition and general appearance of Tom Sayers was the theme of admiration; there was not an ounce of superfluous flesh upon his body: he appeared all wire and muscle. His phiz wore a good-humoured smile of con-fidence, and there was a ruddy glow upon his cheek which told of good health and condition. His attitude was graceful and firm, and to a good judge it was apparent that if he was as good as he looked the Borough Champion had his work cut out. Grant seemed not quite up to the mark; his arms, it is true, were muscular and brawny, and his good-tempered mug looked healthy; but there were certain accumulations of fat upon his chest and ribs which suffi-ciently indicated that his exercise had not been so severe as it might have been, and we were informed that, instead of weighing about 10 stone 2 pounds, he turned the scale at 10 stone 6 pounds. Notwithstanding his lustiness, however, he appeared to look upon the result with confidence, and to hold his adversary at a very cheap rate. His position indicated the old tactician, the arms well up, and not too far from his body; his head back, and his eye fixed upon that of his adversary, who stood well over him, and was longer in the reach. After a little dodging, Grant, who was anxious to begin, led off with his left, slightly reaching Tom's forehead, and jumped away from the return. Sayers followed him up, when Grant tried to repeat the dose on the forehead, but was prettily stopped. Sayers at length got home with his right on the ribs, which was followed by heavy counter-hits, Grant on the left cheek, and Sayers heavily on Grant's nose. Ditto repeated, when Sayers gained "first blood" from a cut over that organ. Grant then went in to force the fighting, but Sayers stepped back, jobbed him again on the nose, cleverly stopping the return. Counter-hits succeeded, Sayers catching a nasty one on the left side of the head and in getting back slipped down.

2. Grant tried to lead off several times, but was on each occasion well stopped. He returned the compliment by twice stopping Sayers, and then lunged out his right, catching Sayers heavily under the left ear. Tom countered him with effect on the nose, and a close following, both were down; Sayers under.

3. Grant took the initiative, but Sayers jumped away smiling; he, however, came again directly and led off with his left, but was stopped. He was more successful a second time, and reached Grant's damaged nose. Grant closed for the fall, but Sayers would not struggle, contenting himself with fibbing Grant on the nose and left ear until both rolled over.

4. Mutual good stopping, after which Sayers delivered his left heavily on Grant's ribs and jumped away. Counter-hits with the left followed—Sayers on the nose, and Grant on the ribs. A close, and some sharp fibbing. A break away, and at it again, Grant delivering his heavily on Tom's left eye. Slight exchanges, Grant again getting it on the nose, and Sayers slipped down.

5. Both, on coming up, looked flushed. Sayers smiled, while Grant looked grim. The latter led off, but was twice stopped. They then got to work; sharp counter-hits were exchanged, Sayers receiving heavily on the left cheek, and Grant on the nose and jaw. A close and struggle for the fall ended in Grant being thrown, but not heavily.

6. Sayers tried to lead off, but Grant was wary, and stopped him. He was not to be denied, however; he made another attempt, and again reached Grant's smeller, getting well away from the return. Sayers then repeated the dose heavily with both hands, and followed this up by one or two punches in the ribs. At length Grant swung round his dangerous right, and caught Master Tom a tremendous whack on the left ear, which staggered him. Grant then closed, but Sayers declined to struggle for the fall, and fibbed away at his man until he allowed him to slip down.

7. Sayers showed the effects of Grant's visitation to his left ear, which was considerably swelled. Grant looked flushed from the taps on the nozzle. The latter led off, but was quite out of distance, and Sayers followed his example by delivering too high to be of any

service. Exchanges then took place, each catching it on the right eye, Sayers' delivery appearing to be the heaviest. In getting away Sayers slipped down.

8. Grant took the lead, but was again stopped, and caught an awkward one on the left listener for his pains. He then succeeded in planting his left on Tom's forehead. Grant then bored in, but Sayers stepped back, administering an upper-cut, which led to a rally, in which some sharp hitting took place, and Sayers scrambled down.

9. Both slightly blown. Tom stopped Grant's attempts to plant on him, and then delivered his left on the nose twice in succession. Grant again made his right sound against the left side of Tom's head, and then sent in a heavy one on the ribs. Sayers, nothing daunted, was at him again, popped in his left on the cheek and his right on Grant's left ear, and this bringing them to a struggle, Sayers let himself down easy.

10. Grant tried to force the fighting by boring in, but got it on the left eye rather heavily. Sayers, however, had not the strength to stall him off. He, again went in, caught Sayers on the left eye, and in a struggle which followed the latter again slipped down to avoid being thrown.

11. Grant led off, got well home on Sayers' left ear, and then closed, and both rolled over together.

12. Sayers' left ear and left side of his head were much swollen; still he smiled, and calmly awaited the attack, which was not long in coming. Grant dashed in, and commenced hitting away with both hands; he drew blood from Tom's mouth by a heavy spank from his left. Sayers delivered on the left cheek, and the round finished by both falling together at the ropes.

13. Grant made his right with a severity on the ribs, getting away from Sayers' return. Sayers followed him up, and some sharp hits were exchanged left and right, both catching it on the nose and cheek, and Grant at length got down.

14. Grant dashed in resolutely, but twice was well stopped. Sayers then delivered his left and right on the nose and left eye. Grant, not liking this, bored in, made his right on Tom's left cheek, closed, but Sayers catching well hold of him, threw him a cross-buttock and fell on him.

15. Both, anxious to get to work, led off at the same time, and each got it on the left eye. Grant was then neatly stopped twice in succession, but at length-closed, and some sharp in-fighting took place, Sayers catching it on the left eye, and Grant on the left ear. The round ended by both going to grass. (Forty minutes had now elapsed, and those who had backed Grant to win in an hour began to look blue.)

16. A capital round. After some excellent stopping and manœuvring on both sides, they got close together, and some sharp exchanges took place, each catching it on the nose and left cheek. A close ensued, followed by a break away, and both at it again, left and right, until Grant got down, somewhat blown, his want of condition evidently beginning to tell.

17. Somewhat similar to the last each catching it severely on the

side of the head. The hitting appeared rather in favour of Grant, who drew more claret from Tom's mouth. Both were eventually down.

18. Grant dashed in and closed for a fall, but Sayers declined the struggle, fibbed him severely on the left ear several times, and Grant slipped down. He lay on his back where he fell, blowing like a grampus until time was called, when he was carried to his corner, from whence he walked to the scratch.

19. Some good exchanges, Sayers on the right eye, and Grant on the nose, removing the bark, and drawing a fresh supply of the ruby. Quick exchanges, but both apparently hitting open-handed, were followed by Tom getting down cleverly.

20. Grant, whose left ear had been lanced, came up bleeding from that organ, which was much swelled from the blows in the 18th round. He rushed in, but Sayers caught him heavily on the damaged listener. Grant, still determined, persevered, caught Tom on the left side of the head twice in succession; exchanges followed in favour of Grant, and at last Tom got down.

21. Sayers' left eye began to show symptoms of adopting the early-closing movement. He tried to lead off, but was stopped by Jack, who made his left again on the closing peeper, and then closed. Sayers fiddled away at his left ear until both were down.

22 and 23. Both slow but steady, and the rounds ended after a few exchanges in the men slipping down at the ropes. In the latter round Grant pursued Sayers, who ran round the ring until he got to his own corner, when he turned sharp round, caught Grant left and right on the nose and left eye, which led to the close and fall.

24. Grant came up bleeding from a cut over his left eye. Sayers attempted to take the lead, but was well stopped, Grant making his right heavily on his left ear, and Sayers fell through the ropes.

25. Sayers was again neatly stopped, and in stepping back from Grant's return, caught his heel and fell.

26. Mutual good stopping, Sayers evidently the more active; he caught Grant again on his left ear, which was terribly swollen, received a heavy thump on the ribs from Grant's right, and dropped on his south pole.

27. Grant dashed in with his left on the mouth, and then his right on the side of Sayers' head. Exchanges—Grant drawing blood from Tom's nose. Some good in-fighting in favour of Sayers, and Grant got down.

28. Good counter-hits, each catching it heavily on the nose. They now went to work in earnest; the hitting on both sides was tremendous, but owing to the excellence of Sayers' condition, he did not show it much, while Grant, who received principally on the left ear and nose, looked considerably the worse for wear. Eventually Sayers slipped to avoid Jack's friendly hug, and Grant, who fell over him, cleverly avoided touching him with his spikes.

29 to 32. In these rounds Grant led off, but his want of condition prevented his being as quick as he otherwise might have been, consequently he was often stopped, and of course exhausted himself by throwing away his blows. When, however, they got at it, he gave as good as he got, and the rounds ended by Sayers

slipping down. In the 32d, however, Grant threw Sayers, and fell heavily on him.

33. Grant came up bleeding from the mouth and left ear; he tried to lead off, but was stopped. Sayers popped in his left and right on the mouth and throat, getting it in return on the nose heavily, more of the bark being displaced, and in the end both were down.

34. Grant planted both hands, but the steam was gone; Sayers returned on the mouth and left eye. A rally, Grant delivering on the damaged cheek-bone of his adversary, and receiving another gentle tap on his nose, which drew more fluid. A close struggle for the fall, and both down, Sayers under.

35. One hour and a half had now elapsed, and both appeared fatigued from their exertions. Grant stopped several well-intentioned deliveries, and returned on Tom's left eye and nose, drawing blood from both. Good exchanges led to a close, when both were down.

36. Sayers came up weak, while Grant had slightly recovered. The latter led off, was twice well stopped, but ultimately sent home his right on Sayers' left cheek, and the latter slipped down.

37. Sayers, whose left cheek and eyebrow were much swollen and discoloured, led off, and caught Grant on the left eye and nose, but not heavily, and in retreating fell.

38. Grant took the lead, but was propped in the throat by Tom's right. Grant, however, found out the side of his head with effect. Exchanges followed, both receiving on the nose; but Sayers, who was weakest, got down on the saving suit.

39. Grant dashed in with his right on Tom's left cheek, who closed, fibbed him heavily on his damaged ear, and then slipped down.

40 to 42. In these rounds but little mischief was done, both sparring for wind, and eventually Sayers got down cleverly.

43. Grant, who seemed to have got second wind, led off quickly, but Sayers jumped away. Grant followed him up, caught him on the ribs heavily with his right, and then on the nose with his left. Sayers returned on the throat, and some heavy deliveries on both sides took place, both standing and hitting away for some time without an attempt at stopping, and there appeared to be no decided advantage on either side; at length Sayers slipped down exhausted. This was unexceptionably the severest round in the fight. The men appeared to think it was the turning point, and each wished to make some decided impression on his game adversary.

44. Both were the worse for their exertions in the last round. Grant's left ear bore marks of having been again severely visited, and we believe his seconds again found it necessary to lance it. Sayers did not show such decided marks of Grant's handiwork, but this was mainly accounted for by his excellent condition. His left eye was, however, closing, and his left cheek much swollen. Both unwilling to begin, and some slight blows having been exchanged, Sayers slipped down.

45. Grant went in to mill, but napped it on the left ear and nose with severity. Good exchanges followed, and Sayers again slipped down.

46. Grant still first to fight; but was cleverly stopped by Sayers, who was getting more active. They quickly got to in-fighting, when after a few exchanges, they rolled over, and Grant excited the admiration of all by the careful manner in which he avoided falling on his man with his feet or knees.

47 and 48. Grant took the lead in both these rounds; but was stopped in each instance, and received deliveries from Sayers's right on his left ear. He nevertheless succeeded in each round in planting on Sayers' left ear with his dangerous right; but the blows had not that vigour we have seen him exhibit on former occasions. Both were down in these rounds.

49. Some rattling exchanges took place in this round; Grant getting it on the throat and ribs, and Sayers on the chest and mouth, and eventually slipping down.

50. Sayers made play on the ribs with his left heavily, Grant returning on the nose with his left; Grant then stopped two attempts on the part of Sayers, made his left and right on the nose and left cheek, and Sayers slipped down.

51. Grant again popped in a spank on Tom's nut, receiving in return on the smeller heavily, and losing more claret. Good exchanges followed, when Grant rushed in and bored his man over the ropes.

52. Sayers attempted to make the running, but was stopped by Grant, who went in to mill, and planted both hands, one on the nose, and the other on the left side of the head heavily. Another on the nose succeeded, which opened the claret jug again. Sayers only planted his left once on the nose, and slipped down. This round was decidedly in favour of Grant.

53. Sayers made his left on the ribs, and tried to plant the same hand on the nose, but was well stopped. He received one from Grant's right on the side of his head; this brought on a rally, in which he caught it on the eyebrow heavily, and slipped down.

54. Grant, thinking the game was now his own, again brushed in; but Sayers was with him, and in the exchanges which followed he visited Grant's left ear with great severity, catching it slightly on the side of the head, and then getting down cunning.

55. Grant again first, but stopped; he, however, made good his right on the ribs directly afterwards, and then his left on the right eye of Sayers, who sent home his right on the neck, and his left on the left ear. Grant bored in again, received one on his left ear, which bled freely, and Sayers slipped down.

56. A close, and Sayers got down.

57. No mischief done. Some slight exchanges, and Sayers slipped down.

58. Sayers caught Grant as he came in on the nose and throat, and then on the mazzard heavily, drawing more of the ruby. Grant then closed, struggled, and both fell heavily to the ground—Sayers uppermost.

59. Grant, who seemed weak and exhausted, was twice stopped; but in a third attempt caught Sayers on the left ear with his right, and the latter slipped down.

60. Grant led off, reached Sayers' left eye, received one on his damaged listener, and slipped down.

61. Grant appeared determined to finish the matter off hand, rushed in left and right on Sayers' cheek and nose. Sayers put in both hands on the left eye and nose; a rally, close, and short struggle; both again coming to the ground heavily—Grant under.

62. Sayers tried to lead off, but was short; Grant just contrived to reach his nose, but the blow had no steam in it, and Sayers in getting back slipped down.

63. Both slow to the call of time, and both evidently exhausted. Grant was first up, but he looked much flushed; his face was much swollen, his nose anything but Roman in its appearance, and his left ear presenting an unpleasant spectacle. He rushed in, but Sayers, whose good-natured mug still bore the ghost of a smile, although nearly on the wrong side of his mouth, stopped him cleverly and got away; Grant followed him up, got home with his right on the side of his head, receiving, in return, on the left ear. A close, and long struggle for the fall, which Grant got, throwing his man, and falling heavily on him.

64 and last. Grant came up looking very groggy. The falls in the few last rounds had evidently shaken him. He appeared to be suffering from cramp, but still was determined. He led off, getting slightly home on Sayers' left cheek bone. Tom retaliated on the left ear. A few sharp exchanges were succeeded by another struggle for the fall, and ultimately both came very heavily to the ground—Grant being undermost—Tom falling across his stomach. Both were immediately picked up and carried to their corners, and on time being called, Jemmy Welsh, on the part of Grant, threw up the sponge in token of defeat. On our inquiring as to the cause of this rather unexpected termination of the affair, we were informed that Grant was severely suffering from cramp, and had moreover injured some part of his intestines in such a manner that it was feared he was ruptured, and he was in such pain, that he could not stand upright. Sayers went up to his fallen but not disgraced adversary and shook him kindly by the hand, and was proclaimed the victor amidst the shouts of his friends. Grant was conveyed on a railway truck to a small public-house in the neighbourhood, where every attention was shown to him, but he continued in great pain for some time afterwards. The poor fellow was not actually ruptured; but he had received a severe internal strain, which caused him considerable uneasiness for some time. Grant met with an accident some time before at Manchester, which always rendered him weak in the muscles of the stomach, and he considered that being not fully up to the mark, he was more than usually susceptible of injury. The fight lasted exactly *two hours and a half.*

Remarks.—The great length to which our account of this "model mill" has already extended imposes upon us the necessity of being brief in our usual accompanying remarks. Tom Sayers by this victory has established for himself a reputation as a man of science, courage, and endurance, for which few were disposed to give him credit. The manner in which he stopped the determined attacks of his adversary, and the judgment with which he extricated himself from difficulty, and continually refused to struggle for the fall with a man much stronger than himself, proved that his head-piece

was screwed on the right way, and that although comparatively a
novice within the Prize Ring, he is perfectly acquainted with the
theory of his art, and only wants the occasion to arise to put that
theory into practice. He is a very hard hitter, and managed to get on
to his opponent so frequently, that even Grant's iron mug displayed
such bumps and contusions as the gallant hero has seldom exhibited
in his former engagements. Sayers is a good tempered, well-behaved
young fellow, and bears a high character for honour and integrity.
He is by this victory nearly at the top of the tree, and we trust that
by his future conduct he will show that prosperity has not in his
case, as it has in many we could name in the same profession, had
the effect of destroying his good principles, and lowering him in
the eyes of those through whose support he has arrived at his
present position. Grant, although not destined on this occasion to
wear the crown of victory, has not disgraced himself by his fall.
He manfully disputed every inch of ground with his clever opponent, and showed that his qualifications as a sparrer were quite
equal to those of Sayers. His stopping and wrestling were univer-
sally admired, while the manliness and care with which he avoided
falling upon his adversary in such a way as to cause any dispute, obtained for him the repeated plaudits of the surrounding throng.
The fight, as we have before observed, was conducted throughout
in a way to leave nothing to be desired, and we sincerely hope that
the example which has been set may be followed in all future encounters. If such be the case, the members of the Prize Ring may
rest assured they will find that the love of the art is by no means
extinct among the upper classes, and that the sole reason for their
continued absence from the ring side has been the disgraceful manner
in which the combats of late years have been carried out.

Tom now remained idle until January of the following
year, 1853, when a game, resolute fellow, named Jack
Martin, who had disposed of several countrymen, and
grown into high favour with Ben Caunt, was brought
forward by "Big Ben" to uphold the honour of "The
Coach and Horses." Tom's standing challenge was accordingly accepted for £50 a side, and Wednesday, January
26, 1853, named as the day of battle. A foggy trip per
steamer landed the voyagers in Long Reach, and, the preparations being made, the men stood up and shook hands;
Alec Keene and a friend, for Sayers, and Tom Paddock
and Jerry Noon as seconds for Martin, joining in the
friendly ceremony.

THE FIGHT.

Round 1. On toeing the scratch it was clear to all that Sayers
was a bigger man than his adversary; and, if possible, in better
condition. His eye had resumed its brightness, and there was a

hardness in his general appearance which made him look all over a perfect gladiator. Martin, who was shorter in the reach than his opponent, showed great muscularity of arm and thighs, but elsewhere he was not nearly so well furnished. He was pale, but there was a good-humoured smile on his mug, which showed that the word fear was unknown in his vocabulary. Little time was lost in sparring—Sayers led off, catching Martin slightly with his left on the nose. Martin immediately rushed to in-fighting, when some heavy hits were exchanged, each catching it on the left eye, and each showing claret at the same moment from cuts on the brow. After a few random shots both were down together. "First blood" was claimed by each party, but was decided by the referee to be a drawn event.

2. Both bleeding from the left eye, Sayers appearing to have the worst of it. He was undaunted, smiled, led off with his left, catching Martin on the right cheek. Martin again went in, and commenced pegging away with both hands. Sayers was with him, hitting with most precision, and the round ended in both again falling together.

3. Sayers commenced the ball, caught Martin a spank on the right cheek, received slightly on the body, and then catching Martin full with his left on the nose, sent him to grass a clean "knock down blow," and thus won the second event.

4. Martin came up bleeding from the nose, but with a smile of confidence. Sayers led off, but Martin jumped cleverly back. He then stepped in, caught Sayers on the damaged optic, drawing more of the ruby. Heavy exchanges followed; Martin delivered his right heavily on the ribs, Sayers returning with effect on the nose. A close at the rope followed, and both were quickly down.

5. Martin attempted to take the lead, but was neatly stopped; he then swung round his right at the body, and immediately closed for the fall. Sayers, instead of struggling, fibbed away at Martin's head until Martin forced him down.

6. Sayers led off on the nose with his left; Martin countered on the side of the head. A tremendous rally followed, the hits on both sides succeeding each other with great quickness. Each caught it on the side of the head, but the blows of Sayers, from his superior reach, told with most force. In the end both were down.

7. Martin led off, was well stopped, and received a nasty one on the nose; he then closed, but Sayers refused to struggle with him, and got down, Martin following suit.

8. Sayers commenced by planting his left on Martin's nose with effect, and immediately repeating the dose. Martin returned on the left eye heavily, enlarging the old cut; and Sayers, in stepping away, slipped down.

9. Martin showed a bump on each side of his nose from the heavy blows in the last round. He tried to take the lead, but was well stopped. Ditto repeated. After which he bored in, Sayers catching him heavily on the left cheek. Martin succeeded in reaching Sayers' damaged brow; good exchanges followed, Sayers getting, however, on Martin's right eye, and Martin on the ribs with his right. Another tremendous rally followed, each getting heavy pepper, Martin, however, having the worst of it, and receiving on

the mouth and left eye with great severity. At last they got close together, and, after a short struggle, Sayers eased himself down, and Martin fell on him.

10. Martin, on coming up, showed marks of the efficacy of Sayers' handiwork in the last round. His right eye, which was previously "all serene," was now completely closed, and his right cheek much swollen, while Sayers appeared little the worse for wear. Sayers led off, but was short; Martin then made an attempt, but failed in like manner. Counter hits followed; Sayers again reached the right ogle of his adversary, who took all in good humour, and still smiled with one side of his face. He now dashed in, and more exchanges took place, Martin succeeding in inflicting a cut over Sayers' right eye, which had been hitherto unscathed. At length, after some sharp in-fighting in favour of Sayers, Martin slipped down on one knee. Sayers, who might have hit him, laughed and walked away, amidst cries of "Bravo" from both sides.

11. Sayers led off with his left, reaching the side of Martin's nose. A rattling rally followed, at the end of which Sayers threw his man and fell heavily on him.

12. Martin came up bleeding at all points, but still the same good-humoured fellow as ever. Sayers led off short, ditto Martin, Sayers in on the ribs with his left. Counter hits, Sayers on the nose, and Martin on the cheek, drawing more of the ruby fluid. A close followed, and some more heavy in-fighting, after which, Martin contrived to swing Sayers over.

13. Sayers on coming up was bleeding rapidly from a severe cut on his left hand, evidently inflicted against Martin's teeth. The men quickly got to it, counter hits were exchanged, Martin on the ribs and Sayers on the right cheek, followed up by two spanks, left and right, on the nose and mouth. More heavy pounding in favour of Sayers, who hit at points, while Martin hit round, and principally at the body. At length they closed, and both were down, side by side, each looking at his adversary and smiling benignly.

14. Martin led off with his left, but was out of distance. Sayers with great quickness let go his left and reached his opponent's mouth. Martin merely grinned at the visitation, bored in, but only to receive another severe prop on the right eye, and a spank on the nasal organ. Still he was determined, and again went at his man, who, in getting away, slipped down.

15. Martin's phisog in anything but picturesque condition, his right cheek much swollen and bleeding, and his mouth completely out of kissing condition. After a few passes, slight counter hits were exchanged, Martin getting home on the body, and Sayers on the left cheek. Martin, not to be stalled off, rushed in and delivered a heavy round hit on the ribs with his right; Sayers was with him, and visited his damaged smeller with severity. This led to another good rattling rally, in which Sayers inflicted more heavy punishment on poor Martin's nose and right eye, while Martin only succeeded in delivering some sounding punches on his ribs. They broke away, again got at it ding dong, and finally, in the close, both were down. Martin apparently as strong on his legs as his opponent.

16. Good counter hits with the left, each catching the other on the mazzard. Sayers now stopped one or two attempts on the part of his adversary very neatly, and returned heavily on the nozzle. An attempt to repeat the dose was unsuccessful, Martin quickly jumping back. Martin came again and swung round his left on the ribs, but napped it again on the nose for his imprudence. More mutual punching in favour of Sayers followed, but still Martin's deliveries were occasionally severe. A close, in which both fibbed away hammer and tongs, Sayers reaching Martin's remaining optic, but not with sufficient force to put up the shutter, and Martin drew more claret from his opponent's left ogle. A break away, and at it again, until Martin slipped down on one knee; Sayers, again, walking away smiling. This round, which was one of the best fighting rounds we have seen for many a day, elicited universal applause.

17. Martin came up piping, and rather slow, but still smiling, as well as his damaged phiz would allow. He endeavoured to lead off, but was easily stopped. In a second attempt he reached Tom's left cheek, but Sayers countered him on the left eye heavily, his superior reach giving him the advantage. Martin, not to be cowed, popped in a heavy right-hander on the ribs; received again on his left eye, and, in retreating, slipped down.

18. Sayers let fly his left, but was short: both appeared fatigued from the quickness with which they had worked, and sparred a few seconds for wind. Sayers at length again led off, and caught Martin on the left eye, Martin returning on the same suit with considerable quickness. Both were now short in their deliveries. Martin at length bored in and reached Tom's ribs with his right. Sayers returned on the right cheek, and both slipped down.

19. Sayers again out of distance. He soon crept closer, however, sent out his left, was neatly stopped, and cleverly got away from Martin's return. Martin followed him up, caught him on the left cheek, and then on the body, receiving a nasty one in return on the left eye. In the close which followed he succeeded in throwing Sayers heavily, amidst the cheers of his friends, who did not think he had so much strength in him.

20. Sayers led off, caught Martin on the mouth, was unsuccessful in a second attempt, and then caught a heavy right-hander on the ribs. Martin sent out his left and was stopped, Sayers returning with effect on the right eye, and then on the left, from which he drew more claret. Martin, whose head was much swollen, again planted a rib-bender, closed, and after a short struggle both were down.

21. Martin took the lead, but Sayers jumped away laughing; Martin returned the grin, and again sent out his left, which was easily stopped. Sayers once more reached his adversary's blind side, and Martin slipped down weak.

22. Any odds on Sayers, who was as fresh as possible. Martin made an effort to turn the tables, but was stopped several times; he at length reached Tom's ribs, and the latter stepping back, steadied himself, waited for Martin's rush, and then sent out his left with terrific force, caught poor Martin on the right jaw, and

the latter tumbled over on his face apparently out of time. It was thought all over, and the poor fellow was carried to his corner, but when time was called, to the surprise of all, he came up for round 23, and last. He was evidently all abroad, and staggered about the ring. Sayers went up to him, delivered his left on the right cheek, inflicting another cut, and following this up with a heavy right-hander on the nose, down went Martin for the last time quite insensible, and Sayers was proclaimed the winner after fighting 55 *minutes.* Sayers, although severely handled about the mug, was still fresh on his pins; both his eyes were fully open, and it was evident that, had it been necessary, he was good for many more rounds. Martin, on being conveyed to his corner, was laid upon the ground, and every effort was made to restore consciousness, but it was fully five minutes before he could be made to understand what had happened. As soon as possible he was conveyed on board the steamboat, and made as comfortable as could be expected under the circumstances.

Remarks.—A few more such battles as that we have just recorded, would go far to restore the fallen fortunes of the Prize Ring. It was in truth, as we have styled it above, a mill of the old school. More punishment was inflicted in 55 minutes than we have seen in two hours in any encounter during the last few years. There was not a single appeal to the referee, nor was there a single action on the part of either man throughout the fight at which the greatest stickler for fair play could take exception. Both had evidently made up their minds to a fair and manly struggle for victory, and their friends ably supported them in their laudable resolution, by rigidly abstaining from any interference. In fact, the only thing at which we felt inclined to cavil was, the manner in which Jerry Noon seconded the losing man. He was evidently not up to his business, and in cleaning his charge used the sponge so roughly, as in our opinion to do more harm than good. He also once or twice wiped the blood away from Martin while he was fighting, which, strictly speaking, is against the rules of the Ring. On the present occasion, however, it was not calculated to assist the man he wished to serve, but, on the contrary, was the very best course to pursue if he wished to confuse him, and put him off his guard. Noon should remember that a good second always remains quiet until the round is over, and then picks his man up, carries him to his corner, and cleans him as tenderly as possible. The slightest degree of roughness, or the slightest interference during the round, does but tend, as we have before said, to confuse a man's ideas and lead him into jeopardy. As to the merits of the men, we should think there cannot be two opinions. Martin was clearly over-matched. He was opposed to a taller, longer, and, in our opinion, a stronger man, and, moreover, one possessing far greater knowledge of the art of self-defence than himself. That he (Martin) is a game, resolute fellow no one will deny. A greater glutton we have seldom seen. He is also an exceedingly fair fighter, scorning to take the least advantage, and is possessed of that greatest of all requisites to a boxer—unwavering good temper. Although defeated on the present occasion, he has earned for himself a char-.

acter among the gentlemen who were present, which we have no doubt will stand him in good stead at a future day. The terms of praise in which he was mentioned by all, clearly showed that his conduct was appreciated as it deserved to be. We have no doubt that words will not be the only reward of his unflinching courage, but that he will receive a golden salve for his wounds, which will prove a more lasting encouragement to persevere in the line of conduct he exhibited on Wednesday. Of Tom Sayers, and his manly good-tempered style of fighting, we have before spoken in the highest terms, and it is only necessary for us to state that his conduct was as upright and his tactics were as fair as ever. He on several occasions refrained from punishing his adversary when he was down on one knee only—a position in which he was perfectly entitled to strike him, and one in which he might have administered pepper with excellent effect. He used his left hand with greater precision than in his battle with Grant, and his deliveries appeared altogether heavier than in that encounter. He has greatly improved since that time, and we fancy that he will prove a teazer to any one near his weight who may have the temerity to encounter him. As we have before observed, the ring was exceedingly well kept throughout, and all had an uninterrupted view of the encounter from its commencement to its conclusion. As soon as possible after the event was decided, the crowd that had assembled took its departure —some returning by the boat, while others, who did not fancy a return trip up the river in the dark against an ebb-tide, struck across the marshes to Dartford, and then reached town at seven o'clock by the North Kent Railway. Among the latter was our eccentric friend, Bendigo, who quite put out the pipe of the milling orator and poet, Charley Mallett, as, while waiting at the station, he composed and sung a long extempore poem, descriptive of the day's sport, and laudatory of the heroes and of himself, which elicited uncontrollable laughter and applause from his Corinthian auditors, and sent all back to the great metropolis in perfect good humour, caused as much by the ready wit and "hanky panky" performances of that eccentric individual—as by the extraordinary treat they had enjoyed on the field of battle.

CHAPTER II.

Nat Langham Champion of the Middle Weights.—Sayers' first
Defeat.—Langham refuses a Second Meeting.—Sayers' easy
Defeat of Sims.—His desperate Battle with, and Victory over,
Harry Poulson.—Aaron Jones; his Pretensions.—Drawn Battle
with Aaron Jones.—Defeat of Aaron Jones.—Sayers claims the
Belt.

THE year 1853 was marked by the first defeat of the
gallant Tom. His conqueror, Nat Langham, claims
a few paragraphs in this place.

Nathaniel Langham, "at this present writing" mine
host of the " Mitre," St. Martin's Lane, Leicester Square,
first saw daylight at Hinckley, near Leicester, in 1820.
His early battles were with men about his own weight
for Nat is of that unlucky size, 11 st., which is most'
difficult to match when accompanied with first-class
pugilistic capabilities. Too heavy for light men (whose
average is 9st. to 9st. 7 or 10lbs.), and too light for real
big ones, provided they have any sound pretensions to
skill and game, men of this size can only find a fair match
among men of their own stamp and qualifications. Nat's
early combats, then, as we have already said, were with
heavy ones, and his only defeat, as will be seen by the
subjoined list, was by Harry Orme, who, by an unlucky

throw, so spoiled Nat's science in the early part of the fight as to obtain the victory; but only after 117 rounds, when the sponge was thrown up by his seconds at the close of one of the bravest battles the modern ring can boast.

CAREER OF NAT LANGHAM, HEIGHT 5 ft. 10 ins., WEIGHT 11st.

Beat Ellis, 12st. 4lbs., £5 a side, 8 rounds, Hinckley, Leicestershire, February 2nd, 1843.

Beat T. Lowe, purse, 43 rounds, 50 minutes, Long Reach, May 7th, 1844.

Beat D. Campbell, 11st. 10lbs., £5 a side, 27 rounds, 35 minutes, down the river, June 12th, 1845.

Beat Gutteridge, 11st. 10lbs., £25 aside, 85 rounds, 93 minutes, Bourne, Lincolnshire, September 23rd, 1846. Received forfeit in a second match.

Beat W. Sparkes (the Australian champion), £50 a side, 67 rounds, 63 minutes, Woking Common, May 4th 1847.

Beaten by Harry Orme, 11st. 8lbs., £50 aside, 117 rounds, 2 hours, 56 minutes, Lower Hope Point, May 6th, 1851.

Beat Tom Sayers, 10st. 10lbs.

Fought Ben Caunt, 14 st., £200 a side, 60 rounds, 1 hour, 29 minutes, on an island in the River Medway, September 22nd, 1857.

The details of these battles will be found in PUGILISTICA, to which work we must refer the reader: suffice it to say that Langham, from the time of his defeat by Orme (May 1851), when he went into business as a publican at Cambridge, under the warm patronage of many of the collegians, although anxious for another match, could not find a competitor. Two years had passed away, during which Sayers had risen rapidly in the esteem of his friends, more especially by his defeat of Grant, and not a few already prophesied him as "the coming man." At this juncture, when Nat seemed upon the shelf, Tom, whose motto was "Excelsior," made overtures to Nat for a cool hundred and the Championship of the Middle Weights. The controversy was ended by "Ould Nat," as he was already called, picking up the gauntlet of the redoubted Tom, whose rashness was blamed by the "knowing ones," who reasonably asked in what respect—skill, weight, or game —Tom was Nat's superior? The one accident of youth excepted, they maintained that all the points were against Sayers. The match went on smoothly, articles having been signed for £100 a side, and the money posted. The men were confined to 11st., and Nat had great trouble to reduce himself within the stipulated weight; indeed, his friends declared he had got off the last few pounds at the expense of a diminution of strength. Sayers, on the other hand, at 10st. 12lbs., was all 4lbs. heavier (at this time) than he should have been, and consequently it was "bellows to mend" with him early in the fight. The battle-ground was Lakenheath, Suffolk; the day the 18th of October, 1853. Langham was seconded by Jemmy Welsh and Jerry Noon, Sayers by Alec Keene and Bob Fuller the pedestrian; and four more accomplished esquires never waited upon two knights in "a gentle passage of arms" than those whose names we have here written.

All being in apple-pie order, the men stood up, the seconds shook hands across, the principals did the same, with a good-humoured smile on each of their bronzed faces; "Ould Nat's" partaking somewhat of a grin, from his "front railing" having partially departed; still his friends were justly confident, and laid 6 to 4 on him.

THE FIGHT.

Round 1.—On facing each other there was a wide contrast between the men. Langham was long and lathy; his frame was evidently that of a man who had seen severe work, and to all appearance incapable of sustaining long-continued exertions. There was a smile of good-humoured confidence on his mug, however, that showed how little he feared the result of the coming struggle. He was, as we have already said, in excellent condition, though "a thought" too fine. Sayers, some two inches shorter, looked broad, strong, and burly, but was clearly overburdened with flesh; his cheeks were puffy, and it was apparent that he could well have spared several pounds of superfluous matter. There was a breaking-out upon his chin and face, which, we were informed, was the result of a cold, but to our mind it did not betoken the highest state of health. There was also an anxious look about his eyes which we do not recollect on former occasions. Neither man struck us as being very artistic in his position. Their legs were too far apart, and their guard inelegant. A good deal of sparring took place for an opening, and at length Langham let go his left, but did not quite get home. Caution was again the order of the day, until Langham again got within distance, and tried his left a second time, just reaching Tom's chest. Sayers now tried to draw his man, but Langham was not to be had. Sayers, therefore, approached him, when Nat popped in his left on the cheek, and then the same hand on the nose, and got away. Sayers followed him up, and Langham, as he retreated, again sent out his left on the cheek. More sparring now took place, and at length counter-hits were exchanged, Langham catching Tom on the chin, and drawing "first blood" from a pimple below his mouth. Sayers now bored in and caught Nat a nasty one on the forehead, from the effects of which Nat went to grass. "First knock down" for Sayers. Little merit, however, could be attached to it, as the ground was in such a state as to render it difficult for Nat to keep his legs.

2.—Langham feinted, and, as Sayers threw out his arms wildly, led off with his left on the mouth, but with no severity. Sayers returned on the frontispiece, and Langham slipped down.

3.—Langham led off, but the blow fell short on Tom's chest. A second attempt was more successful, as he got home a heavy spank, on Tom's snorter, from which the ruby was instantly visible. Left-hander counter-hits followed, each getting it slightly on the cheek, and Nat, in getting back, fell.

4.—On getting within distance, both went to work. Tom made his left on Nat's cheek, and his right heavily on the ribs. Heavy counter-hits followed in favour of Nat, whose superior length was of great advantage. Tom napped it again severely on the smelling organ, and returned it on the side of Langham's nut and his short ribs, the latter heavily with his right. Langham now retreated, and, as Tom followed him up, pinked him twice in succession with effect on the nozzle, drawing more claret. Sayers returned slightly on the ribs, and again was met by Nat on the mouth and left eye. Sayers continued to persevere, occasionally getting in a little one on Nat's ribs; but Nat in this round appeared to have it all his own way; he propped his man repeatedly on the nose and mouth, and then on the dexter eye. Again and again did Sayers go to it, but Nat jobbed him with severity on the old spot, and at length finished the round by going down, Sayers walking away, his face brightly crimsoned by Nat's handiwork.

5.—Nat, on getting near his man, let go his left with great quick-ness on Tom's nose, completely over his guard. Sayers then went to in-fighting, and got home his left on the side of Nat's know-ledge-box, and, after a slight rally, both went down. A claim of foul was made, that Sayers had hit Nat while down, but it was not allowed, the men being on the ropes when the blow was delivered.

6.—Tom came up grinning, but his mug was in anything but grinning order. Langham, as usual, led off, but Tom jumped away. Tom now feinted, let go his left on Nat's jaw, and then repeated the dose without a return. Some rattling exchanges followed in favour of Sayers, and in the end Langham fell.

7.—Langham attempted to plant his left, but was out of distance. Two more efforts were frustrated by Tom jumping away. Nat was not to be denied; he went in, and some rattling exchanges took place in favour of Sayers, who got home on Nat's cheek and ribs with severity, and received one or two on the kissing organ, from which more pink was drawn, and Langham, in getting back, fell.

8.—Langham dodged his man, and again popped in his left with great quickness over his guard, turning on the tap. Sayers returned slightly on the cheek, and, on trying to improve upon this, was countered heavily on the mouth. This led to some rapid exchanges in favour of Sayers, who got home heavily on the ribs and jaw, and received on the nasal promontory. The round finished by Langham going to the earth weak.

9.—Langham, as usual, led off on Tom's mouth. Sayers returned left and right on the canister and ribs, received another little one on the nose, and then lunged out with his right a tremendous spank on the ribs. Langham retreated, and was followed up by

Tom, who caught him on the mouth with his left, and Langham, after an ineffectual attempt to return, fell.

10.—Langham stepped back, to draw his man, who came for it, and again napped an awkward one on the snout. Sayers tried a return, but was short, and got another smack on the nose for his pains. Counter-hits followed, Nat getting it rather heavily on the left eye, and Tom on the nose. Nat, after placing a little one on the nose, fell on his south pole.

11.—Langham opened the pleadings by another well-delivered spank on the proboscis, from his left, over Tom's guard. Left-handed exchanges followed, but Sayers appeared to hit short. Langham delivered again with severity on the bridge of the nose, when Sayers made a one, two (the left on the side of the head, and his right on the ribs), and Langham got down on the saving suit.

12.—A pause now took place, and some mutual feinting and dodging, it being "bellows to mend" on each side. Langham at length tried his left, which was prettily stopped. Sayers now went in, made his left and right on the nose and ribs, but not heavily. Langham retaliated on the nose, which led to some slight exchanges, and a close, at the end of which both fell, Langham under.

13.—Sayers attempted to take the lead, but was propped heavily on the snuff-box. He, however, got in his right with severity on the ribs, and then his left on Nat's cheek. Nat's returns were rendered abortive by the activity of Tom, who again visited his ribs very heavily with his right, and ¦Langham fell, Tom falling over him.

14.—Langham resumed his lead, and got well on to Tom's damaged nose and mouth. Tom countered him heavily on the cheek and ribs, and Langham fell, Tom on him.

15.—Sayers went to his man, planted his left on the side of Nat's brain-pan. Langham returned on the neck with his right, a round hit, and fell in getting away.

16.—Langham sent in his left, over Tom's guard, upon his nose heavily, and again turned on the main. Good counters followed, Nat on the nose, and Tom on the neck heavily. Exchanges, in which Tom got on to Nat's left cheek, and Langham got down, Sayers falling over him.

17.—Langham was short in two attempts with his left, and a third was stopped, when Sayers dashed out his left, getting heavily home on the ribs. Langham returned with good effect on the nose, and both fell.

18.—Long sparring until Nat let fly his left on the old spot. Tom made his right on the ribs, but again got a nasty crack on the side of his cranium, and Langham got down.

19.—Langham was again short in his lead. Tom was more successful, got home his right on the ribs, and Langham was again down.

20.—Langham tried his left, but Tom jumped well away; in a second attempt Nat got slightly home on the chest, and then on the nose; Sayers countered him on the mouth, and then some exchanges took place, in which Nat hit straightest, Tom's blows appearing to be open-handed. Sayers now went in, but got it heavily on the nose from Nat, who fought on the retreat. Sayers followed him up, got well home on the jaw, and then on the nose and left ogle, knocking Langham off his pins.

21.—Langham's left eye and nose showed the effects of the blow in the last round. Tom immediately led off, got in his left and right on the nose and ribs without a return; then closing, he threw Langham a back fall, and fell heavily on him.

22.—Nat led off, getting well on to Tom's olfactory organ; Tom, nothing daunted, let go his left on the mouth, and Nat, in stepping back, fell.

23.—Sayers now seemed to have the best of it; he was full of confidence; he opened the ball by popping in his left heavily on Nat's kisser. Langham retreated, but was followed by Tom, who again reached the mouth, and avoided Nat's return. Counter-hits now followed, in which Nat reached Tom's scent-bottle, received on the potatoe-trap, and then fell weak. Odds of 5 to 4 on Sayers were now freely offered.

24.—Tom again led off on Nat's left cheek, and Nat retaliated on the nose heavily. Tom retreated, and, on going to it again, popped in his right on Nat's bread-pan. He tried a repetition of this, but napped it severely on the snout for his pains. A pause ensued, at the end of which Tom reached Nat's ribs, and Nat got down in his own corner.

25.—Sayers, first to begin, delivered a little one on Nat's nose, but the blow wanted steam; Nat retreated, and, as Tom followed him, Nat jobbed him on the nozzle, again disturbing the cochineal, and, on receiving a little one on the chin, Nat dropped.

26.—Langham attempted to resume his lead, and was successful; he got home heavily on Tom's left cheek, which led to exchanges in favour of Langham, who repeatedly met Tom on the nose. Tom got in one or two on the ribs and chest, and one on Nat's left peeper, but not heavy. Nat returned on the mazzard, and, in retreating, fell.

27.—Sayers went to his man, but was met with great straightness on the nose, his cork again being drawn. He got in a little one on the ribs in return, and Nat fell, Sayers on him.

28.—Langham, in leading off, misjudged his distance, and was short, the blow falling on Tom's cheek. Tom sent out his left on the nose, but got a very heavy one on his mouth in return. Some heavy exchanges followed, in which Tom got home well on Nat's nose, from the effect of which Nat fell. One hour had now elapsed.

29.—Langham was again short in his lead, and Sayers, after returning on the left cheek, closed and threw his man, falling on him.

30.—Langham's left once more fell short of its destination, when Tom let out his left and caught him on the mouth; Langham returned quickly on the nose, from which once more the ruby trickled. Slight exchanges followed, and Langham fell evidently weak.

31.—Sayers led off, caught Nat a heavy cross hit with his left over the left peeper, inflicting a deep cut and drawing the carmine; he in return had his cork drawn from his snout by Nat's left. Some exchanges followed, in the course of which Tom again opened the cut over Nat's left ogle by a heavy hit from his left, and Nat fell.

32.—Langham's left peeper looked much the worse for wear, but he came gamely up, and as Tom led off he countered him on the nose. Some exchanges followed in favour of Sayers, who got well on Nat's left cheek, and received on the nose. They now got to work in earnest, and some ding-dong fighting took place, as if each thought this the turning-point of the battle. Each got it heavily on the frontispiece, Sayers reopening the cut over Nat's left eye, and receiving one or two awkward reminders on the cheek and nose. A break away followed, and then Langham again went up to his man, who met him on the left eye another heavy spank. Nat returned on the nozzle, and immediately afterwards received another reminder on the sinister peeper, and fell. This was a capital fighting round, and elicited much applause.

33.—Sayers led off, got home slightly on the throat, and received a heavy one from Nat's left on the right cheek. Excellent counter-hits followed, Tom on the cheek and Nat on the right peeper, and Langham then got down.

34.—Long sparring, Langham evidently wanting wind, and Tom not much better. At last Langham went to work, got well on Tom's damaged nose with his left, and stopped Tom's return. Sayers tried again, and succeeded in reaching Nat's throat, when the latter again fell.

35.—Good counter-hits, each receiving on the left eye. A break away and more counter-hitting, Sayers on the left peeper, and Nat well on the nose. Langham now lunged out his right with great force, but luckily for Tom the blow missed its destination, and Langham overreaching himself, fell.

36.—Nat, on coming up, showed his left peeper in deep mourning, and nearly closed; he was evidently very weak, and the friends of Sayers were up in the stirrups. Sayers feinted, and let out his left, which reached the damaged optic, reopening the claret-jug. Langham was very short in his return. Sayers twice got home his left on the throat, and was stopped in the third attempt; he afterwards succeeded in reaching Nat's left cheek, and the latter, after an ineffectual attempt to return, fell.

3

37.—Langham, first up and at it, sent out his left; but Tom jumped quickly away, and, as Nat followed him up, caught him on the left ogle. Langham returned heavily on the forehead and body, and then got down.

38.—Both let fly at the same time, but were out of distance. Sayers then got nearer, and put in a little one on the left eye. Nat retreated, and, on being followed by Tom, who delivered slightly on the mouth, got down weak.

39.—Langham tried to lead off, but was stopped. Sayers attempted to return, but Nat sent out his left very straight on the left eye, and on Sayers again coming in he delivered the same hand on Tom's damaged smeller, which was much swollen, and drew more claret. Tom made his left slightly on the cheek, and Nat got down.

40.—Tom let go his left, got slightly home on the chest, and Nat, after returning with his left on the forehead, again got down.

41.—Langham on coming up appeared to be getting stronger. Sayers tried to take the lead, but Nat jumped quickly away; Sayers followed him up, when Nat met him with a sharp tap on the left eye, and then another left-hander on the cheek. Sayers persevered until he got home his right on Nat's ribs, when the latter fell.

42.—Langham, all alive, led off, caught Tom heavily on the left cheek, and then on Tom's brow. He tried to repeat the visitation, when Tom caught him sharply on the os frontis, just over the right optic, and Nat got down.

43.—Sayers rushed in, but Nat countered him on the left peeper. Sayers got in his right heavily on the bread-basket, and Nat fell.

44.—After a little sparring, they got close together, and some sharp counter-hits were exchanged, Tom getting well on to Nat's damaged left peeper, and receiving on the right cheek. Nat now attempted another delivery, but again overreached himself, and fell.

45.—Sayers let go his left, caught Nat again on the cheek, and the latter, who was again "in queer street," fell, sick.

46.—Sayers was short in two attempts to deliver his left, and Nat, after a short scramble, again eased himself down.

47.—Sayers, whose mug was a good deal swollen, came up determined to do or die. He led off, caught Nat over the left ogle, and this led to some counter-hits, in which Langham got home heavily on Tom's right peeper, which was now pretty nearly closed from the repeated hits on the nose and exposure to the bright rays of the sun. Langham received a little one on the left cheek in return, and fell.

48.—Tom led off, but was countered by Nat on the left eye. In a second attempt Nat stopped him, and then propped him heavily on the nose. Nat succeeded in planting another heavy hit on the left peeper, and Tom fell.

49.—Sayers came up bleeding; his eyes had been artistically

lanced while in the corner to prevent his going blind. He dashed
in, aware that, although much the stronger man on his legs, he must
be in total darkness if he did not finish his man soon. Slight
exchanges took place, Tom getting it on both eyes slightly, and
returning, but without effect, on Langham's mouth, and in the end
got down.

50.—Sayers once more dashed in, but was met by Nat on the left
peeper. Tom returned slightly on the body, and Langham again
went to grass, apparently very weak.

51.—Tom rushed in, delivered his left heavily on the conk, and
then his right on the ribs without a return, and Nat dropped.

52.—Tom again went to work, caught Langham on the side of
his nut; Nat returned on the left peeper, and then slipped down.

53.—Tom led off, got home on Langham's left eye, but the blow
lacked force, and Nat fell, Sayers falling over him.

54.—Sayers stepped in with his left, but was short; he tried it
again, catching Nat on the waistband. Langham attempted a
return, but Sayers jumped away. Langham again lunged out, but,
overreaching himself, fell.

55.—Langham now shook himself together, went up to his man,
led off with his left on the right cheek, and got away. Sayers
followed him up, when some sharp exchanges took place, Nat
reaching Tom's damaged snout, and once more turning on the tap.
Tom returned the compliment on the left ogle, and Langham fell
weak, Tom falling over him not much better off.

56.—It was now clear that Tom's peepers had not many minutes
to remain open, and he therefore at once led off, but was out of
distance; in a second attempt he caught Nat over the left peeper,
but received another hot one on the nose in return. He would
not be shaken off, however; he followed Nat, and let fly his left
on the jaw. Sharp counter-hits followed, Sayers on the mouth
and nose, and Langham on the right ogle, and Langham fell.

57.—Tom at once rushed in, but was stopped. His next effort
reached Nat's mouth, and the latter got down.

58.—Both were nearly pumped out, and it was evident that a
chance hit would finish Langham, while Sayers, if he could not
deliver that hit, must soon "cut it." They let fly simultaneously,
each getting it on the frontispiece. A break away followed, after
which Tom reached Nat's left eye, but not effectively. A close, in
which Tom caught his man with his right as he went down, and
then fell on him.

59.—Langham went to his man, delivered his left heavily on the
nose, and received a little one on the jaw. He then rushed at
Sayers, who stepped back, and Nat, missing his mark, fell.

60.—Tom, all but blind, rushed in open-handed. Nat stepped
on one side, met him as he came on the left peeper and then beside
the nose. Tom persevered, but Langham easily avoided him, and

then propped him on the mouth heavily. Tom continued to bore
in, and delivered a round·hit on the side of the head, when Nat
popped in his left heavily behind the ear, and both fell, Sayers all
abroad.

61 and last.—Tom, on coming up, was very groggy, and his
friends cried out "Take him away;" but he persevered. He lunged
out, but was not within distance. Nat coolly waited for him, and,
as he came again, caught him heavily on the right eye, completely
closing the account on that side. Tom lunged out wildly, and Nat,
stepping back, met him, as he came, with a well-directed left-hander
on the left eye, which knocked him down and put up the last
shutter. Poor Tom was now quite in darkness; Alec Keene, seeing there was no hope for him, threw up the sponge; and Nat
Langham was proclaimed the victor, after a gallant struggle of *two
hours and two minutes.* So delighted was the gallant Nat at his
good fortune, that, although he was previously extremely weak on his
pins, new strength seemed to come upon him, and, after having
shaken hands with his fallen opponent, who shed tears of disappointment, he cleared the ropes at a bound, and throwing his
hands above his head as if waving a cap of victory.

REMARKS.

The length of our account of this gallant struggle entails upon
us the necessity of being brief in our comments. It was, as our
readers will have gathered, a determined, manly struggle for pre-
eminence, in which the adage "Youth will be served" was for once
set at nought. The superior length of Nat Langham bid defiance
to the strength and freshness of Tom Sayers. The repeated visitations received by Nat upon the ribs, where, it will be remembered,
he was so severely punished by Orme, evidently told a tale, and he
was on several occasions reduced thereby to the greatest distress,
which nothing but his unflinching game and perseverance enabled
him to overcome; and, had he not been in first-rate fettle, the result
might have been widely different. Tom Sayers persevered in getting
home upon the place most likely to find out Langham's weak point,
and, although at one time this method of proceeding brought the
palm of victory almost within his grasp, still, as he was compelled
to give his head in order to reach Nat's body, and as that head,
moreover, was in such a state as to be more easily swollen than it
ought to be, the quickness of Nat, and his straight deliveries on the
nose and optics, gradually, but surely, shut out the daylight, and
added one more to the list of his conquests. It is imagined by
some that, had Sayers adopted another system, the "boot might have
been on the other leg." Opinions vary, however. That he *is* a
game, resolute fellow, and took his licking like a man, no one will
deny; and that his conduct throughout the fight was entitled to

all praise the fact that nearly £50 was collected for him in the train on the way home sufficiently testifies. He did his best to win, and we are sure that the untoward result will have no effect in diminishing his friends. It must be recollected that his opponent was a 7 lbs. heavier man, and we are inclined to think that there are few, if any, men in the P. R. at the present day of his own weight who would stand a chance with him. We opine that this will be Langham's last appearance in the P. R., and that his friends will now start him in a business which will prove more profitable to him than his late crib in the town of Cambridge. He could not retire at a better moment. He has the good wishes of all, and we doubt not, if he pursues the upright course in private life that he has invariably displayed in the P. R., he will have nothing to desire in the way of patronage. Everything being brought to a satisfactory conclusion, the travellers harked back to the special, which was in waiting, and, after half an hour's delay, started on their return to the metropolis, which was reached in safety about eight o'clock, all being in high glee at the treat they had experienced, and at the orderly way in which everything had been conducted, thanks to the establishment of the Pugilistic Benevolent Association.

The suggestion contained in the remarks just quoted was promptly acted on, and Nat shortly opened the "Cambrian Stores," in Castle Street, Leicester Square. Here he decorated his lamp with an inscription: "Nat Langham, Champion of the Middle Weights." At this period our hero also had ripened into a publican; for your pugilist is the publican in chrysalis, so sure as the caddis shall become a May-fly in due season. Tom, then, having set up his rest at his favourite locality of Camden Town, at the appropriate sign of the "Bricklayer's Arms," demurred to Nat's inscription. He urged that he was entitled to a new trial, or the title of Champion on his lamp. "Here I am," said he, "ready for all comers, Nat Langham included. He has been beaten by Harry Orme*, who has retired, and I have been beaten

* Harry Orme had retired, and become landlord of the "Jane Shore," Shoreditch, where he still hangs out his sign.

by him. I do not believe myself conquered on my merits, but by inferior condition, and claim the Championship of the Middle Weights." Nat had espoused the niece of Ben Caunt (who also kept a public—the "Coach and Horses"—hard by, in St. Martin's Lane), and, considering himself settled down, did not see why he should risk all by trusting what Captain Godfrey calls, in his sketch of Jack Broughton, "a battle to a waning age." Langham's health, too, was not at this time A 1, and he prudently preferred leaving off a winner, as disposing of such a boxer as Tom Sayers was by no means what betting men would call "a safe thing." He therefore declined Tom's cartel, and told him he might assume the title and style of Middle Weight Champion if he chose, but that he had won it, should wear it, and would not consent to transfer it from the "Cambrian" to the "Bricklayers' Arms." Sayers, having made good his title, was now on the look-out once again for some competitor, on whom he might visit the defeat he had sustained at the hands of the accomplished Nat. But Tom's reputation had become higher, even by his defeat, and in vain, throughout several months, did he "propose:" none of the provincials of 10 st. and upwards would listen to his suit. At length an evening's "chaff" ended in a challenge from George Sims, who offered 25 sovs., all he could raise, if Tom would post £50. Sayers was getting "blue mouldy," and he caught eagerly at the chance to keep his hand in. The day being fixed for the 2nd of February, 1854, the parties and their friends took a trip, per steamer, to Long Reach, below Gravesend, where they soon confronted each other. Sayers's weight on this occasion was 10st. 6lbs., and he looked remarkably well.

Sims, who stood over him, was 5 ft. 10 in., and stated at 10st. 7lbs., but we doubt if it was so little, despite his leanness. Sims was waited upon by Jemmy Welsh and Harry Orme, so that he had talent behind him; Sayers had Jemmy Massey and Bob Fuller as counsel. 7 to 4 and 2 to 1 on Sayers.

THE FIGHT.

Round 1.—Sims, although much taller than Sayers, seemed quite a lath before him, and, as soon as he held up his hands, displayed such extreme awkwardness that it was evidently "sovereigns to passingers" on Sayers, and Dan Dismore immediately offered 4 to 1 on him, which was taken by Jem Burn on the off chance. Sims, after a little unartistic squaring, lunged out awkardly, and caught Tom on the chest with his left. Tom, who was evidently waiting to find out what his adversary could do, returned smartly on the mouth, and in getting back fell on his corybungus.

2.—Tom grinned, dodged his man, and, on the latter wildly sending out his left, countered him on the nozzle heavily. Sims immediately closed, and Tom, seizing him round the neck, pegged away with his right at the ribs and left eye until both fell.

3.—Sims led off, evidently without any settled plan; he caught Tom slightly on the mouth, and the latter again countered him heavily on the nose, deciding the first event in his favour by producing an excellent supply of the best crimson dye. Sims did not like this, and again closed, when Tom fibbed him heavily on the proboscis, drawing more of the ruby, and then on the left eye, and both again fell.

4 and last.—Sims, on coming up looked much flushed; his left ogle winked again as if it saw so many bright stars as to be perfectly dazzled. He attempted to lead off, but was countered with the greatest ease by Tom on the left eye and mouth. He retreated as if bothered, and then went in again, when Tom let go both hands, the left on the smeller, and the right with terrific effect over the left brow, inflicting a deep cut, and drawing a copious supply of the best doubled-distilled. Sims was evidently stunned by the hit; for, as Sayers caught hold of him, he fell back and rolled over him. It was at once perceptible that it was all over: poor Sims lay perfectly insensible and motionless. His seconds did their best to stop the leak in his os frontis, but for some time without effect; and, as for rendering him capable of hearing the call of "Time," that was quite out of the question, and Tom Sayers, to his own astonishment and the disappointment of those who had expected

a rattling mill, was declared the conqueror, after a skirmish of exactly
five minutes. Sayers was so bewildered that he could not make
it out; he evidently did not know he had made so decided a hit,
and displayed considerable anxiety to ascertain the fate of his less
fortunate opponent. A medical gentleman was present, who soon
did the needful for the poor fellow, and in about five minutes more
he was himself again, and was able to walk about. He was quite
dumbfounded as to the result, and expressed a strong wish to be
thrown into the river; but, after some persuasion from his friends,
became more calm, and thought it " better to live to fight another
day."

REMARKS.

A few words are all that are called for in the shape of remarks on
this mill. Sims was from the first overmatched. He is a civil,
well-behaved lad, and may perhaps, a few years hence, arrive at a
higher position in the P. R. than he at present enjoys; but he
must bide his time until his frame becomes more hardy and his
experience more matured. Tom Sayers and his tactics are too well
known to require comment. He on Tuesday did all that was required of him, and left the ring without a scratch. We never saw
him in better fettle; and if he ever had a day on which he was
better than he ever had been before, that day was Tuesday. An
easier job never fell to man's lot; and the best wish that his friends
can express is, that he may never have a worse.

This brief episode left Sayers literally without a chance
of continuing the main story of his battles, of which this
could hardly be reckoned more than " un affaire," as
French *militaires* would call it. Tom looked round and
round, he sparred, and challenged, and travelled, but he
was not fancied as a customer by either Londoners or
provincials. He was too good a horse, and handicapping
him was not so easy. There was much " talkee,
talkee" about a match between himself and Tom Paddock, then claiming the championship, and a proposal for
Paddock to stake £200 to Tom Sayers's £100, Paddock
weighing 12st. 8lbs. to Tom's 10st. 8lbs., or there-
abouts. It came to nothing, however; and Tom, in
despair, announced his intention of going to Australia.

Harry Poulson, of Nottingham, whose three tremendous battles with Paddock, in the first of which he was victorious, though defeated in the second and third encounters, had raised his fame deservedly, was now talked of, and Tom was induced to match himself against him. Here, again, Sayers was giving away "lumps of weight;" for Poulson, though an inch shorter than Sayers (namely, 5 ft. 7½ in.), was a perfect Hercules in the torso, weighing 12st. 7lbs. in hard condition. He had thrashed in provincial battles all comers, and was known as one of the coolest, most determined, and game fellows that ever pulled off a shirt. True he had come into the London ring rather late in life, having been born in 1817, but his endurance and strength were considered an overmatch for Sayers. So, too, thought Jem Burn, a staunch friend of Poulson, and he proposed to stake £50 on his behalf. Sayers accepted it, and Bendigo, who was Poulson's friend and adviser, snapped at what he declared to be "a gift" for his townsman Harry.

Many of Tom's friends were displeased with the match, which they considered presumptuous on his part, and declared that he was completely overmatched, as it was known Poulson could not fight under 12st., and Sayers to be well ought to be more than a stone under that amount. At first he had some difficulty in finding supporters, but that was happily got over by the influence of one of the staunchest Corinthian fanciers of modern times. After he was matched, Sayers remained longer in town than was prudent, and, as a natural consequence, was too much hurried in his preparations. He was not quite a month at country quarters, and on arriving in London looked fleshy, and had evidently done insufficient work. Had

he been about five pounds lighter he would have been all
the better. He was, nevertheless, extremely sanguine of
success, and assured his backers that he would fully
justify the confidence they had placed in him. He was
at Nat Langham's, the "Cambrian," on Monday evening,
and was surrounded by an extensive circle of the upper
crust supporters of the P. R. His weight was about
10st. 12lb. or 13lb.

Poulson, after his last defeat by Paddock, had remained
at Nottingham, where he followed his laborious occupa-
tion as a navvy until informed of the proposed match,
in which, as already stated, he was taken in hand by Jem
Burn. That facetious worthy determined that no pains
should be spared, summoned Bendigo to his assistance,
and under the able tutelage of that eccentric but pains-
taking ex-champion did Harry get himself into very first-
rate trim. Every muscle in his powerful frame was beautifully developed, and there did not seem to be an ounce
of superfluous meat in any place. As the men were not
tied to weight, no scaling took place at the last moment
on which dependence could be placed. He was certainly
not less than 12 st., and might have been a pound or so
more. His height 5ft. 7¼in., and in figure and general
appearance, although shorter and thicker set, marvellously
like "the renowned" Bendigo. On the Monday before
the battle Poulson took up his quarters under the hos-
pitable roof of "My Nevy," at the "Rising Sun," where
he was greeted by an admiring circle, including many
patricians. He retired to his "flea pasture" at an early
hour; but the eccentric Bendy kept the company at the
"Rising Sun" in a perpetual grin until the approach of
the small hours reminded him that he too had work to do

early in the morning, upon which he at once retired to
roost, as did the host himself, who, although suffering
from gout, had made up his mind to be present. The
betting, at both Jem's and Nat's, varied between 6 and 7
to 4 on Poulson—odds which the superior strength,
weight, and condition of the countryman fully justified.
The betting was tolerably brisk, but there were more
layers of odds than takers.

By six o'clock in the morning all the fancy were astir,
and great was the difficulty in getting cabs. A hard
frost had set in, and most of the vehicles were detained
at home to get the horses " roughed." Several, owing to
this unforeseen occurrence, were unable to catch the
train at eight o'clock; and, had it not been for the oppor-
tune arrival of the drag of an old friend, Sayers would in
all probability have been left behind. As it was, he cut
it so fine that he only arrived as the station-doors were
closed. The journey down was performed by eleven
o'clock, and within half an hour the ring was ready at
Appledore. The men lost no time in entering its precincts, Poulson attended by Bob Fuller and Bendigo, and
Sayers receiving the friendly assistance of Nat Langham
and Jemmy Massey. Umpires and a referee were soon
appointed, and at six minutes to twelve the men toed the
scratch. The betting now was tolerably brisk at 7 to 4
on Poulson — odds which at one period of the fight
advanced to 3 to 1, which was laid by Tom Paddock,
whose confidence in his old opponent's tried game
and resolution tempted him to overstep the bounds of
prudence in his investments.

THE FIGHT.

Round 1.—The disparity in weight was very perceptible, as was also the superior condition of Poulson. Sayers, however, had the advantage in height and length. Poulson threw himself into the old-fashioned attitude, with both hands held somewhat high, and planted firmly on both pins. Sayers, on the contrary, assumed an elegant position, resting most upon his left foot, his right arm across the mark, and the left well down. He fiddled a little, until Poulson went in and let go his left and right. The former was stopped; but with the latter he got home on Tom's nut. A sharp rally instantly took place, which brought them to close quarters, in which Sayers fibbed his man very cleverly, catching him heavily on the conk, and in the end both were down, Poulson under.

2.—Both were flushed from the rapid in-fighting in the last round, which had evidently been severe. Poulson tried to lead off, but was too slow for his active opponent. He persevered, and at last got home with his right over Tom's left ear. This led to more heavy exchanges and a close, in which Poulson caught Sayers round the neck. Sayers hit up, but without doing any damage, and in the end was down, Poulson on him.

3.—Sayers came up smiling, but cautious. He fiddled his man until he got within distance, when he lunged out his left on the right brow, but too high for mischief. Poulson returned heavily on the ribs with his right, when Tom retreated. Poulson followed him again, let go his left and right, was beautifully countered, but again too high and on the side of the nut, and Poulson slipped down.

4.—Sayers feinted and let go his left on the nose, but not heavily. Poulson was wild and missed his return, whereupon Sayers put in his left very neatly on the right cheek. Poulson now went in ding-dong, but his blows wanted precision. He got close, when Sayers caught him on the right peeper and the right lug, from each of which there was a tinge of blood. Tom then closed and then threw his man, very neatly falling on him. "First blood" for Sayers.

5.—Sayers again feinted to draw his man, who came in, and Sayers sent his left over his shoulder. Poulson then closed, threw, and fell on him.

6.—Tom, after one or two feints and dodges, again let fly his left, but was well stopped. Poulson, however, missed his return with the right at the body. He now rushed in determined, and some tremendous punching, left and right, ensued, in which Sayers was straighter and oftener, but Poulson heavier with his right, which paid some heavy visits to Tom's nut.

7.—Sayers again feinted and succeeded in drawing his man, who let go both hands, but out of distance. Sayers with quickness returned on the forehead, but was too high. Heavy counter-hits followed to a close, in which the fibbing was severe, Sayers receiving on the left side of his head and returning on the mouth.

8.—Both, much flushed on the dial, came up laughing. Poulson lunged out his right, catching Tom heavily on the ribs and then on the cheek. Tom instantly closed, and, after a sharp struggle, in which it was thought Poulson had the best of it, Sayers cleverly back-heeled him, throwing him heavily and falling on him.

9.—Poulson tried again to deliver his right on the ribs, but Sayers was well away. Harry rushed after him, slinging out both hands, when Tom ducked and escaped. Poulson persevered, and at last caught him with his right on the ribs, when some more severe in-fighting in favour of Poulson took place. In the end both were down.

10.—On coming up Tom's nose showed that Harry had been there in the last round; his ribs, also, were unmistakably bruised. He feinted to draw his adversary, and let go his left, which was stopped, and Poulson returned on the ribs. Sayers, with great quickness, countered him as he delivered this blow, and sent him to grass by a sharp left-hander on the right temple. "First knock-down blow" for Sayers.

11.—Poulson came up slow, as if posed by the blow in the last round. Sayers dodged with his left, and popped it over Harry's right peeper, getting quickly away from the return. Poulson followed him up, but missed his right; he persevered until they got to close quarters, when Sayers again knocked him down by a heavy right-hander on the jaw. (Loud cheers for Sayers, the Poulsonians looking blue.)

12.—Tom came up, smiling and all alive, dodged, and put in his left very straight on Harry's nasal promontory. Poulson instantly rushed in, but napped it on the right side of his nut and slipped down.

13.—Poulson, who had been called on to fight with his left, waited for Sayers, and, on the latter coming near, caught him heavily with that hand on the proboscis, staggering him. Tom soon came again, and retaliated by a heavy delivery on the mouth with his left. After some mutual sparring, Harry was short with his left, and Tom countered him with the right on the left peeper, and then with the left bang on the olfactory organ. Some sharp exchanges ensued, in which Poulson drew the ruby from Tom's snout, and Tom slipped down.

14.—Both got quickly to work. No stopping; and, after one or two harmless cracks, Sayers got down.

15.—Poulson again attempted to fight with his left; but Sayers was too quick for him, and nailed him on the right cheek. Harry tried it again, but was stopped; and Sayers then let drive with his left on the smelling-bottle very heavily; he retreated, feinted, and, by putting the double on, succeeded in delivering another smack on the same organ. Some very heavy exchanges followed, in which Sayers got home on the right eye and Harry on the sneezer; Sayers slipped down.

16.—Tom came up filtering the juice from his beak. Poulson tried to plant his favourite right, but was stopped. He then tried his left, but was out of distance. After several more wild efforts, Sayers caught him with his left heavily on the right cheek; and retreated. Poulson followed him to the corner and let go his left and right, whon Sayers countered him on the cheek. Poulson retaliated on the mouth very heavily, and Tom slipped down.

17.—Tom was now bleeding from the mouth and nose. He was as steady as ever, and planted his left on the side of the head. This led to some sharp in-fighting, without material damage, and in the end Sayers slipped down, tired.

18.—Poulson bored in, let go his left, which was stopped, and Sayers was out of distance with his return. The same thing was repeated on both sides; but, on their getting closer, some good counter-hits were exchanged, Poulson getting it on the jaw and Tom on the damaged nose. Tom retreated, followed by Harry, who let go both hands, but was prettily popped on the nozzle. Some more sharp exchanges followed, Tom getting it heavily on the left eye, and in the end Tom was down.

19.—Tom's left peeper showed signs of closing. Poulson, seeing this, bored in, but was propped on the forehead and cheek. He persevered, when Tom succeeded in planting a very straight nose-ender, which removed the bark from Harry's proboscis. The force of his own blow staggered Tom, who slipped down.

20.—The gnomon of Harry's dial was by no means set straight by these visitations. He tried his dangerous right at the body, but missed. Sayers nailed him again on the snout, and got down.

21.—Tom again put in his favourite double on Harry's os frontis and nose, and, on receiving Poulson's right on the ribs, fell.

22.—Harry, in his usual style, lunged out his right at the body, but was short; Tom returning on the right peeper, and getting cleverly away. Poulson followed him up, and, after innocuous exchanges, Sayers went down.

23.—Poulson again led off, but was propped neatly on the forehead and nose. This led to sharp counter-hitting in favour of Poulson, and Sayers was again down.

24.—Tom tried his double and got home, his left on the portal bone, to the detriment of his knuckles, but again too high to be effective. Poulson pegged away at the ribs and the side of his head very heavily, the latter blow knocking Tom off his pins.

25.—Tom seemed much fatigued; he nevertheless led off, but without effect. Poulson tried to return, when Tom met him on the nose with his left, and then on the forehead. Poulson once more reached Tom's nose with his right, and Tom was down.

26.—Harry tried his left, and succeeded in reaching Tom's right peeper, but not heavily. Tom returned on the forehead, and then delivered his left on the snout. He retreated to draw his man, and as he came caught him a tremendous spank on the potatoe-trap with his right, but in retreating caught his foot against the stake and fell.

27.—Harry's mouth much swollen from the hit in the last round. He rushed in, when Tom caught him on the nasal organ heavily with his left, and got away. Poulson now tried his left, but was short; and Sayers caught him once more on the lips, renewing the supply of carmine. Poulson rushed after him, and Tom in getting away again caught against the stake and fell heavily.

28.—Tom, smiling, dodged and popped in his left on the mouth, and then on the nose with great quickness, drawing more gravy. Poulson rushed after him, but missed his right; some slogging punches followed on both sides to a close, in which both fell, Sayers under.

29.—They immediately closed, and, after some sharp fibbing, in which Sayers was the quicker and straighter, both were again down. One hour had now elapsed.

30.—Tom led off, and again reached Harry's nose. It was a long shot, and not heavy. Poulson missed his return, whereupon Sayers planted his left twice in succession on the nose, and, after receiving a little one on the chest, slipped down.

31.—Poulson led off with his left, but was stopped, and Sayers was short in his return. Harry then missed his right on the ribs, and napped a hot one on the kisser from Tom's left. This visitation Tom repeated, and then got on Harry's nose. Harry rushed at him, and Tom slipped down, the ground being in a dreadful state.

32.—Sayers feinted and again got well on the mug and nose with his left, and Harry was short with his return. Tom drew him, and as he came got home on the right eye. Harry now reached his left cheek heavily, and Tom got down.

33.—Tom planted his left slightly on the dexter ogle, and then in the mazzard, getting cleverly away from the return. Poulson followed him up and delivered another terrific smack with his right on the nose, drawing a fresh supply of the sap. A close followed, in which Tom slipped down, bleeding from his proboscis.

34.—Poulson tried both mawleys, but was short. He then rushed in again, missed, and Tom, in getting back, fell. He was evidently weak, and it was now that Paddock laid 3 to 1, thinking, no doubt, that Poulson, who from his fine condition showed scarcely a mark, would tire him out.

35.—Poulson went to work, missed his left, but caught Tom with his right on the larboard cheek, which was much swollen, and in the close which followed Tom was down.

36.—Tom led off with his left on the nose, but not heavily. Harry returned on the nose and the side of his head, and Tom slipped down.

37.—Harry let go, and planted his right on the nose. Exchanges followed in favour of Poulson, and Sayers got down.

38.—Tom collected himself, waited for his man, and nailed him twice in succession on the right eye. Slight exchanges followed, and they fell opposite to one another on their knees, the ground being more slippery than ever, and their spikes almost useless.

39.—Tom dodged, put in his left and right on Harry's optics ; the latter then went to work, and some heavy exchanges ensued in favour of Poulson, who nailed Tom with effect on the left eye, and Tom fell. His left eye was nearly closed.

40.—Tom still took the lead, caught Harry on the snuff-box heavily, and in retreating slipped down.

41.—Tom busy with the left on the right eye, and then on the mouth. Poulson returned heavily on the left goggle, and then bored Tom down through the ropes, his left daylight being quite extinguished.

42.—Sayers tried his left on the mouth, but was stopped, and Poulson dashed in, nailed him with the right on the mouth, closed, and fibbed him until Tom was down.

43.—Tom, although evidently tired, came up smiling, feinted, and let go his left on the right cheek. Poulson dashed in, when Tom met him heavily over the left eyebrow. Poulson still followed him as he retreated, and Tom nailed him on the nose. In the end Tom got down in his corner.

44.—Tom "put his double on,".but it wanted steam. Poulson then bored in, closed at the ropes, and, after a short struggle, both were down.

45.—On getting close, some heavy counter-hitting took place, Tom getting on to the right peeper, and Poulson on the mouth, renewing the supply of crimson. Tom retreated, came again and caught his man on the temple, and then on the mouth. Poulson returned on the latter organ and ribs with his right.

46.—The left side of Tom's nut was much swollen, and his nose all shapes but the right. He came up undaunted, let go his left well on the right ogle, which at last began to show signs of a shut-up. Tom retreated, followed by Poulson, and, as the latter let go his right, Tom countered him bang on the right eye. Poulson returned slightly on the nose.

47.—Sayers once more tried his double with effect, and got on the right eye. Poulson rushed after him, when Tom slipped down in rather a questionable manner, but there was no appeal.

48.—Tom crept in and popped his left on the nose. A close followed, in which Tom got down on the saving suit.

49.—Poulson tried to take the lead, but was too slow for the nimble Tom, who got quickly away. Harry persevered, and got well on the ribs twice in succession very heavily.

50.—Tom evidently felt the effects of the visitations to the ribs ; for his left arm evidently did not come up with the same freedom as before. Poulson went in, delivered another rib-bender, and Tom got down.

51.—Harry tried to improve his advantage; but Sayers propped him beautifully on the nose, received another little one on the ribs, and dropped.

52.—Poulson once more swung out his right; but Tom got away, and, as Harry followed, planted his left on the smeller. Poulson then bored him down, and, falling himself, carefully avoided dropping on Sayers by placing a knee on each side of him. This manly forbearance on the part of Poulson elicited loud applause on all sides, the more particularly as it was not the first time during the fight.

53.—Poulson again let go his left and right, but Tom was away, planting his left on the jaw as Harry came after him. Poulson succeeded in delivering his right slightly on the cheek, and Sayers got down.

54.—Poulson led off left and right, but was stopped, and he, in turn, stopped Tom's attempted deliveries. Tom then made his left on the throat and mouth by one of his clever doubles, and, after napping a little one on the proboscis, dropped.

55.—Poulson popped his right on Tom's damaged peeper, and then on the jaw very heavily. Heavy exchanges followed, each getting it on the side of the cranium, and in the end Sayers was down.

56.—Tom feinted, put his double on the mouth and throat, and, as Poulson followed him up, he took advantage of a slight hit to go down.

57.—Poulson dashed his right on the left cheek, and Tom was again down, evidently requiring rest.

58.—Harry got well on to Tom's conk with his right, and then with his left, and Tom dropped.

59.—Harry again led off, but the blow was of no effect; he followed it by another on the nose, and a third on the side of the head, and Tom went to earth.

60.—Harry made his left and right, but they were very slight, and Tom got down.

61.—Sayers was now recovering his wind, and, waiting for his man, countered him very straight on the right eyebrow as he came in, inflicting a cut, and drawing the carmine. Exchanges in favour of Sayers followed, who again caught his man over the right peeper, and, in the end, Tom got down, the Poulson party asking why he did not stand up, and claiming a foul, which was not allowed, there being no ground for it.

4

62.—Tom led off, but missed, and napped a heavy smack on the whistler from Poulson's left. On getting close, a tremendous counter-hit with the right was exchanged, Sayers getting it on the jaw, and Poulson on the right eye, each knocking his adversary down.

63.—Both slow to time, the counter in the last round having been a shaker for each. Poulson was bleeding from the right ogle, and Tom from the mouth. Tom again got on to Harry's right eye, and, on getting a little one on the mouth, once more fell.

64.—Tom, again very weak and tired, waited for his man, caught him slightly on the left cheek, and slipped down. Another claim that he went down without a blow disallowed, the ground being very bad; the referee, however, cautioned him to be careful.

65.—Tom tried his left, which was easily stopped, and Poulson nailed him on the mouth. A close and fibbing followed, when Tom, having all the worst of this game, got down.

66.—Poulson led off with his right, which was stopped, and Sayers missed his return; Poulson then caught him a little one with his right on the side of his nut, and Tom, glad of the excuse, got down.

67.—Harry tried his left, and succeeded in reaching Tom's right cheek. Heavy counter-hits followed, Poulson on the nose, and Tom on the left cheek; and Tom, in turning, after getting another crack on the side of his occiput, dropped.

68.—Poulson dashed out his left, but Sayers got cleverly away. He tried it again with the same result, and, on making a third essay, Tom countered him well off on the right ogle. He then made his left twice on the left eye, and, as Poulson rushed at him, got down. Two hours had now passed, and the punishment was pretty equally divided. Poulson's right eye, like Tom's left, was completely closed, and each of their noses was much out of shape. The right side of Tom's face was unscathed, but his ribs bore heavy marks of punishment. Poulson had a mouse under his left eye, but was much stronger on his legs than Sayers, and it was still thought he must wear him out. Many also imagined that, as Tom was getting slower, Poulson would knock him out of time with his dangerous right.

69.—Tom tried to lead off with his left, but was stopped twice in succession, and Poulson nailed him on the snorer. Tom returned the compliment by a tidy smack with his right on the mouth, drawing more of the cochineal; slight exchanges followed, and Sayers got down.

70.—Tom's left was again stopped, and Harry was short in his return. Tom then feinted and popped his double on the nose and right cheek, which he cut slightly.

71.—Poulson let go his left, but did not get home. On Sayers attempting to return, Harry popped him on the nose, and Tom got down.

72.—Poulson's left was stopped easily; he then tried a one, two, and reached Tom's mouth with his right; the left, however, did not reach its destination (the unscathed side of Tom's phisog). In the end Tom got down.

73.—Sayers stopped Poulson's one, two, and then got home on the right eye. Poulson returned on the chin. Some rapid exchanges followed, Tom making both hands on the mouth and left cheek, and Poulson getting on the nose. Poulson closed, when Tom caught him heavily on the mouth, and Poulson got down.

74.—Tom put in a well-delivered left-hander on the blind peeper. Slight exchanges followed, and Tom got down.

75.—Tom getting more lively every round, and Poulson's head at last beginning to swell. Tom let go his left on the throat; good counter-hits followed, Poulson on the mouth, and Tom on the side of the head. Poulson then dashed in with his right on the ribs, leaving marks of his knuckles. Tom retaliated on the right eye, and a determined rally followed, in which each got heavy pepper; but Sayers was straighter in his deliveries. In the end he was down. The Poulson party began now to look serious; their man was gradually going blind of both eyes, and Sayers appeared to be no weaker than he was an hour ago, added to which, he had still a good eye.

76.—Both came up piping from the effects of the last round. Poulson tried his left twice, but Sayers got away, and, as Harry came after him, met him well on the mouth, and then on the right eye, and in the end both fell side by side.

77.—Sayers came up smiling as well as his distorted mug would allow; he dodged, and then got well over Poulson's guard on to his left eye. Harry instantly returned on the chin, when Tom once more popped his left on the mouth heavily, and got away. He played round his man, and at last sent home another left-hander on the left eye—a cross hit. Poulson just reached his jaw with his right, and Tom got down.

78.—Tom made play with his left on the right ogle, and avoided the return. Poulson persevered, and at last Tom got down in his corner.

79.—Poulson dashed in his right on the nose, but not very heavily; Sayers returned on the right gazer, and napped a heavy right-hander on the cheek, from the effect of which he went down very weak.

80.—Tom steadied himself, crept close, and popped his left on the left eye. Poulson rushed at him, and heavy counter-hits were exchanged on the jaw, both coming to the ground side by side.

81.—Tom missed two attempts to deliver, and received another heavy thwack on the bread-basket. Heavy exchanges ensued in favour of Poulson, who was always best at close quarters, and Sayers got down.

82.—Tom came up a little stronger, and let go his left, but not heavily, on the right cheek. Poulson tried a return, but Tom, who gradually retreated, propped him, as he came in, on the right eye and nose. Poulson, determined, if possible, to make a decided turn in his favour, persevered, and some rattling ding-dong fighting took place, each getting it heavily on the dial, and in the end both were down.

83.—Both looked all the worse for the last round, but Poulson's left eye was fast following suit with his right, and it was evident to all that if Sayers kept away it was a mere question of time. Sayers feinted, put in his double very neatly on the mouth, and then got a hot one on the left cheek. Good exchanges at close quarters followed, in which Poulson's visitations to Tom's snout were anything but agreeable, while Tom was busy on the right eye. This was another ding-dong round, and astonished every one after the men had fought so long. In the end Sayers got down, and Poulson fell on his knees at his side.

84.—Tom's double was once more successful, and he got well on Harry's smeller. Poulson once more reached the left side of the nut, just by the ear, and Tom fell.

85.—Poulson led off with his left, getting well on Tom's nose. Good counter-hits followed, Tom getting it on the mouth and Harry on the left eye. Poulson now dashed in, but got one on the right eye; he, however, nailed Tom on the right ear, drawing claret. Another desperate rally followed, in which Jack was as good as his master, and in the end Sayers got down. Two hours and thirty minutes had now elapsed.

86.—Poulson dashed in, but Sayers stepped nimbly back, popping him as he came on the left eye. Harry at last made his right on the left ear, and Tom got down.

87.—Poulson again rushed in, but Sayers, after propping him over the right eye, dropped. Another claim of foul not allowed.

88.—Tom tried his left, but was short; Poulson then rattled in, caught him on the left side of his knowledge-box, and Tom dropped.

89.—Poulson, after being short with his one, two, made his right on the ribs, and Tom fell.

90.—Poulson again hit out of distance; he persevered, and eventually nailed Tom slightly on the nozzle, and that hero wisely got down, by way of a rest, finding that Harry was still dangerous at close quarters.

91.—Tom stopped Harry with great neatness, and then planted his left on the throat; heavy exchanges followed in favour of Poulson, who again reached Tom's left ear very severely, drawing more of the Burgundy, and Tom fell very weak.

92.—Tom, who staggered up, received a heavy one from Harry's right on the brow, and got down.

93.—Neither very ready at the call of "Time," but Tom slowest; he nevertheless came up steady, and, as Poulson rushed in, planted his left very heavily, first on the right eye and then on the nose, and got away, followed by Poulson, who forced the fighting. Heavy exchanges followed, Harry on the ribs and Tom on the forehead, and Tom down.

94.—Poulson for the first time got on to Tom's right eye, but not heavily; he then popped his right on the ear, and also on the ribs very heavily, staggering Tom, who evidently winced under the latter visitation. Tom, however, shook himself together, and some sharp exchanges took place, which ended in Sayers dropping to avoid a fall.

95.—Poulson's right neatly stopped. He tried again with a rush, but Tom cleverly ducked and got away. Poulson followed him up, and napped a sharp reminder over the right brow; Poulson returned on the chest, and Tom got down.

96.—After some harmless exchanges, Sayers got down, amidst the groans of the Nottingham party.

97.—Poulson was again neatly stopped, and Tom returned heavily on the mouth, turning on the main once more. Poulson made his right on the ribs, and then on the left cheek, and, after one or two harmless passes, Tom got down.

98.—Sayers put in his double on the throat, and Poulson rushed to a close, and, after a brief struggle, Sayers fell; Poulson again, in the most manly way, avoiding falling on him.

99.—Tom, evidently the best man, dodged, and put in his left on the side of Poulson's head; Harry wide of the mark with his return. Tom came again, dodged him, and whack went his left on the smelling-bottle. Slight exchanges followed, and then Poulson, as Sayers was retreating, caught him a heavy right-hander on the jaw, which knocked him down.

100.—The Poulsonians anxious for the call of "Time;" but, to their surprise, Tom came up quite steady. He dodged his man, popped in his double on the nose and left peeper, without a return, and then on the throat, and, in getting back, fell.

101.—Poulson, nearly blind, dashed in with determination, and heavy counter-hits were exchanged, Tom getting well on the mouth and Harry on the nose; and Sayers slipped down. Three hours had now elapsed.

102.—Sayers drew a fresh supply of the ruby from Harry's right cheek, and, in retreating, fell. Another claim of foul.

103.—Poulson went in and made his right on the side of Tom's head. Tom retreated, advanced, making his usual feint; but, on seeing Poulson coming at him, he tried to get back, and, his legs slipping apart, he could not get himself into a defensive position, and fell. Another claim of foul was here made; but the referee, who had not seen the round, owing to the interposition of the bodies of the seconds and backers of Poulson, pronounced fair; and in his decision we decidedly concur, as, in our opinion, the fall on the part of Sayers was entirely unpremeditated and accidental. It was some time before order was restored; and the delay was of the greatest advantage to Sayers, while it had an opposite effect on Poulson, whose left eye was now all but closed.

104.—Tom came up gaily, dodged his man, who came towards him, and then nailed him heavily on the proboscis and left peeper. A close followed, and Sayers got down.

105.—Slight exchanges, in which no damage was done, and Sayers slipped down.

106.—Poulson dashed in to make a last effort, and heavy counter-hits were exchanged. Sayers caught him on the left eye, and received a heavy rib-bender and then a crack on the left ear, where-upon he dropped.

107.—Sayers, bleeding from the left ear, came up slowly and feinted in his usual style; caught Harry on the right eye, and then on the mark. Poulson popped his right heavily on the ribs, and another give-and-take rally followed, at the end of which Sayers, who was still weak on his legs, got down.

108.—Poulson's face was now much swollen, and there was scarcely a glimmer from his left peeper. He was, however, still strong as ever on his pins. He rushed in, knowing he had no time to spare, and caught Tom heavily with his right on the left ear. Exchanges followed, Sayers being straightest. Poulson bored in, and got home heavily with his right on the ribs, when Tom delivered his left heavily on the jaw, and knocked him down.

109, and last.—The last blow had evidently been a settler for the gallant Poulson: he came up slowly and all abroad. The game fellow tried once more to effect a lodgment, but missed, his head came forward, and Tom delivered the *coup de grace* by a heavy right-hander on the jaw, which again knocked the veteran off his legs, and, on being taken up, he was found to be deaf to the call of "Time." He recovered in a few minutes, and shed bitter tears of dis-appointment at the unsatisfactory and unexpected termination of his labours. Sayers walked to a public-house adjoining the field of battle, and of course was vociferously congratulated by his friends and admirers upon his triumphant success. Poulson was also con-veyed to the public-house, and, after taking some refreshment, be-came himself. He was quite blind, and his mug otherwise much battered, but beyond this had sustained no injuries whatever. Sayers complained a good deal of the punishment about his body, and the repeated visitations to the side of his head, but of course the fact of his being the winner went far to allay the physical suffer-ing he endured. Both were enabled to return to town in the same train with their friends, and arrived at their respective houses about half-past nine o'clock. The fight lasted three hours and eight minutes.

REMARKS.

Owing to the minute details which we have given of all the material incidents in this really extraordinary battle, we may spare our readers the trouble of reading many observations upon the respective merits of the men, of which the account of the different rounds will have enabled them to form as correct an opinion as ourselves. Tom Sayers, by his quickness on his legs, his steadiness and excellent judgment, not only astonished his adversary and his backers, but completely took his own friends by surprise. He has evidently much improved, in every possible way, since his defeat by Nat Langham, and is destined ere long to prove a teaser to yet another of the great guns of the day. Great fault was found with him for his too constant resort to the dropping system; but for this he has every excuse: he scarcely ever went down without having had a bustling round, and once only during the battle did we observe anything at which an impartial man would cavil. This was at a period in the middle of the fight when he was extremely weak, and at the time no appeal was made by the friends of Poulson. It must be taken into consideration that Tom was anything but himself, and the ground was far from favourable for keeping on his legs and getting out of the reach of his powerful adversary. It has been urged that the ground was as much against Poulson as Sayers; but this was hardly so. Poulson is a steady, ding-dong fighter, of the squarest build, who does not depend much on his defensive tactics, and makes little use of his legs; while Tom had to be continually jumping back, and, when opposed to such superior weight, would of course find proportionate difficulty in keeping on his pins: indeed, many times when he fell he came to the ground with such a "thud" as must have shaken a good deal of his strength out of him. We are aware that since the present match has been made many things have occurred to harass Tom's mind, and that he had difficulties to contend with which, we trust, will not exist in future matches; and this, again, must be taken into consideration. He does not want for friends, and, we doubt not, with steadiness and good conduct, he may now easily find himself on the high road to prosperity. Of Harry Poulson's gallantry and manliness we cannot say too much. He fought from first to last in a game, straightforward manner, with an evident determination to do his best to win in a fair and honourable way. He scorned to take advantage of many opportunities of falling heavily on his man, when he might have done so with perfect fairness, and otherwise comported himself in a manner that reflects the very highest credit upon his character as a man and a demonstrator of the noble art of self-defence. Although evidently annoyed at being unable to get home as he expected, he still never allowed his temper to get the better of him; and often when Tom, from his shifty tactics, evaded what had been intended

as a finisher, he stood and shook his head at him, as much as to
say it was too bad, but not once did he allow a harsh or angry
expression to escape him.   He is truly one of the gamest of the
game; but he is too slow, and depends too much on his right hand,
to have much chance of success against a really finished boxer.   We
do not consider that his age had anything to do with his defeat, for
he is as fresh as most London boxers who are ten years his juniors.
His bravery and universal good conduct cannot but secure him the
respect and support of all admirers of such good qualities.

The conquest of Poulson was unquestionably the
greatest achievement of Sayers's pugilistic career.   He
was now established as a man with whom the men under
12st. on the boxing list must not meddle; at any rate,
none other were likely to get backers against him.

From this period the name of Tom Sayers mixes itself
with every question of the belt and the Championship.

In the year 1853 a proposition was set on foot by a
number of patrons of the ring, to raise, by subscription,
a sum of money to purchase a belt of greater intrinsic
value than anything of the kind previously presented, in
lieu of the belt which had "gone astray" during the
squabbles between Bendigo, Caunt, and the Tipton
Slasher.   Lists were opened, and before long a sum of
nearly £100 was collected.   To Mr. Hancock, of New
Bond Street, was intrusted the manufacture of the
trophy, and from that gentleman's establishment was
produced the elegant badge of the highest fistic honours
which Tom Sayers so well and so worthily won.   On the
belt being ordered, the committee who undertook its
management issued the following as the conditions on
which it should be held:—"That it should not be handed
over to any person claiming the Championship until he
had proved his right to it by a fight; that any pugilist
having held it against all comers for three years, without

a defeat, should become its absolute possessor; that the holder should be bound to meet every challenger of every weight who should challenge him for the sum of £200 a side, within six months after the issue of such challenge, within the three years; that he should not be bound to fight for less than £200 a side; that at the final deposit for every match within the three years the belt should be delivered up to the committee until after the battle; and, finally, that on the belt being given to the winner of any Champion-fight, he should deposit such security as should be deemed necessary, in the hands of the committee, to ensure the above regulations being carried out."

No sooner did it become known that the belt was ready for whosoever could win it, than there was a general stirring up of the decaying energies of the big men who had retired, or were thought to be about to retire, from the ring. Harry Broome shook himself together; the Tipton Slasher roused him from his lair; Tom Paddock's hair stood on end between hope and fear of disappointment; while Aaron Jones, who about this time (1855) had fought the second of two tremendous battles with Paddock, and, though defeated, had entirely removed any impressions as to his want of pluck caused by his battles with Harry Orme, also pricked up his ears, and issued a sort of defiant grunt. The only man among the recent combatants for Champion's honours who made no sign was Harry Orme, who was content to rest upon his well-earned reputation. At first it was thought there would not be found one man sufficiently venturous to tackle the "Ould Tipton," but this was soon seen to be a fallacy; for not one only, but each and every of the aspirants sent out a defiance to the crooked-legged hero of the hardware districts. The first cartel that reached him was that of Aaron Jones, and with him preliminaries were at once arranged.

The challenges of Broome and Paddock arriving afterwards, the Slasher informed them that they must wait the issue of the struggle with Jones. Broome and Paddock seemed both disinclined to wait for this event, and neither was desirous of postponing his claims to those of his co-challenger, and, as a natural consequence, a good deal of badinage took place between them, which ended in their being matched for £200 a side, to ascertain which should have the preference. While they were in training Aaron Jones was compelled to forfeit to the Tipton Slasher, through meeting with an accident during his training; so that there appeared a clear course for the winner.

The fight between Broome and Paddock took place on the 19th May, 1856, and was won by Tom Paddock with ease in 51 rounds, and 68 minutes; it being at once apparent that, though Harry Broome had all the will and the courage to do deeds of valour, the power had deserted him, and he had become prematurely old and stale.

Soon after Paddock's defeat of Broome, he obtained the acme of his desires; viz., a match with his old opponent, the Slasher; but when £80 a side had been staked Master Tom allowed his temper to get the better of his judgment, and, having offended his best friends, had to forfeit, through a scarcity of "ochre." This was not only a disappointment to himself, but also to his opponent, who was thus foiled in his efforts to get hold of the belt, which could not be obtained without a mill, and which he had made sure of winning from Tom Paddock. Just previous to this mishap Jones had recovered from his accident, and, to the surprise of all, had been matched with the "coming man," Tom Sayers; so that even here the "Old 'Un" was again done out of an opponent, and the belt still remained in abeyance, to abide the issue between Sayers and Jones, the winner to meet the ponderous Tipton for the coveted trophy. The fight, which took place on the banks of the Medway, on the 19th February, 1857, we now propose to narrate.

Owing to the Puritanical persecution to which the ring had been for some time subjected, a line of country had to be selected which had for a long time been untried, so that there was every prospect of matters being adjusted in that quarter without let or hindrance. Although bills were circulated, stating that a train would leave the Great Northern station at King's Cross on Tuesday at nine o'clock, it was at the eleventh hour considered that this locality would on the present occasion be too "warm," and therefore an alteration was deemed prudent. This alteration could not be made public at so late a period, and it was only those who happened to consult the initiated at the benefit of the Pugilistic Benevolent Association, on the previous Monday evening, who got a clue to the real state of the case. The consequence was that on Tuesday morning, at the Fenchurch Street station, there were at the utmost 130 persons, including a considerable number of patricians and a very small proportion of the professors of the noble art, while of the "roughs" and other noisy demonstrators there was an almost total absence. These gentry and some few unfortunates of the

higher class hastened to the Great Northern terminus at
the hour named in the handbills, and great was their
disappointment, and loud their indignation, at finding
themselves sold.

The start from Fenchurch Street took place at eight
o'clock precisely, and by nine o'clock Tilbury was reached,
where all at once embarked in a vessel provided for the
purpose, and by twenty minutes to ten were safely on
board, and, greatly to the credit of the managers of the
expedition, a start was at once effected. In order to
throw dust in the eyes of the Blues, it was determined to
proceed straight to the mouth of the river, and, in the
face of a stiff gale from E.N.E., the journey to the Nore
was effected in excellent style. The lumpy water in this
locality had, as may be imagined, a most unpleasant
effect upon many of the voyagers, whose stomachs, unac-
customed to salt water, and anything but improved in
tone by their nocturnal vigils (as they had sat up all
night in order to be early in the morning), were turned
inside out; and the consequence was that swabs and
buckets of water were in strong demand. After about an
hour's tossing among the billows, "'Bout ship" was the cry,
the river was re-entered, and the vessel sped homewards
until a spot was reached not far from Canvey Island,
where Freeman and the Tipton Slasher fought. With
some difficulty a landing was effected, and Tom Oliver,
Callas, Pug, &c., proceeded to form the lists, although
it was not without extraordinary exertions that anything
like a favourable spot could be found, and even this was
rough and extremely uneven from the late heavy weather.
Numerous were the mishaps of the company on landing,
but by no means equal to those they experienced on

attempting to regain the vessel after the battle was over, when thick darkness overspread the land, and led many an unwary traveller into mud and mire of the most consistent character. The ring was pitched by half-past twelve o'clock, and a tolerable outer ring was established; but, as usual when the attendance is small, the difficulty of preserving this outer circle intact was very great, and towards the close of the fight, notwithstanding the exertions of some of the ring-keepers, the spectators crowded close to the ring, but, fortunately, did not disturb the ropes and stakes.

The combatants, who had made a sort of demi-toiletto on board the steamer, quickly entered the ring, Sayers attended by Jemmy Welsh and George Crockett, Jones advised by Alec Keene and Mike Madder. The stake was £100 aside. Before, however, the men set to, we will devote a few lines to Tom's youthful antagonist.

Aaron Jones, a Shropshire youth, first saw the light in March 1831. He therefore had the advantage of Sayers in age by five years; his height 5 ft. 11¼ in., and his weight 12 st. His first encounter, with Harry Orme, came off December 18, 1849. It was for £20 a side, and lasted two hours and forty-five minutes. It was won by Orme. On the 24th of September following Jones achieved his first and only conquest, his opponent being the veteran Bob Wade, whom he fought for £25 a side, and whom he licked in forty-three rounds, lasting sixty minutes. After this Jones remained on the shelf for nearly two years, and then he came out with the avowed intention of redeeming his lost laurels by a second bout with Harry Orme. The latter was nothing loth, and they fought for £100 a side. The police were very officious on the occa-

sion, and the men were much harassed. They fought a
few rounds at Bourne Bridge and a few at Newmarket,
Orme getting the advantage at the former place, and
Jones at the latter. The referee then named a third
place, where the ring was once more pitched, but Jones
declined to renew the contest, and the stakes were
awarded to Orme. Jones's reason for this refusal was
never fathomed. It was at the time set down to a want
of heart; but we are more inclined to attribute it to weakness of constitution, as his two battles with Tom Paddock
and the encounters we are about to chronicle amply re-
deemed his character from any charge of want of courage.

Jones, after the above battle, was again on the shelf for
a period of two years, and he then came out with a challenge to Tom Paddock, which was accepted, and the men met
July 13, 1854, at Long Reach, for £100 a side, and, after
as gallant a struggle as was ever witnessed, Jones became
blind, and his friends gave in for him, after fighting 121
rounds in two hours and twenty-four minutes. So satisfied were his backers on this occasion that they at once
expressed their willingness to make a fresh match.
After some little time articles were entered into, and they
went into training for the second mill. This affair came
off at Mildenhall on the 26th of June, 1855, and was
another display of manly courage and perseverance on
both sides. Towards the close Jones, who for some time
had the best of it, fell off very weak, and Paddock, who,
like his opponent, was much punished and exhausted, saw
that his time was come, and, shaking himself together, he
rattled away in style until poor Aaron was once more
compelled to cry "a go," after a contest of sixty-one
rounds, in one hour and twenty-nine minutes. Jones

after this was matched with the Tipton Slasher, as we have already stated, but this went off; and this brings us to the present meeting.

·On entering the ring both men were loudly cheered, and both looked equally confident. No sooner had they put in an appearance than speculation began. The Sayers party originally stood out for 6 to 4, but, being unable to get on at that price, they reduced their demands to 5 to 4, at which price considerable business was done, and a bet of £10 to £8 was made and staked between the men. It was piercingly cold, and, the ground being in a moist state, all looked anxious for business, in the hope that the excitement of the combat would dispel some of the shivering-fits to which the spectators, one and all, notwithstanding their Crimean-looking outfits, seemed to be subject. Little time was lost by the men in denuding themselves of their remaining outer-garments, and,.the handkerchiefs having been tied to the stakes (a light grey and white for Sayers, and a neat white and blue check for Jones), at one o'clock precisely "Time" was called, hands were clasped, and the men began

THE FIGHT.

Round 1.—On baring their forequarters to the piercing breeze, a perceptible shiver ran through the carcasses of the combatants. Sayers looked in perfect condition; every muscle was perceptible, and we doubt whether there was an ounce of superfluous flesh about him. There was a smile of confidence on his lips and bright sparkle in his eye that betokened extraordinary health and spirits. His attitude was artistic and firm, yet light. Of course he stood on the defensive, and eyed his heavier opponent. There did not appear to be that disparity of size that really existed; for Jones stooped rather on throwing himself on guard, and thus reduced his height almost to a level with that of the gallant Tom, who was upright as a dart. Aaron's condition did not seem to us so first-rate as the first glance at him had led us to suppose. His muscles,

though large, were too well covered, while his back and chest also
displayed much superfluous meat, and we should say that his
weight could not have been less than 12 st. 4 lb.   He, like Sayers,
looked confident, but was far more serious in his demeanour.   They
both commenced the round with the utmost caution, sparring, and
attempting to draw one another into something like an opening;
but for a long time neither would throw a chance away.   At length
Jones dashed out left and right; but the blows passed-over Tom's
shoulders, and Tom with quickness tapped Aaron on the face, but
without force.   Sayers now let go his left, but Jones retreated.
Tom persevered, and was cleverly stopped.   In a third attempt,
after more dodging, he got heavily on Aaron's mouth and stepped
back without a return.   Jones now assumed the offensive, but was
stopped, and Tom, after another dodge or two, planted his left
heavily on the mark, and then the same hand on the side of Aaron's
nut, but not heavily.   Jones returned heavily on the right peeper,
and shortly after made a second call at the same establishment.
More stopping and dodging, until Sayers paid another visit to
Aaron's kisser, Jones missing his return.   Each now stopped a lead;
but immediately afterwards Jones popped in his left on the snuff-
box, a heavy hit without a return.   Tom grinned a ghastly grin;
but the crack evidently made him see stars.   Jones attempted to
repeat the dose; but Tom got well away, and, as he retreated,
popped his left on the neck.   More excellent stopping on both
sides, and, after a few harmless exchanges, Tom tried a double with
his left and got on the throat, but the blow lacked steam.   Jones
returned with quickness over the left peeper, inflicting a cut and
drawing the claret.   " First blood " for Jones.   Tom, although
staggered, was undaunted, and went at his man with determination.
He once more got on the bread-basket heavily.   Good counter-hits
followed, in which Jones again reached Tom's damaged peeper,
drawing more of the essential, and Tom delivered a straight one on
the snout, removing a small portion of the bark.   Tom then got on
the left eye, and, after some sharp punching at close quarters, both
fell.   This round lasted exactly half an hour.

2.—Tom came up much flushed, and the crimson distilling from
his damaged eye.   After a little dodging, he tried his double, but
did not get it home.   He tried a second time, but was stopped, and
Jones returned on the left eye.   This led to very heavy counters,
each on the larboard goggle.   Jones now feinted, and popped his
left on the nose.   They got hold of one another, swung round,
broke away, and Sayers then popped his left again on the left eye.
Severe exchanges followed at close quarters, and both, in the end,
were down.

3.—Sayers quickly led off with his left, and was stopped.   He
then tried his double, but was short.   In a third essay he got home
on Aaron's nose, but not heavily.   Twice again did he pop in gentle

taps, but he now napped another rattler on the left eye. Severe exchanges followed, Aaron again turning on the stream from Tom's left brow, and Tom tapping his opponent's snuff-box. More exchanges in favour of Jones; and in the end both fell in a scrambling struggle, Jones under.

4.—Tom's left brow and the left side of his canister were much swollen, but he was still confident, and led off, Jones countering him well on the mouth. Heavy exchanges followed, Tom on the nose, and Jones on the left cheek, and both again slipped down, the ground being anything but level.

5.—Tom let fly his left, but was neatly stopped; Jones returned on the side of the brain-pan, and got down.

6.—Sayers came up, looking very serious, and it subsequently turned out that he was suffering from severe cramp in the stomach and lower extremities. He went in, feinted, and got well home on Jones's left eye. This led to sharp exchanges and a close, when both were down, Jones being underneath. Aaron had now a bump on his left peeper, which was apparently closing.

7.—Aaron lost no time in sending out his left, which fell on Tom's chest. Heavy counter-hits followed, Jones on the nose and Tom on the mouth. More exchanges in favour of Sayers, who again got on Aaron's damaged optic, and the latter got down.

8.—Sayers went to his man, and tried his double, the second blow dropping on Aaron's sneezer, and Tom then got cleverly away from the return. Exchanges ensued, Tom on the mark, and Aaron on the mazzard; Aaron then got home his right heavily on the left side of Tom's knowledge-box, then his left on the left eye, and in the close Sayers was down.

9.—Aaron led off, but was well stopped, and this led to some sharp exchanges, Jones on the bad peeper, and Tom on the left brow. Sayers tried another double, and once more visited Aaron's nose, but not heavily. More mutual stopping, and Jones, at length, in getting away, slipped and fell. One hour had now elapsed.

10.—Tom planted his left on the beak, and received a little one in return on the forehead. Jones now let fly his left and right, but was cleverly stopped. In a second essay he got home on the left cheek. Heavy exchanges followed, Tom getting on both peepers, and Jones on the side of Tom's cranium with both daddles, and Tom fell.

11.—Aaron had now a mark on each peeper, the left fast closing. Tom's left, too, appeared almost shut up. Jones tried to take the lead, but missed; Sayers, likewise, missed his return. Exchanges followed in favour of Jones, who, in the end, closed, and in the struggle both fell, Jones uppermost.

12.—No time lost; both quickly at it, and some sharp exchanges took place in favour of Jones, who got heavily on Tom's nose. Tom made his left on the body heavily, and they then pegged away wildly at close quarters until Jones got down.

13.—Aaron dashed in and pegged away left and right, but without precision, and ultimately bored his man down.

14.—Jones feinted and popped his left on the left eye, without a return. Tom then let go his left, but was short, and Jones, in dashing at him in return, slipped and fell.

15.—Aaron led off, left and right, but Tom got away. He came again, and tried to plant his left, but was short. He then tried his double, but Jones got away. Both now sparred and dodged, but nothing came of it. At last Jones dashed in, and heavy exchanges took place in favour of Jones, who, however, in the end, fell.

16.—Both at once went to work, and heavy exchanges took place, each napping it on the left ogle, and both fell through the ropes.

17.—Tom's forehead and left eye much disfigured. Jones let fly his left and right on the sides of the nob very heavily, and both again fell through the ropes.

18.—Tom came up slowly, and was nailed on the damaged peeper. In return he caught Aaron on the brow, but not heavily. Jones then made his left and right on the side of the head and left eye, and Tom retaliated on the nose a little one. A close followed, and in the end both were down, Jones under.

19.—Tom dodged and got home on Aaron's smeller with his left, and Aaron then made both hands on the left side of Tom's wig-block. A close and sharp struggle, when both fell, Tom under.

20.—Jones dashed in and let go both hands on the head. Tom returned on the left brow, and both fell backwards.

21.—Aaron again dashed in. He missed his right, closed, and both fell, Jones under.

22.—Tom now led off, but missed, and Jones caught him heavily with his right on the frontispiece, and knocked him down. "First knock down for Jones."

23.—Tom, on coming up, showed the effect of the last blow on his forehead. He attempted to lead off, but was very short. He tried again, with a like result; and Jones, in letting go both hands in return, overreached himself and fell.

24.—Aaron rattled in, planted his left and right on the scent-box and left ear, the latter very heavy, and bored Tom down.

25.—Tom came up bleeding from a severecut on the left lug, and his gnomon much out of straight. He tried to lead off, but Jones caught him on the right brow, but not very heavily. Tom then got home on the body, and tremendous counter-hits followed, in favour of Jones, who, in the end, slipped and fell, Tom catching him, just as he reached the ground, on the side of the head.

26.—Jones went in left and right, closed, and both were down. Sayers was now very weak, and the Jonesites were in ecstasies.

27.—Aaron led off, getting well on the side of Tom's nut with his right. Tom missed his return, and Jones then planted his left and right on the top of the skull; closed at the ropes, where Tom managed to throw him, but not heavily.

28.—Jones led off, and got well on Tom's nose with his left, and Tom returned on the side of the head. After a little dodging, Jones popped his left on Tom's left peeper, and his right on the jaw, again flooring Tom and falling on him.

29.—Tom, who was excessively weak, came up slow, but determined; he tried his left at the body, but was short. Jones then let fly his left in return, but was countered on the mouth. He then planted his left and right on Tom's damaged listener, and in the end fell.

30.—Aaron, after a few dodges, once more popped a little 'un on Tom's ear. Tom thereupon dashed in, but got a little one on the nose, and another on the side of the head, and Jones, in getting away, fell, laughing.

31.—Jones attempted to lead off, but Tom got away. Jones followed him up, caught him again on the side of the nob, closed, and both rolled over together.

32.—Jones dashed in, planted both hands on the brain-pan, closed, and forced Tom down.

33.—Jones again rushed in, but inflicted no damage, and again bored Tom down.

34.—Jones still forced the fighting, and caught Tom, who seemed very tired, on the side of the head, and, in the end, both slipped down.

35.—Sayers was forced down, after getting a gentle reminder on the side of his damaged figure-head.

36.—Tom, a little refreshed, sparred about for wind, until Jones went in, and heavy exchanges took place, in favour of Jones, when both fell backwards.

37.—Tom, recovering a little, tried his double, but Jones got away, and, as Tom came, he nailed him on the left brow. Tom then made his left on the mark, but again napped it heavily on the left eye. Aaron now got on the nose with his left—a heavy spank—and, in getting back, he staggered and fell.

38.—Jones dodged, and planted his left on the mouth heavily, and his right on the side of the head. Tom returned slightly on the nose, and, after slight exchanges, both fell.

39.—Very slight exchanges, and Sayers slipped down.

40.—After a little sparring they got close, and exchanges took place, each getting it on the mouth. Sayers then tried his left at the mark, but Jones got away. Tom followed him up, and was caught by Aaron, left and right, on the side of his head, and fell.

41.—Tom came up, shook himself, and rattled in, but he got it on the top of his cranium. Jones, in stepping back, fell. Two hours had now expired.

42.—Jones, steady, let go his left on the side of Tom's head, and

then both mawleys on the same spot. Tom followed him up, but
got it again on the brow. He, however, got home on Jones's body,
and, in retreating, slipped and fell.

43.—Long sparring for wind, and at length Jones again made
play on the left side of Tom's occiput, and then on his snout. Tom
returned on the latter organ, but not heavily. He now tried his
favourite double, but did not get home. In a second attempt he
got heavily on Aaron's proboscis, and got away. Exchanges followed, in which Tom again got heavily on the nose with his left,
and in the end Jones dropped.

44.—Tom was now evidently recovering from his exhaustion. He
came up steadier, and sparred shiftily until Jones commenced the
attack, when he stopped him neatly. Heavy counter-hits followed
on the jaw, after which Tom tried the double once again, but was
stopped. More good counter-hits, Tom getting well on Aaron's
left eye, and receiving on the mouth. Aaron's left eye all but
closed.

45.—More sparring, until Jones let fly his left, but Tom got
away. Exchanges followed, Tom on the whistler, and Jones on
the nose, but not heavily. More sharp counter-hitting, Tom once
more getting on the left eye heavily. Jones returned, but not
effectively, with both hands on the side of the head, and in getting
away from the return he fell.

46.—Jones succeeded in planting a spanking hit from the left
on the left ogle, and then another with the same hand on the left
cheek. In a third attempt he was stopped. Heavy counter-hits
followed, and in the end Jones fell, Sayers falling over him.

47.—Aaron feinted with his loft, and got well on Tom's nose ; a
very straight hit. Tom, in return, tried his double, but was short.
After some more ineffectual attempts they got to it, and tremendous
exchanges took place, each getting it on the nose and left eye, and
in the end Jones got down. Two hours, fifteen minutes.

48.—Tom tried to lead off, but was stopped, and Jones planted
his left on the cheek. Tom now stopped two of Jones's hits, after
which heavy exchanges took place, Tom getting well on to the left
eye, and Jones on the nose. More sharp exchanges, left and right,
each getting pepper in earnest, and the favours mutually divided.
A break away and to it again, ding-dong, and Tom drew the crimson from Aaron's left peeper, which was now effectually closed.
In the end Jones fell. It was now anybody's battle ; Tom had
quite recovered his wind, and was nearly as strong as his heavier
opponent.

49.—Both much punished. Sayers sparred until Jones tried to
lead off, when he got away. Jones followed him up, but was short
in his deliveries. In the end they closed, and as they were falling
Tom popped his right sharply on Aaron's back.

50.—Jones, after sparring, led off, and got home on the nose, but not heavily ;(Tom returned on the right peeper, and some pretty exchanges, left and right, took place, followed by a break away, and Jones then stopped Tom's left ; Tom, in return, stopped Aaron, and planted his left on the mark, and then on the left eye, and Jones got down.

51.—Jones led off, but was stopped. He persevered, and a good give and take rally followed, Jones getting on the left eye and Tom on the left cheek heavily. Tom next got on the mouth, drawing the Burgundy, and then on the nose and left cheek. Another sharp rally followed, after a break away, and in the end both down.

52.—Sayers visibly improving, while Jones fell off. Jones was short in his lead, and Tom returned on the smelling-bottle, and got away. Jones followed and dashed out his left, but Tom ducked his head. Tom then got home on the mouth and nose, and drew more of the ruby from the latter ornament. Jones succeeded in returning a little 'un on the left eye, and Sayers slipped down.

53.—Jones, who was bleeding from the left eye and mouth, led off, but was well stopped. He then missed his left, but in the end heavy exchanges, left and right, took place, Jones on the side of the nut and the neck, and in getting back he fell.

54.—Tom now essayed a lead, but was stopped. A second attempt reached Aaron's body, but not heavily, and Jones returned on the nose. Tom tried his double, but missed, and Jones popped a little one on the mouth, and then his left on the left eye, and fell in the corner.

55.—Tom dodged about until he got within distance, and then got home heavily on the mark. Jones returned on the jaw with his right, but not heavily. After some more sparring, Jones dashed in, when Tom met him very heavily on the right cheek-bone with his left, and Aaron fell all of a heap. He was carried to his corner, where it was with the utmost difficulty he could be got round at the call of "Time."

56.—Jones came up all abroad, and Tom popped in another spank on the same spot, whereupon Jones again fell. It was thought to be all over; but, by dint of shaking him up, Aaron was again enabled to respond to the call.

57. Tom rushed at his man to administer the coup de grace, but, going in without precision, he contrived to run against Aaron's left, which was swung wildly out, and the blow, which alighted on Tom's nose, regularly staggered him. He quickly recovered himself, and went in again, but Jones fell weak.

After this, the battle continued to the 62nd round, Jones getting gradually blind, and Sayers becoming very tired. At length, in the 62nd round, after some slight exchanges, the men, who were much exhausted, stood still, looking at each other for some time, their seconds covering them with rugs. At length the referee and umpires called on them to go in and finish. Both went to the scratch, but on Sayers approaching Jones, the latter retreated to his corner, and Tom, in obedience to the orders of his seconds, declined going to fight him there. It was getting dark, and it was clear that Jones and his friends were determined not to throw a chance away. The referee once more called on Jones to go to the scratch, which he did, but with precisely the same result; and the referee seeing that Tom was not strong enough to go with prudence to finish on his adversary's ground, and that Jones was unwilling to try the question at the scratch in his then exhausted state, ordered the men to shake hands, leaving the motion as to further hostilities to a future day. Both were severely punished; each had a peeper closed; Jones's right was fast following his left, and his right hand was injured; so that a second meeting the same week was not to be thought of. The fight lasted exactly three hours. The men and their friends now hastened to regain the vessel, and it was dark long ere the last of the company were safely on board. Of course there were many laughable accidents in the mud, through which all had to wade; but, luckily, nothing occurred of a serious nature to mar the pleasures of the day, which, although in some measure clouded by the fact that the battle was not finished, still left sufficient impression on the minds of the spectators to cause them to remember this brilliant passage of arms, which formed so hopeful an opening to the pugilistic year 1857. The vessel conveyed the company with all due speed to a convenient place for debarkation, whence they obtained a passage by railway to the metropolis, which was reached in safety by nine o'clock. Numerous complaints were made by the disappointed ones who went to the Great Northern Railway at the manner in which they were deceived; but the only consolation is that we are sorry for those whom we should have been glad to welcome at the ring side, but who have themselves alone to blame for not finding out the final fixture as many others had done; while, as to others of a certain class, who are always more free than welcome, we can with truth say their room was better than their company, and we rejoice, with others who were present, that they were so completely sold. Some unlucky wights got a sort of hint as to the fixture, and arrived within a few miles of the spot at a late hour in the afternoon, and were landed, but, unluckily for them, on the wrong island, and here the poor fellows had to remain all night, and sleep under a haystack. The boats that landed them had departed, and they could make no one hear; so that, cold, hungry, and thirsty, they had to weather the cold, severe night in the best way they could.

REMARKS.

In reports of prize battles of importance, it is usual to add a few remarks upon any features the battle may present worthy of note. But as the above battle was so near a thing, and as the men will meet again shortly to decide the moot point, it is only fair to both parties to avoid prejudging the merits of the affair, and postpone remarks until the fight is decided.

The renewed battle, which was for £200 and an additional bet of £100, was fixed for Tuesday, the 10th February, 1857, on the same spot as the previous gallant encounter. On this occasion Sayers was seconded by Jemmy Massey and Bill Hayes, with Jemmy Welsh as bottle-holder; Aaron Jones by Alec Keene and Jack Hicks, Jack Macdonald taking care of the restoratives. 7 to 4 on Sayers.

THE FIGHT.

Round 1.—On tossing the scratch the condition of both men struck the spectators with admiration. In our opinion it was perfect on both sides, but the development of muscle was decidedly in favour of Sayers, who is better ribbed up, and has his thews and sinews laid on in the right place. He looked brown, wiry, and healthy, and, for a middle weight, seemed wonderfully big. Jones, who is of fairer complexion, was altogether more delicate in appearance than Sayers, and, although so much taller, heavier, and longer, did not loom out so much larger as might be expected. He is a fine-made, muscular young fellow, but still there is an appearance about him which at once leads to the conclusion that his stamina is scarcely fitted for the wear and wear of gladiatorial encounters. He is about twenty-six years of age, and in height is over 5 ft. 11 ins., while Tom Sayers is thirty-one, and is little more than 5 ft. 8 ins. It was soon seen that Sayers intended to pursue different tactics to those he adopted on the previous occasion. He dodged about for a few seconds, and then let go his left and right with great quickness; but Jones stopped him neatly, and in getting back fell.

2.—Tom came up smiling, feinted with his left, and then tried his favourite double; the first hit was stopped, but the second caught Aaron on the chin. This he repeated, and got away without a return. After trying his double once more without success, he planted his left very heavily on the mark. Jones at once went to close quarters, and some quick in-fighting took place in favour of Sayers, who got well on to Aaron's snuff-box with his left, drawing "first blood." Jones got on the left side of Tom's head, but not heavily, and at length both fell.

3.—Both quick to the call of "Time," and Sayers at once went to work with his left, Jones countering him heavily, each getting it on the forehead. Tom then popped his left on the mark, and Aaron returned, but not heavily, on the nose. Tom now again planted the left on the mark, and was stopped in a second effort. Heavy exchanges next took place, Tom once more drawing the cork from a cut on Aaron's sniffer, and receiving on the left ear. After a few dodges, Tom again approached, and made a heavy call on Aaron's bread-basket, and then planted a stinger between the eyes, and got away laughing. He attempted to repeat the dose, but was stopped. Another effort was more successful, and dropped on the mark, staggering Jones, who, however, recovered himself, and popped his left on the chest, and then on the left cheek, but not heavily. Sparring until Tom got within distance and shot out his left heavily on the proboscis, without a return, Jones being a little wild. Tom now essayed his double, but Jones got away, and returned on the mouth. Tom persevered, and napped a little 'un on the left eye for his pains; still he would be at work, and got well on Aaron's left peeper, drawing the ruby. Heavy exchanges followed, Jones getting on Tom's left brow, and Tom turning on the home-brewed from Aaron's nasal organ. After two or three slight exchanges in favour of Sayers, he again put the double on, reaching the left cheek and bread-basket. Next he popped another hot one on the victualling department, receiving a slight return on the forehead. After a break away he stole in, and bang went his left on Aaron's damaged eye, drawing more of the ruby. A merry little rally followed in favour of Sayers, who at length broke away, and sparred as if blown from his fast fighting. Jones approached to take advantage of this, when Tom propped him on the brow, and then on the forehead. Jones returned with both hands, but not heavily, on the brow and body, and another bustling rally came off, Tom getting home on the left ogle and throat heavily, and Aaron on the larboard cheek. Another break away, and Tom, on getting himself together, resumed the double and got on the mark very heavily, and then popped his right on the left side of Aaron's nob; he got away laughing, and as Jones tried to follow him up he warned him off by a pop on the left eye. A heavy rally at last took place, in which Jones got sharply on the left ear, and Sayers on the left eye, and this protracted and well-fought round was concluded by Tom slipping down.

4.—Sayers, on coming up, showed a mark on his forehead, and another on his left ear, while Aaron's left eye and nose were much out of the perpendicular. Tom lost no time in going to work, and planted his one, two, the left on Aaron's right eye, and the right on the left jaw, knocking Aaron off his pins. "First knock-down" for Sayers. Jones seemed all abroad, and it was with the greatest difficulty that he was got round to the call of "Time."

5.—Sayers at once went in left and right, but he was too anxious to finish his handiwork, and the blows lacked precision. He reached the side of Aaron's nob, and Jones returned slightly on the same spot, and after mild exchanges both fell. This gave Jones time to get round, and by the commencement of the next round he had shaken off the nasty one he got in the fourth.

6.—Tom tried his double, but missed, and Jones rushed in to close, when Tom caught him round the neck and punched him heavily on the left peeper and nozzle, drawing more of the ruby. In the end both fell, Sayers under.

7.—Aaron came up with his left eye all but closed. Tom let go his left, but Jones returned on the nose. Tom tried again and got on the ribs; Jones returned merrily left and right, but did little damage, and Tom fell in his corner.

8.—Jones dashed in and pegged away with both mawleys on the left side of Tom's knowledge-box; Tom returned on the left brow and closed, when both fell, Tom under.

9.—Jones again dashed in, and some sharp in-fighting took place, followed by a close, in which both fell, Jones this time being underneath.

10.—Tom's dial seemed flushed, but his eyes were still uninjured. Jones rattled in to close, some quick fibbing took place, followed by a long struggle for the fall, which Sayers got and fell on his man. In drawing his legs away, he brought one foot in smart contact with Aaron's leg, which was claimed as a foul kick, but disallowed by the referee, being evidently accidental.

11.—Jones again took the initiative, and let go both hands on Tom's forehead, and then his left on the nose. Tom returned on the left eye, and then a squasher on the mark. Exchanges, and Sayers fell, evidently fatigued by his fast fighting.

12.—Jones persevered in his forcing system, and got on the left side of Tom's cranium, Tom returning very heavily on the nose. Jones again went in, and planted his left under the left optic, closed, and both fell, Tom under.

13.—Jones rushed at Tom, and pegged away at him in his corner. It was a rambling, scrambling round, and both fell, no mischief being done.

14.—Jones again led off, but Tom propped him well on the left eye, and Aaron fell on his face.

15.—Good exchanges on the left cheek, after which Jones got well on Tom's throat, closed, and both were down.

16.—Jones dashed at Tom, popped in his left and right on the frontispiece and nose, and bored Tom through the ropes.

17.—Jones again opened the ball, got on to Tom's left ear, closed, and both were down.

18.—Aaron led off on Tom's nose; Tom returned on the left eye very heavily, and Aaron fell.

19.—Tom resumed the initiative, and reached Aaron's nose—by his favourite double. Jones returned, but not heavily, on the forehead; after which Tom cross-countered him prettily on the left peeper, and this led to exchanges in favour of Jones, when Sayers fell.

20.—Both quick to work; good exchanges, and in the end Jones floored Tom by a heavy right-hander on the jaw. (Loud cheers for Jones.)

21.—Jones, elated, rushed in, but Tom steadied him by a straight 'un on the left cheek, and Jones dropped.

22.—Aaron missed both hands, and after some sparring Tom caught him heavily on the left ogle, and Jones dropped; Sayers also fell.

23.—Tom, who seemed getting fresh wind, rattled in, and planted his double on the nose and mouth. Jones rushed at him, and in the scramble Sayers was bored over.

24.—Tom popped a left-hander on the "grubbery," received a little one on the nose, and fell.

25.—Heavy exchanges, Sayers on the left eye, and Aaron on the nose. Jones slipped down.

26.—Jones led off with both hands, but not heavily, and Tom returned severely on the nose and left eye, which was now quite closed. Jones fell.

27.—Jones rushed to close quarters, and after a brief struggle fell.

28.—Tom feinted, and popped his left twice on Aaron's damaged peeper. Jones returned on the mouth, and Tom fell.

29.—Jones went to work, catching Tom over the right eye, and Sayers, in getting back, fell.

30.—Both went to work with good will, and, after sharp exchanges in favour of Sayers, Jones got down.

31.—Aaron tried to lead off, but was well stopped, and Tom returned on the mark. He next popped his left on the left cheek, and in getting away slipped down, just escaping a heavy upper cut.

32.—Tom feinted, and then got well on to Aaron's nose with his left, and retreated, Aaron pursuing him. At length they got close, and Tom sent in a stiffener on the scent-box, receiving a right-hander on the left ear, which opened a cut received in their former fight, and both fell.

33.—Tom again seemed tired, and sparred for wind. Jones came to him, when Tom let go his left on the jaw, closed, and both fell.

34.—Tom slowest to time. He tried his left, but was stopped ; Aaron closed, and Tom fibbed him on the left eye as they fell.

35.—After a little dodging, they got close, and heavy counters were exchanged. They now closed, and, as they fell, Tom again put a little one on Aaron's left eye.

36.—A close and a struggle, when both fell, Jones under.

37.—Tom led off, but was stopped, and, after a wild scramble, Tom fell. One hour and five minutes had now elapsed.

38.—Jones dashed in, but Tom steadied him by a left-hander on the left cheek, and Aaron got down.

39.—Jones still first let go left and right on the mouth and left cheek. Tom returned on the blind eye and got down.

40.—Jones let fly his left, but missed. Slight exchanges to a close, and both down.

41.—Jones on the forcing system, planted his left on the jaw and then on the left ear, and as he was pursuing his man he fell on his face.

42.—Jones missed his left. Tom returned open-handed on the back, and Jones dropped.

43.—Jones dashed to a close at the ropes, where they pegged away smartly but ineffectually until they fell.

44.—Tom got home on the left jaw. Aaron missed both hands, and fell.

45.—Jones went to work, but without precision, and, as Tom retreated, Jones fell on his face. It was clear that Tom was carefully nursing himself, while Jones, feeling that both his ogles were going, was forcing the fighting, in order to tire out his opponent before he became blind.

46.—Jones rattled in and caught Tom on the left cheek, but not heavily. Tom returned on the left peeper, drawing more claret, and Jones dropped.

47.—Aaron, in his anxiety, missed both mawleys, and Tom caught him a heavy right-hander on the proboscis, whereupon Jones dropped.

48.—Jones went to his man, who nailed him on the left ogle, and, as Jones persevered, he caught him heavily on the throat, and Jones fell.

49.—Tom tried to lead off, but was short, and Jones returned heavily on the ribs with his right. He then attempted to close, but, on Sayers catching hold of him, he fell.

50.—Tom tried his double, but Jones stopped him, and in getting away slipped down.

51.—Slight exchanges ; Jones on the mouth and Tom on the nose, and Jones down.

52.—Jones led off and was neatly stopped. Tom missed his return, and Jones fell forward.

53.—Tom led off and got on Aaron's blind eye. Jones returned very slightly on the nose, and fell.

54.—Tom planted his left heavily on the mark, which led to mutual exchanges, and Jones fell.

55.—Tom feinted and popped both hands slightly on Aaron's good eye, which began to tell tales. Jones returned on the left ear, but it was too long a shot to do damage, and Sayers fell.

56.—Aaron opened the ball, and planted his left and right on the nose and ear twice in succession. He then rushed in, when Tom stopped him by a straight one on the blind eye, and Jones down.

57.—Jones again went to work, but Tom was too quick on his pins, and got out of harm's way. Sayers missed his return, and Jones fell.

58.—Tom, still on the nursing system, kept himself quiet, waiting for the attack. Jones went in, but Tom stepped back; slight exchanges ensued, and Jones down.

59.—Jones let go his left; Tom ducked his nut, and the blow went over, when Jones fell. A claim of foul that Jones fell without a blow. The referee said, "Fight on."

60.—Jones popped his left on the chest; Tom returned on the left cheek, and Jones fell. One hour and a half had now elapsed.

61.—Jones, still first to begin, got on Tom's nose, and fell, Tom falling over him.

62.—Jones planted his left very slightly on the side of Tom's nob; Tom just touched him on the smeller in return, and Jones down again.

63.—Jones rushed in, caught Tom on the chin, and Tom fell. The blow was not very heavy.

64.—Jones missed both hands, got a little one on the side of his nut, and fell.

65.—Jones got home, left and right, heavily on the ribs; Tom retaliated on the mark, and Jones down.

66.—Jones let go his left, but Tom avoided the force of the blow by stepping back. He returned on the neck, and Jones got down.

67—71.—In all these rounds Jones led off, but did no mischief, from Tom's quickness on his pins, and in each Jones was down.

72.—Tom still waiting and resting himself; Jones came in and planted his right on the ribs. Tom returned on the right ogle, but not heavily, and Jones down, his right eye going fast. Sayers, though much tired, had both eyes well open, and his face presented no very serious marks of punishment.

73.—Heavy exchanges, and Jones fell on his face.

74.—Jones tried to lead off, but was stopped. Counter-hits, Sayers on the nose, and Jones on the cheek, and Jones fell.

75.—Heavy exchanges, in favour of Sayers, and Jones down.

76.—Jones, who saw he must do it quickly or not at all, dashed in recklessly, but was stopped. Tom popped a little one on the nose, and Jones down.

77.—Jones was again stopped, and Tom got well on his good eye, and Jones fell.

78.—Sayers stopped Aaron's rush, and again got on to his good peeper. Jones instantly fell on his knees.

79.—Aaron delivered his left on the nose, and, in trying to repeat it, fell on his face. Another claim that he had fallen without a blow not allowed.

80.—Heavy exchanges, Tom getting again on Aaron's good peeper, which was now all but shut up, and Jones down.

81.—Jones led off, but wofully out of distance, and fell forward.

82.—Exchanges, in favour of Sayers, and Jones down, weak.

83.—Tom, who saw his time had arrived, went in, planted his favourite double on Aaron's good peeper, and Jones fell.

84.—After a little fiddling, Tom crept close again, dashed out his left on the good eye, and then on the cheek, and Jones down.

85 and last.—Jones made a last effort, was easily stopped, and as he turned round Tom caught him with his right a terrific half-arm hit on the right eye, and knocked him off his pins. It was evidently a finisher. Poor Aaron's nob fell forward, and it was at once apparent that his remaining daylight was closed; and his seconds seeing this, of course threw up the sponge, Tom being proclaimed the winner, after a gallant battle of exactly *two hours*. Sayers at once went to shake hands with his brave antagonist, and then repaired on board the vessel, whither he was soon followed by Jones, whose damaged peeper was at once looked to by a medical friend. The poor fellow was very severely punished, but he did not seem to feel this so acutely as he did the bitter disappointment of having to play second fiddle to one so much smaller than himself. The expedition quickly got under way, and all reached the metropolis by nine o'clock. As soon as Sayers was dressed he went round among his fellow passengers and made a collection for his fallen antagonist, which reached the sum of £8. Beyond fatigue, and a few trifling bruises on his forehead and nose, he was unscathed, and he certainly could scarcely be said to have a black eye.

REMARKS.

We have little doubt that many of our readers will have anticipated the remarks that we feel called upon to make respecting the two game encounters between these men. On the first occasion it was obvious that Sayers felt he had a great undertaking before him, and he was therefore naturally cautious in the outset not to throw a chance away which might at once put the victory beyond his reach. Jones was known to be a very heavy hitter with his right, as was proved by the severe punishment he dealt out to Tom Paddock in both their mills. Sayers accordingly

78 TOM SAYERS,

"played possum," and in the first few rounds allowed him to take
the initiative, in order that he might measure his powers carefully
before he exposed himself to danger. Tom proved himself extremely quick on his pins, and by his agility he to a certain
extent neutralised the effects of Jones's severe lunges. True, he
got hit occasionally with effect, as witness the cut over his left eye,
and also on his left ear. Jones, to his surprise, found before him
a man clearly his superior at outfighting, and one, too, as he soon
discovered, but little his inferior in bodily strength. For the first
hour and a half, it will be recollected, he had apparently the advantage, Sayers suffered severely from cramp, and having to depend
principally upon his legs to keep him out of harm's way; but after
this he gradually recovered, and Jones, as was the case in his
fights with Paddock, after the said hour and a half, gradually fell
off, and became languid in his exertions. Tom, of course, improved
the occasion, and showed such superiority in hitting that many
thought he would have won with the greatest certainty had not
darkness come on. We must confess that, although we did not
say so at the time, we entertained a similar opinion, and we at the
same time thought that the darkness was in other respects an
unfortunate circumstance for Sayers, believing as we did that Jones,
profiting by experience, would at the next meeting have resorted
to a different system of milling, and, by at once going to close
quarters, have reduced his adversary to such a state in a few
rounds as to render victory certain. It seemed to us that this
would have been his game in the first fight, instead of trusting to
long shots, at which he found Sayers as good as himself, and we,
in common with others, were fully prepared to see him adopt the
system. There is no harm now in making known our opinion
that Aaron's performances on the first occasion disappointed us not
a little. We all along thought Sayers had overmatched himself, and
it was not until the conclusion of the first round that we changed
our mind. Many shared our belief that the man who could maul
the game and resolute Paddock as Jones had done must prove too
much for an antagonist so inferior in size and weight as Sayers, and
many blamed the latter for his presumption. Among this latter
class we do not number ourselves, for it is our practice never to
blame a man for soaring at high game when he really feels confidence in his own powers. Ambition, when kept within bounds,
is a praiseworthy quality, and Sayers merely followed the example
of other middle weights who had preceded him, in essaying to raise
himself to a higher level when he could not find an antagonist
worthy of his fist in his own sphere. How fully he was justified
in his confident aspirations the result has proved. On Tuesday
last, as may be gathered from our account of the fight, Jones fought
even less "judgmatically" than at the first merry meeting. Instead
of forcing the fighting at once, as he had expressed his intention of

doing, he allowed Sayers to open the ball, and in the very onset to inflict such punishment upon him as to shake the confidence of his friends very materially; and not only did he allow his adversary to take extraordinary liberties with him, but he seemed to have lost his precision in returning, and for some time made not the slightest impression upon Tom's wig-block. The exceedingly clever performance of Sayers in the third round, and the apparent impunity with which he got home upon all parts of Aaron's dial, took his own friends by surprise, and the fear expressed was that he was fighting too fast for a long day, and that the strength and length of his opponent must tell with fearful effect when he became tired. He was cautioned as to this, but requested to be allowed to fight his own way, as he knew what suited him best. The blow on Aaron's jaw in the fourth round was very severe, and nearly decided the event, and this we are induced to believe had some effect in stopping his rushes later in the fight, when, had he been capable of continuing the offensive with effect, the result might have been very serious to Tom, who for a long period was exceedingly fatigued, and had to nurse himself in the most careful manner in order to bring himself through. The improvement he (Sayers) displayed in every way, since his last match, was extraordinary. His system of leading off is almost perfect, and his quickness on his legs would have delighted the late Mr. John Jackson, whose opinion on the subject of this qualification is well known. He had little recourse to stopping, trusting to his activity to keep him out of harm's way, and the success with which his manœuvring was attended was proved by the fact that he had scarcely a black eye, and, beyond exhaustion, had nothing to complain of. In addition to his quickness in defence, he seems also to have acquired greater facility in pursuing the offensive, and the weight with which many of his blows fell upon his opponent proved that his hitting was as effective as that of most 12 st. men. As usual, he stood up in the gamest, most resolute manner, and faced his adversary throughout with the utmost good humour, but, at the same time, with determination. By many it was expected he would have adopted the dropping system, as he had done with Poulson; but we were delighted to perceive that on neither occasion did such a notion enter his head; and indeed we are told that even with the bold Nottingham man he would not have had recourse to it, had he not been terribly out of condition, and altogether in such a state as to be incapable otherwise of resisting the onslaughts of so powerful an opponent. We understand that Tom has now an intention of looking still higher in the scale for an opponent worthy of his powers, and both Tom Paddock and the Tipton Slasher are talked of as his next antagonists, but that he will first rest on his oars awhile to recover from his recent fatigue. How far this may be true we know not, but we presume time will show. Of this, how-

ever, we are confident, that whoever the Middle Weight Champion
may next pick out, that worthy must look to his laurels, and leave
no stone unturned to get himself fit for the fray; for, big as he may
be, he will have a hard day's work before him. At the same time,
we are sure Tom himself will pardon us for warning him of the perils
of too high a flight, and calling to his mind the words of the immortal
bard (not Charley Mallett), who says—

> " Vaulting ambition doth o'erleap itself,
> And fall on t'other side."

Of Aaron Jones we must say that his exhibition on each day
disappointed us, and fell far short of what we expected after his
extraordinary encounters with Paddock. True it is that he never
once flinched from punishment, and when severely hit persevered
in the most manly way to turn the scale in his favour. Not a word
can now be said against his character for gameness and gluttony,
for both which qualities he had already earned for himself sufficient
fame in his passages with Paddock to · remove any stigma that
his meetings with Orme might have cast upon him, but in
other respects we think he has fallen off. There was a want of
steadiness and precision in his hitting which we were not prepared
to witness, and his right hand on Tuesday last appeared entirely
to have forgot its cunning, for only once did he plant a smack
likely in any degree to make a change in his favour. Most gamely
did he persevere while Sayers was fatigued to force the milling and
to wear out his antagonist; but, owing to the great quickness and
judgment of Tom, his efforts recoiled upon himself; and, being unable
to effect any punishment, he did but reduce himself below the level of
the gallant Tom, and thus fall an easy prey to his superior judgment
and tactics. We were sorry to see him resort so constantly to the
dropping system, but, as it might be in some degree owing to the
slippery nature of the ground, we will say no more about it than to
remark that the clumsy way in which he often fell must have tended
more to his disadvantage than if he had stood up and battled it out
manfully with his adversary. As we have often before observed, and
as we now more emphatically state, there appears to be a want of stamina
about him which renders him unfit to undergo the fatigue of a
lengthened encounter. He can sometimes make a very excellent fight
for an hour and a half, but almost invariably after that time he appears
to fall off weak and languid, and to become incapable of anything like
extraordinary exertion. We cannot help thinking that the prize
ring is not his vocation, and that if he only can get a situation as a
gamekeeper, or something of the kind, he will do well to stick to it,
as more congenial to his constitution and habits. He is a thorough
sportsman in every way, a civil, obliging young fellow, and we have
no doubt in this capacity will give satisfaction. We do hope, however, that he will take our advice, and refrain from wooing fortune

any further in a circle where he is never likely to make a show beyond mediocrity. He has, by his last few encounters, recovered the imputation of want of pluck, and he may safely retire from the roped arena with credit. We have been informed that early in the fight he injured his hands very severely, and was thus to a great extent prevented from administering punishment. If this be so, it is an additional reason why he should retire from a profession where strong, firm hands form two of the principal necessaries. We are glad to hear that the friends of Tom Sayers who put down the money for him have promised to present him with the whole of the stakes. This is but a fitting tribute to the gallantry and daring of the man.

CHAPTER III.

Fight with the Tipton Slasher for the Championship—Beats the
Slasher—Beats Bill Benjamin—Tom Paddock, his career—Vic-
tory over Paddock—Second fight with Bill Benjamin—Conquest of
Bob Brettle.

WE closed our last chapter with the arduous conquest
of Aaron Jones by his little opponent; we open the
present one with Tom's yet aspiring aim at the Championship. His next step was to challenge the redoubted
13-stone Tipton Slasher, then claiming the belt, having
received forfeit, in 1856, from Harry Broome, who
retired; and in the year 1857 from both Tom Paddock
and Aaron Jones. Never since the memorable battle
between Caunt and Bendigo, in Sept. 1845, had there
been a match which excited such general interest beyond
the circle of regular supporters of true old British boxing.
Here was a man, the acknowledged champion of the middle
weights, boldly throwing down the gauntlet to the equally
acknowledged Champion of England, and daring him to
combat for the title and reward to which for so long a
time he had laid claim without meeting an adversary
of his own weight and inches daring enough to deny his
pretensions. Not a semblance of ill feeling was there
existing between the men, and we are glad to state that
throughout, even up to the very contest itself, they maintained towards one another the most kindly sentiments.
The only matter at issue between them was, whether a

man of 5 feet 8½ inches, and under 11 stone in weight, possessed of considerable science, could contest, with any chance of success, against one topping the 6 feet by half an inch, and weighing not less than 14st. 6lb. The Slasher himself laughed at the idea of defeat, and stated to us his firm belief that on entering the ring [he would, in addition to other advantages, be found the cleverer man of the two. He said he had made up his mind not to run all over the ring after his younger and more active opponent, but to take his stand at the scratch, and await the onslaughts of the gallant Sayers. This we (who knew the bold Tom's capabilities) deemed a sound determination; how far the burly Tiptonian adhered to it on entering the ring will appear in the sequel. Sayers also to some measure made us his confidant as to his intentions on the day of battle, and intimated that he believed the Slasher was perfectly worn out and incapable of anything like prolonged exertion. He had fully made up his mind, he said, to keep him on his pins, and lead him about the ring, by forcing the pace until he should be so exhausted as to be somewhat nearer his own mark. He, like the Slasher, scorned the idea of defeat, and felt such intense confidence from the very day the match was made, that he invested almost every penny he possessed upon the result of the encounter. The excitement in all quarters increased week by week from the time the match was made, and in every sporting circle the match was made one of the great themes of discussion. The general feeling at first appeared to be that Sayers had by his victory over Aaron Jones got above himself, and that his overweening confidence would lead him into unexpected difficulties, if, indeed, as was in many quarters anticipated, the match did not end in a forfeit on his part. As the time approached, however, and it was found that both men were in active work, and evidently both meaning mischief, the doubts as to the match going on vanished, the only point remaining for discussion being the foolhardiness of Sayers, and the overweening confidence of his friends in allowing the match to go on. The Sayers party, however, maintained their own opinion, and from first to last contended that the Slasher must be stale and out of practice; that he was destitute of scientific acquirements, and so slow that any want of size and weight on the part of his adversary was fully. compensated for by these deficiencies. We believe they never refused to take 6 to 4, and finally accepted 5 to 4 against their pet.

A glance at the doings of Tom's gigantic opponent may here be acceptable, and lead to the perfecting of our biography of his conqueror.

Bill Perry (the Tipton Slasher), according to his own account, was born at Tipton in 1819, and, if correct in this statement, must have commenced his career as a pugilist at the early age of 16, as we find it recorded that on the 3rd Nov. 1835, he defeated one Dogherty, at Chelsea. He then weighed about 10 st. 10 lb. On the 27th December, 1836, he defeated Ben Spilsbury, for £10 a side, in 19 rounds, at Oldbury; and on the 22nd of November, 1837, he obtained his third victory in a battle with Jem Scunner (the Gornel Champion), many years afterwards gamekeeper to the Earl of Stamford. This fight lasted 60 minutes, and 31 rounds were fought. It was several years after this that the Tipton was brought up to town by Johnny Broome, who attempted to bring

about a match between him and a man called the Dorset-
shire Champion, who was a *protégé* of Jem Burn.
Johnny, it is said, took the Slasher with a chain round
his neck, and showed him to " my nevvy," pretending
he was a sort of wild man of the woods; but ould Jem
did not like his looks, and declined to back his champion against him. The Slasher was then matched by
Broome against Deaf Burke, then stale, and in failing
health; but by some mistake on the part of Johnny, a
forfeit occurred, when only £15 a side was down, and the
Deaf-un never gave away another chance. The Slasher,
however, was not doomed to remain long without a customer, for about this time Caunt returned from a tour
in America, bringing with him Charles Freeman (the
American Giant), who was forthwith pitted against the
Slasher, and they met for the first time Dec. 14, 1842, at
Sawbridgeworth, and after fighting 70 rounds in 84
minutes, with pretty equal advantages, were stopped by
darkness, and the fight was finally brought to an unsatisfactory conclusion on the 20th of December, in Cliffe
Marshes, below Gravesend, Freeman being proclaimed
the victor through the Slasher falling without a blow in
the 38th round. On the 19th of December, 1843, the
Slasher for the first time met Tass Parker, for £100 a
side, and after fighting 67 rounds in 95 minutes the police
interfered and the fight was postponed to Feb. 27, in the
following year, when Tass, after fighting 133 rounds in
152 minutes, fell without a blow, and the Tipton was
proclaimed the winner. On the 4th of August, 1846,
the same adversaries again met, and our hero was a second time victorious in 23 rounds and 27 minutes. For
three years after this, beyond a futile effort to make a

match with Ben Caunt, he appears to have been shelved,
and in Sept. 1849, we find him forfeiting to Con Parker,
then a promising young big one. On the 17th of December,
1850, he made his first appearance as a *bond-fide*
claimant for the Championship; and met Tom Paddock
for £100 a side, when, after fighting 27 rounds in 42
minutes by moonlight, he won his battle by a foul blow.

The following year his former friend and backer,
Johnny Broome, undertook to find a man to fight him
for the Championship, and on the challenge being accepted,
Harry Broome stepped forward and announced that he
was the Simon Pure. The Slasher was nothing loth, and
a match was the result for £200 a side. It came off Sept.
29, 1851, at Mildenhall, Peter Crawley being referee,
and ended in a verdict against the Slasher on the ground
that he had struck Broome when on his knees. It did
not appear to us at the time to be a wilful foul on the
part of the Tipton, and we always considered that Peter
strained the cord too severely, but the fiat once given
could not be recalled. It was a question of intention,
and we believe that the blow was accidental. A fresh
match was made between the same men, which ended in
a forfeit of £25 to the Slasher in August, 1853, whereby
he regained the title of Champion, as Broome retired
from the Ring, and from that time until the present
match the Slasher has not figured in any way in the pugilistic hemisphere except as the receiver of forfeit in the
previous year of £70 from Aaron Jones, and £80 from
Tom Paddock, both of whom were anxious to wrest his title
from him, but neither of whom appeared able to raise
the requisite amount of sovereigns to complete the stake.
It was thought by most people that the Slasher would

now have retired from the Ring, but the announcement
of the establishment of the new Champion's Belt appeared to have instilled fresh vigour into his constitution, and he announced his intention of defying all
comers who might be anxious to dispute his title to the
trophy.   He was not, as is well known, kept long in
suspense, as almost immediately after the defeat of
Aaron Jones by Tom Sayers the present match was
made for the Slasher by Jemmy Massey.   The Slasher
stood six feet and half an inch in height, and in his best
days fought about 13st, in weight.   From the waist
upwards he at one time possessed one of the finest and
most herculean busts we ever saw, but his pins being
somewhat the shape of a letter K, considerably dete-
riorated from the beauty of his configuration, which, had
his understandings been straight, would have been the
perfection of manly strength.   He was a game, resolute
fellow, but never possessed any very strong claims to
scientific acquirements.   He was a terrific hitter with his
right when he did get home, but always rather slow in
his deliveries.   As soon as the match was made he gave
up his public house in Spon-lane, Tipton, and commenced
gentle exercise, and gradually got off his superabundant
weight.   About six weeks before the fight he betook
himself to the neighbourhood of Box Moor, where by
steady work he got himself as fit as a man of his age and
former somewhat fast habits could be expected to do.
There were all sorts of rumours as to the Slasher's condition, some saying he was as fat as a pig, and others
asserting, on the contrary, that he was as thin and worn
out as a starved greyhound.   As it turned out, however,
the happy medium would have been nearer the mark.

He was certainly not so thin as we have seen him, but
his muscles were tolerably well developed, and there was
a glow of health upon his good-tempered mug which betokened no want of attention to his training. His weight
was somewhat over 14 stone, and on his arrival at Owen
Swift's on the day before fighting, he announced that he
felt quite up to the mark, and was as well as ever he had
been in his life. He felt perfect confidence as to the
result, and pooh-poohed the very idea of defeat. He
left London the same afternoon *en route* for the scene of
action, and was picked up the following morning at
Tilbury.

The stakeholder (Mr. Vincent Dowling) having to
name the place of fighting, originally intended that two
vessels should be hired, one to convey the men and their
friends, and one to convey a select party of Corinthians
alone, who were anxious to witness the sport without
encountering those *contretemps* so general on water excursions; but, owing to the impossibility of procuring boats,
the latter part of the scheme was knocked on the head;
and, up to Friday, it seemed as if no vessel could be
obtained, even for the conveyance of the men. On that
day, however, a gentleman came forward, and offered a
vessel at a very high figure, and then only on condition
that the number on board should be limited to 250 persons.
Under the circumstances, his offer was gratefully accepted,
and it was arranged that the good ship should wait the
arrival of the company at Southend on Tuesday morning, and thence convey them whither they chose to go.
At a meeting at Swift's, on Friday, it was determined
that the number of passengers should be still further cur-
tailed, and, if possible, kept under 200, including ring-

keepers, men, seconds, and all. On arriving at Southend,
it was blowing a gale from the S.E., and there was a
heavy sea on. The boat could not come alongside the
pier, and it was with great difficulty that the passengers
were able to get on board. It was upwards of an hour
before Tom Oliver and the ropes and stakes were got in.

When all were on board, the vessel steamed out to sea,
and rounded the Nore Light. The passage was anything
but enjoyable to bad sailors, and many offered their
contributions to Neptune in the most liberal manner.
The 'passengers in the fore part of the vessel were
drenched with salt water, but they bore the infliction
with stoical good humour. The men entered the ring
between two and three, but just as all was arranged,
the company seated, and the dressing commenced, a bevy
of blues was seen swiftly approaching the ring. *Sauve
qui peut* was the order of the day, and all rushed off to
the steamboats, many, in their anxiety, making for the
wrong vessel, and many mistakes consequently occurring.
All, however, got on board one or the other by three
o'clock, and a move was made some miles farther on to an
island, where a second debarkation speedily took place.
Another ring was pitched, and round it were quickly
ranged some 3000 persons. The movements of the
steamer had put all the frequenters of the river on the
qui-vive, and the water was studded with boats and sail-
ing vessels of various sizes conveying their numerous
freights to the scene of action. The ground selected was
excellent for milling purposes, and the inner and outer
ring were formed with as much expedition as possible,
for fear of further interruption. A good business was
transacted in the sale of inner ring tickets, the amount

realised by which was £47 2s. 6d. The number of
Corinthian sportsmen was the largest we remember at
the ring side, and the spectators most orderly.. At half-
past four the men entered the ring ready for business ;
Sayers attended by Nat Langham and Bill Hayes, and
the Slasher under the superintendence of Tass Parker
and Jack Macdonald, perhaps the best pair of seconds
that could be found in any place. No time was out
to waste in preliminaries; the colours were tied to the
stakes—blue and white spot for Sayers, and the old blue
bird's-eye for the Slasher—and at twelve minutes to five
they were delivered at the scratch, the betting being
6 to 5 on the old one.

THE FIGHT.

ROUND 1.—On toeing the scratch the contrast between the men
was, as may be imagined, most extraordinary. The ould Tipton
topped his adversary at least four inches, and it looked to the un-
initiated "a horse to a hen." His immense frame and ponderous
muscular arms and legs seemed calculated to bear him to victory
against four such men as Sayers. He looked all full of confidence,
and evidently considered he had a very easy little job before him. He
was thinner than we expected to see him, and his condition generally was very fair, but there were the usual indications of age upon
certain points where the fullness and roundness of youth had disappeared from his form. He looked all his age (thirty-eight) ; indeed,
by many he was thought to be far on the shady side of forty. His
attitude was ungainly, but still he was rough and ready, and the
question that suggested itself was "how was Sayers to get at him ?"
Tom Sayers as he advanced to meet his antagonist was the perfection
of manly strength and athletic development. His fine broad shoulders,
small loins, and powerful arms and legs, were all turned in one of
Nature's best lathes, and there was not a fault to find, unless it
was found that he had two or three pounds more flesh than was
necessary about his back and ribs. His attitude for attack or defence was admirable, and however confident the Slasher was, it was
perfectly obvious that Sayers was not one whit behind him in that
respect. The Slasher had evidently made up his mind to set to work
at once and cut his man down in a jiffey. He lumbered in like a

large bear, let go both hands with more vigour than judgment, but did not get home, and Sayers, in stepping back, fell, but at once jumped up to renew the round. The Slasher went at him, put in a little one on the skull, and Tom again fell.

2.—The Slasher came up evidently with greater confidence than ever, and lunged out his right, which reached Tom's ribs, with great force, and Tom countered him sharply on the mouth, drawing *first blood*. The Slasher looked astonished, stopped to consider a moment, and again went in swinging his great arms like the sails of a windmill. Sayers danced lightly out of harm's way, and then, stepping in, popped a tidy smack on the spectacle beam, and got away laughing. After dancing round his man, and easily avoiding several more lunges, Tom again got home on the snuffer-tray, removing a piece of the japan, and drawing a fresh supply of the ruby. The Tipton, annoyed, rushed in, missed his right, and also a terrific upper-cut with his left, and Sayers again dropped in upon the nose. After this, slight exchanges took place, the Slasher too slow to be effective. He now chased Sayers all over the ring, the latter dancing round him like a wild Indian, or fleeing like a deer, to draw him after him. The vicious blows aimed by the Slasher all fell upon the air, and his exertions to catch his nimble antagonist caused him to blow off steam to an indefinite extent. Had one of the intended compliments alighted upon Tom Sayers, it looked as if it would have been all over with him. After Sayers had completed his dance he went to his man, cleverly avoided a good right-hander, and delivered another very hot one on the proboscis (more "Badminton" of the first growth). The Tipton tried his heavy punches again three times, and missed : a fourth attempt was prettily stopped, after which both hit short. The Tipton next got on Tom's right cheek with his left, but not heavily, and some very pretty stopping followed on both sides, after which the Tipton made another rush like a bull at a gate, and found himself once more battling with vacancy, Tom having slipped under his arm, and danced off laughing. The Slasher looked with astonishment, and shook his nut. Sayers again approached, and after one or two feints a good exchange took place, Sayers getting on to the left eye, and the Slasher on the ribs. Sharp counter-hits followed, Slasher on the mouth, and Tom on the cheek. Tom now led off with his double, but the Slasher stopped him prettily twice in succession, when he missed his return. The Slasher again pounded away, principally with his right, but without effect, as Sayers jumped back or stopped every effort. Sayers now planted a stinger with his left on the mark, and stopped the return. The next minute he got sharply home on the nasal organ, and jumped quickly away from a well-intended upper-cut, which looked like a finisher. The Slasher now stopped one or two pretty leads, but his return came so slowly that Sayers was far out of harm's way. This occurred several times, the Slasher rushing about like a baited bull, Sayers skipping and nimbly getting away from every rush. After a little of this entertainment Sayers went in, let go his left, and was stopped neatly, and he in turn stopped two very round hits on the part of Perry. Sayers next feinted, and got home a slashing left-hander on the right cheek, which he cut severely, and drew a plenteous supply of ruby. Another hit fell on the same spot. The Slasher then got a little one on Tom's body, and tried again, but Tom got away. The Slasher retired to his corner to get his mug wiped, and, on coming out again, Tom led him another dance all over the ring, the Old One, with more haste than speed, trying to catch him, and repeatedly expending his strength in empty space. At last Sayers, having given him a good turn at this game, stopped to see whether he was pumped, and some good exchanges followed, Sayers again on the damaged cheek, and the Slasher also reaching the cheek. Mutual stopping followed, and Sayers next got home heavily on the olfactory projection. The Slasher now stopped Tom, and returned, but not heavily, on the top of his nut, which led to exchanges, Tom on the left optic, and Bill on the ribs. After one or two more exchanges, another tremendous counter took place, Tom receiving on the mouth, and the Slasher on the nose, each drawing the carmine. The Slasher having next made several misses went in, and another sharp counter was exchanged, Tom receiving on the brainpan and the Slasher on the beak, from which more home-brewed escaped. Each now had a wipe of the sponge, and Tom treated his opponent to another game of follow-my-leader all over the ring; in the course of which the Slasher caught him a heavy right-hander on the back. He then stopped Tom's left, and heavy counters followed, Tom on the nose and Slasher on the os frontis, knocking him down (first knock down for Slasher). This round lasted nearly half an hour.

3.—The Slasher came up laughing, but he was evidently bent on mischief. Sayers smiled, tried his left, and was stopped, and the Slasher, as usual, missed two swinging right-handers. Tom dodged, popped his left on the mark, and then on the forehead, got a little one on the ribs, and exchanges followed, Tom getting home on the left ogle, and Tipton on the mouth. Some heavy give and take fighting followed, Tom getting more juice from the Slasher's right cheek, and receiving one or two smart ones on the neck and side of his head. Mutual stopping, feinting, and dodging, until Tom got home on the mark, and the Slasher again followed him all over the ring, hitting out of distance, and with no manner of judgment. Finding he could do nothing, the Slasher put down his hands, and retired for another wipe from Jack Macdonald, and then renewed his exertions, when some pretty stopping took place on both sides, after which Sayers got home on the left side of the nob, but was stopped in another essay. The Slasher stopped two more well-intended ones, and then got home on the side of Tom's cranium; Sayers returned now heavily on the proboscis, once more turning on the tap. Tom now dodged, and then got home heavily on the damaged cheek—a tremendous hit, and again did the home-brewed appear. The Slasher retired to be cleaned, and came again viciously, but Sayers pinked him on the smeller, receiving a slight return on the top of the nob. More futile efforts on the part of the Slasher, whose friends called upon Sayers to stand still and be hit, but Tom wisely declined. He had orders to keep his man on his legs and fight him at long shots, and these orders he carried out most excellently. Again and again did the Slasher miss or get stopped. Occasionally he got home a very little one, which did not leave a mark, and now he rushed at Tom, dashed out his right, and very narrowly escaped smashing his fist against the stake—it was within an inch. Sayers lifted up his arms with astonishment, and stood laughing until the Slasher wore round on another tack, and came at him again, when Tom got away, shaking his noddle and grinning. The Slasher followed, and Tom nailed him on the nozzle, stopped his return, and then planted another on the cheek. Sharp exchanges followed, the Slasher getting on Tom's right cheek and just drawing the juice, while Tom left a mark on the Slasher's left eye. The ould 'un, very slow, sparred apparently for wind, and was then stopped left and right, after which each hit over the shoulder. Tom afterwards stopped both hands, and got easily away from a third attempt. Slight exchanges followed, Tom on the nose, and Slasher on the top of the head. More dancing by Sayers, and exhausting efforts on the part of the Slasher, and then, as the Slasher came, Tom caught him a severe straightener on the snuff-box, drawing lots of claret. The Slasher, savage, stood to consider, and then rushing in delivered a little one on the side of Tom's head with his right, and Tom fell. (Time, 52 minutes.)

4.—The Slasher came up grinning, but he was evidently somewhat fatigued by his exertions. He nevertheless adhered to his practice of forcing the fighting, again dashed at Tom, and contrived to plant a little one on the body with his right, but it was not within punishing distance. Slight exchanges followed on the side of the wig-block, after which the Slasher stopped Tom's left. Heavy counter-hits next succeeded in favour of Sayers, who got home on the Slasher's potato-trap, and napped a little one on the nob. After another dance round the ring, Tom stopped the Slasher's right, and the latter then drove him into a corner, and, evidently thinking he had him safe, wound himself up to finish; but when he let go his left and right, he found that Tom had slipped under his arm, and was laughing at him in the middle of the ring. The Slasher, irate that his opponent would not stand to be hit, again lumbered after him, like an elephant in pumps, but it was no go. "No catchee no havee" was Tom's maxim, and he kept to his active tactics. The Slasher persevered, and Sayers stopped his left and right, and then turned away laughing and shaking his noddle. Perry could not make it out, and turned to his second as if to inquire what he should do ; another illustration of the classical adage—*Capit consilium gladiator in arena.* At last he went at it again and got home on the body, receiving in return on the kisser. Some sparring followed, until the Tipton again led off, and was short with both hands. Finding he could do nothing, he retired to his corner, where he stood leaning on the ropes, Tom waiting and beckoning him to the scratch. After a rest the Slasher came out, feinted at Tom, but was quickly nailed on the left cheek. He tried again, and got home heavily on the ribs, and Sayers fell. (Time, one hour and four minutes.)

5.—Perry still adhered to his boring tactics, but Tom was far too quick on his pins, and easily avoided him. Another attempt was stopped, and from a third Sayers got easily away. A fourth was missed, and Tom returned on the left cheek, which led to heavy exchanges on the side of the head, and Tom fell, the Slasher falling over him.

6.—The Slasher came up laughing, and let go his left, but out of distance ; good exchanges followed, Sayers effecting another lodgment on the right cheek, and increasing the cut in that quarter, and the Slasher getting home on the cranium. The Slasher, after another ill-directed rush, again retired to his corner, had a drink and a wipe, and then came again, and Sayers stopped his deliveries with the greatest ease. The Slasher persevered, and Tom led him another morris-dance, but they afterwards got close, and slight exchanges ended in the Slasher falling.

7.—The Tipton, after some boring, just got on to Tom's head, and each then missed a blow. The Slasher persevered, and Tom countered on the left side of his forehead with his right, after which Parry retired to his corner, whither Sayers followed him, and the Slasher at once lunged out at the cheek, but not effectually. He now made another of his wild onslaughts, but only to be disappointed, and he next stopped both Tom's mauleys. Some sparring followed, both being slightly blown, and the Slasher then stopped Tom's left, and returned with his right on the body. After a few more misses they got close, and Tom delivered a heavy spank on the left eye, and fell from the force of his own blow. (One hour fifteen minutes.)

8.—Perry showed a bump under the left peeper, but he came up smiling, and let go his left and right, both of which were stopped. He then stood blowing, until Sayers went to the attack, and some mutual pretty stopping took place, followed by several misses on either side. The Slasher once more retired to rest in his corner, but was fetched out by Sayers, who then got home on the side of the nob, and neatly avoided a return. Both were now rather wild in their lunges, and the Slasher, who pursued his man most vigorously, repeatedly missed his blows. Tom at length caught him on the cutwater, drawing a fresh supply from the best bin, and the Slasher walked off to borrow Jack Macdonald's wipe. Tom followed, and got home very heavily on the mark and then on the mouth, renewing " the cataract from the cavern." Sharp exchanges in favour of Sayers followed, and in the end both fell.

9.—The Slasher came up slowly. Notwithstanding his severe punishment his seconds sent him up beantifully clean, and in fact their attention throughout was beyond all praise. He tried again and again to plant upon the agile Sayers, but in vain. Sayers stopped him at all points, and then delivered a heavy left-hander on the mark. Some sparring followed, and Sayers stopped several heavy lunges, the Tipton in return stopping his left. Tom, in another attempt, got on the damaged cheek, increasing the cut, and the Tipton walked to his corner, whither Tom followed him, but on the Slasher making his usual lunge Sayers jumped back. Perry followed, and some pretty taps and stops, without mischief, took place. The Slasher then hit out of distance several times in succession, but on getting close some neat exchanges followed, Tom on the mark, heavily, and Perry on the cheek, but not effectively. Perry once more bored in, and delivered his right, but it was a mere fly-blow. Tom missed his prop with the left, and the Slasher retired for a drink. Tom thought this an example worth following, and after the inner man was refreshed, they went to work again, and sharp exchanges, all in favour of Sayers, followed ; he kept playing on the Slasher's damaged nose and cheek, his double being very effective, while Perry's blows appeared to leave no mark. Tom now stopped several well-intended blows, and returned heavily on the right cheek with his left. Perry, although getting slower every minute, gamely persevered, put in his right and left on the body, and then hit short with both hands. More mutual stopping ensued, until they got close, when the Slasher dashed his right at the body, but Tom met him with a very straight left-hander on the mouth, drawing more of the elixir of life, and with his right he planted very severely on the nose. Another sharp one on the mouth caused the Slasher to stagger and fall, and Tom fell over him. The Slasher evidently was fast going ; the last three blows, particularly the right-hander, were very heavy, and the game old fellow was almost abroad, and was very slow to time.

10 and last.—The Slasher crawled very slowly to the scratch, and attempted to lead off. It was, however, only an attempt. Tom easily avoided it, and planted a tremendous hit on the mark, stopping the

return with ease. He stopped two more attempts, and then as the
Slasher lunged out a third time he caught him with the left on
the damaged cheek and the right on the mouth, cutting his upper
lip very severely, and the Slasher fell, Tom on him. The Slasher
was carried to his corner, and, with some difficulty, was got round
in time to go to the scratch for another round. His dial, however,
was dreadfully punished, and his lip was so much cut that he presented a piteous appearance. It was evident that he had not the
slightest chance; he was as weak as a kitten, and entirely at the
mercy of his adversary, who was perfectly scathless and apparently
as active as when he began, and Owen Swift, the Slasher's principal backer, seeing the state of things, stepped into the ring, and
with praiseworthy humanity declared that he should fight no more.
Perry was very unwilling to give up without one more shy, but
Owen was imperative. He insisted upon the men shaking hands,
and the sponge was thrown up, Tom Sayers being proclaimed
the winner, and Champion of England, amid the cheers of his partisans, at the expiration of one hour and forty-two minutes.

No time was now lost in getting on board the vessels, the
majority of the spectators making for the larger vessel, for which
they had no tickets, and taking advantage of the absence of the
authorities on shore to scramble on board before demands could
be made upon them to show their credentials. The charterers
of the Widgeon (the companion or rather opposition), did not display
much consideration for their patrons, as they steamed off almost
immediately on the conclusion of the mill, leaving the majority of
their customers to their fate.

It was fortunate for Sayers that he finished his task at the time
he did, for scarcely had the men left the ring when the same body
of Peelers who had interfered before arrived upon the ground, just
in time to be too late to put their kind intentions into effect. It
was only the difficulty in getting a boat that prevented their arrival
at an earlier hour.

As soon as all were on board the regular boat a consultation was
held as to the course that ought to be pursued, and the general
opinion having been taken, it was resolved to make for Strood,
instead of giving the navigators another turn round the Nore, and
by eight o'clock a landing was effected at that town, and nearly
all were enabled to reach town by eleven o'clock in the evening.
On the voyage to Strood, Tom Sayers went round among the
Corinthians and made a collection for his fallen but game opponent,
which amounted to the sum of £22 5s.

REMARKS.—The account of this battle tells its own tale, and calls
for scarcely any remarks. From first to last it was evident that the
Tipton Slasher's star had sunk, and that he was no longer "The
Slasher." He must have felt from the very first that, barring an

accident, he had not the slightest chance. All his quickness and activity had left him, and we could not help thinking that his eyesight also must be failing, for times out of number did he lunge out and attempt to deliver upper-cuts when Tom Sayers was far beyond his reach, and these blows were of such tremendous force that they must have tended to take much of the steel out of him. It appeared to us that from the very beginning he adopted a wrong principle. For a heavy, lumbering man, like himself, to attempt to force the fighting, and pursue a lithe, active fellow, such as Sayers, was perfectly ridiculous, as he evidently felt towards the conclusion of the battle; and we should imagine that he must many times since have regretted that he did not adhere to his original intention of awaiting the attack and depending upon his powers as a counter-hitter to bring him through. That he did his best to please his backers and to bring the fight off in his favour cannot for a moment be denied, and that he took his severe punishment without a murmur was self-evident. He always had the character of being a game man, and that character he carried with him into retirement. The Tipton said that early in the fight he injured his right hip in one of his sudden twists to catch his opponent, and this materially interfered with his powers. Tom Sayers fought strictly to orders throughout, and his coolness and judgment greatly enhanced his reputation among his friends. Some persons present commented upon his retreating tactics, and contended that this was not fair fighting, but as these remarks proceeded from the enemy's camp they are worth but little. Of course it would have been infinitely more pleasing to them had Tom stood and slogged away against an adversary of so much heavier metal until he was disabled by a chance blow, but such a course would have been perfect madness on his part. How his jumping or running away could be called unfair, so long as he confined himself within the ring, we cannot conceive. The ring is always constructed of a certain size for the express purpose of restraining the combatants within certain bounds, and within those bounds a man has a perfect right to retreat and jump about as long as he likes, so that he does not decline to face his opponent; and that Tom Sayers for one moment declined to continue the battle cannot by any one be maintained. How far his jumping about and exertions upon his legs were advisable for his own sake is another question, and we are inclined to think that he might have kept out of harm's way with far less exertion, and reserved much of his strength against any unlooked-for contingency, had he restrained his peristaltic energies within more reasonable bounds. If the Slasher had been younger and more active, it is not improbable that the gallant Tom would have found out to his cost, as the battle progressed, the benefit of such a mode of fighting. As it turned out, however, no harm was done, and

7

as he achieved such an easy victory, none of his friends can for one moment complain. That his retreating arose from any want of confidence is a proposition not to be entertained for a moment. Never in his brilliant career has he shown the semblance of the white feather, and we feel assured that the only causes to which his method of fighting the Slasher can be set down are caution, a desire to please his friends, and an extraordinary exuberance of animal spirits.

The ring throughout the fight was well kept, and, beyond the few vicissitudes connected with the voyage to the scene of action, we heard of nothing calculated to mar the pleasures of the day.

Tom's defeat of the ponderous Tipton was not, however, to leave him in undisputed possession of the belt. Tom Paddock considered himself capable of taking the shine out of such a little one, and challenged Sayers accordingly; but, ere a match could be arranged, was suddenly seized with a rheumatic fever, which completely floored him, and from which it was feared he would not recover. There was now apparently every chance that Sayers would walk over the course, but this did not suit Harry Broome, who, although unable to cope with Tom himself, "thought he knowed a cove wot could," and made a match for an Unknown, to fight Tom for £200 a side, on the 5th of January, 1858. The speculations as to who this unknown could be were extraordinary—he was the bold Bendy, he was Ben Caunt, he was Ould Nat, he was Harry Orme—in fact, he was everybody but himself; and great indeed was the public astonishment when it became known that he was not only actually an Unknown but also a perfect novice, being, in fact, Bill Bainge, or Benjamin, a native of Northleach, 5 feet 10¾ inches in height, weighing 12 stone, of whose prowess rumour had propagated extravagant accounts, while others maintained that, as the Broomes were behind Benjamin, it was a "got-up" robbery, and that Sayers would "chuck it."

Poor Tom was sadly mortified at these insinuations, and indignantly assured the writer, that if he should be beaten it should only be by a better man.

A steamboat conveyed the men and their backers down the river to the Isle of Grain, where at about half-past twelve o'clock the champion made his appearance at the ring-side, and modestly dropped his castor within the ropes, following it at once himself, attended by Bill Hayes and Harry Brunton. He was hailed with loud cheers from all sides. Bill Benjamin was close upon his heels, and stepped into the ropes under the care of Harry Broome and Jemmy Massey. There was a smile upon the face of each man; but we fancied that of Sayers was the genuine smile of confidence, while that of his opponent had somewhat of a nervous twist about it. They shook hands good humouredly, tossed for corners, Sayers proving the winner, and then at once commenced peeling to the bitter frost and south-easterly breeze. The colours, a neat French grey for Sayers, and blue-and-white spots for Benjamin, were now tied to the stakes, the usual preliminaries were quickly settled, and at fourteen minutes to twelve "time" was called. The betting round the ring was very slight, 2 to 1 being freely offered, but takers were scarce at anything under 5 to 2.

THE FIGHT.

ROUND 1.—When the men appeared at the scratch, which they did in the midst of perfect silence, there was a visible contrast in their physical powers. The Novice stood well over Sayers, his muscles were larger and better developed, and altogether he looked, as he undoubtedly was, the more powerful man. His attitude at first was good, and led one to suppose he had studied under a good master. His condition was perfect, there not being a superfluous ounce about him. Tom looked rather fleshy about the chest and shoulders, but in such weather it was perhaps a fault on the right side. His attitude

7—2

was the same as ever—cool, calm, and collected. He eyed his adversary with steadiness, and there was the same unmistakeable glance
of confidence always to be seen on his mug. He had clearly made
up his mind to let the Novice make the first move, and tried several
dodges to draw him out. The Novice, although evidently nervous,
sparred and feinted like an accomplished boxer for a brief period,
and at length tried his left, but Tom stopped him with *nonchalance*,
and returned quickly with the left on the nozzle, and then on the
mark a sharp crack. The Novice stood his ground, and now succeeded in stopping Tom twice, and returning, but very slightly, on
the cheek. Tom next delivered his left and right at close quarters,
on the cheek and jaw, and the Novice dropped. He was conveyed
to his corner, and the look of dismay upon his countenance as he
glanced around was perfectly ludicrous. It was at once patent to
all that he knew nothing of the business he had undertaken, and that
the contest was virtually over, for directly his guard was broken
through he appeared to have no resources. He could not use his legs,
and his arms flew about like the sails of a windmill, so that Tom was
able to put in both hands perfectly at his ease. The celerity with
which he brought his right into play thus early in the fight was
remarkable.

2.—The Novice did not "smile as he was wont to smile," but
seemed to be on the look-out for a place of secure retreat. Tom
walked quietly up, led off with his left and was stopped, but the
Novice missed his return. Tom then popped his left very heavily on
the mouth, knocking his opponent clean off his pins, and filling his
potato-trap with ruby. The Novice lay as if undecided for a second,
and then, turning over, got gradually on his pins, and his seconds
took him to his corner. He shook his head several times, and
appeared extremely undesirous of encountering another of Tom's
heavy shots, but, on time being called, Harry Broome pushed him
forward, and he went reluctantly to the scratch, Massey, in disgust,
having declined to have any more to do with him.

3.—Sayers, evidently bent on making short work of it, quickly
went to work left and right. Benjamin tried to rally with him, but
beyond an accidental touch on the lip did not reach him. Tom
planted heavily on the mouth and jaw, drawing more ruby, and
down went the Novice all abroad. He lay in the middle of the ring,
and nothing could persuade him to come to "time." Broome then
threw up the sponge, and Tom Sayers was once again proclaimed
the conqueror, and still champion, in *six minutes and a half*, the
battle—if battle it could be called where it was all one way—being
the most bloodless we ever witnessed. The Novice, on being asked
to account for his cutting up so badly, said he was hit very hard in
the mark the first round, and, not expecting to be hit there, it had
made him very sick and incapable of exerting himself. Further than

that he knew not. His easy defeat struck dismay into all his friends, and the look of surprise and contempt cast upon him by Jemmy Massey was a study for an artist. Both men at once left the field of action, and repaired on board the boat, where they lost no time in resuming their warm wraps, and taking other means to infuse a little of that caloric into their systems which had been subtracted therefrom during their brief exposure to the outward air.

REMARKS.—We question whether it is not an insult to the understanding of the reader to offer any remarks upon this singular exhibition of incapacity upon the part of the would-be champion. Of Tom Sayers we have nothing more to say than that he did what he was called upon to do with the utmost *nonchalance*, and that he performed his task even easier than he had all along anticipated. The Novice did not exhibit a single point which would entitle him to be called even an "outsider." From the time that he was foiled in his very first move, he cannot be said to have even "tried." All his senses seemed to have left him, and, as far as we were able to judge, the only predominant thought in his mind was how to escape from the dilemma in which he had been placed, with the least damage to himself. Doubtless he was hit very heavily, but still he had not received even half enough to justify him in crying "a go," had he meant winning at all hazards. That he must eventually have been beaten by such a man as Sayers, barring an accident, is a positive certainty, and that he exercised a sound discretion in not submitting to further punishment is equally true; but that he has done more than heap ridicule upon himself and those who brought him out, by his miserable performance, is a proposition not to be disputed for a moment. How such a judge of fighting as Harry Broome could have made the mistake he did we cannot understand, but the task of bringing out a candidate for the championship once undertaken by a man of his known "talent," it is easy to understand how the public were induced to come forward and take the long odds offered on Sayers. Among the deceived was the renowned Jemmy Massey, who, liking the appearance of the man, and being led on by the reports of Harry Broome as to his man's cleverness and gluttonous qualities, took the odds of 2 to 1 to a considerable amount. The whole affair was carried out from first to last in a quiet and orderly way, and there was no fault to find with the partisans of either man for either unseemly language or noisy demonstrations. All that was required to render it a model fight was a little more devil and resolution on the part of the loser. The battle money was handed to Tom Sayers at Owen Swift's, Horse-shoe Tavern, Tichbourne-street, on Wednesday evening, January 13, when he was again adorned with the champion's belt, which, according to rule, was deposited with the stakeholder to abide the event of his next battle for the permanent possession of the trophy.

After this victory Tom appeared in a fair way to rest
upon his laurels, but soon, to his astonishment, as well as
every one else's, it was announced that Tom Paddock had
recovered, and did not intend to let the belt pass without
a struggle.   He issued a challenge to Sayers, in which he
intimated that, it being dead low water in his exchequer,
he was as poor as a church mouse, and that unless Tom
would extend him the hand of charity, and meet him
for £150 a side, instead of the stipulated £200, the
darling wish of his heart could not be gratified.   He
thought he could win the belt, and hoped Tom would not
let a paltry £50 stand between them, and prevent a
friendly mill.   Sayers, like a "brick" of his own laying,
promptly responded to the call, and intimated that the
meeting would afford him the highest gratification.   With
such an old pal he could not allow the paltry "rag" to
stand in the way.   The match was at once made, and
came off on the anniversary of Tom's fight with the
Slasher, viz. on the 16th of June, 1858.   After some
narrow escapes from police pursuit and persecution, the
two Toms met on a place selected as "maiden ground,"
at Canoey Island.

The first to shy his wide-awake into the ring was Tom
Paddock, who was loudly cheered.   He was attended
by Jemmy Massey and that accomplished master of the
art Jack Macdonald, and looked as red as beet-root, and
as strong and healthy as though he had never in the course
of his life assisted at the ceremony of seeing out the gas.
His demeanour was the same as ever, that of extreme
confidence, and the smile on his mug was more that of
one who had merely come out to enjoy a little gentle
exercise than of a candidate for honours preparing to

meet the Admirable Crichton of the P.R. There was, however, nothing of bravado about him : he merely took the affair as a matter of course, which would soon be over. He was not kept many minutes before he was joined by his opponent, who, attended by Bill Hayes and Harry Brunton, was also received with a complete ovation of applause. Tom, like his brother Tom, also looked in rude health, but his good-tempered mug struck us as if anything too fleshy, and in this we were confirmed when he stripped, for it was then apparent that he was some three or four pounds heavier than he should have been under such a tropical sun. The lads shook hands good-humouredly, and while they were completing their half-finished adornments, the betting round the ring was of the liveliest and heaviest description : £25 to £20, £50 to £40, and similar odds to smaller sums upon Sayers were offered, and eagerly accepted in all quarters, and it was as much as the stakeholder could accomplish for some time to collect and enter the names and amounts of perhaps some of the heaviest investments for many years.

We feel it incumbent upon us here to perform an act of justice to Alec Keene, which speaks volumes for his kindness of heart, and without which our account would be incomplete. After the men had been fighting about twenty minutes, Alec, who had followed the belligerents in a tug from Gravesend, made his appearance on the ground, and, finding that things were not going altogether smoothly with Tom Paddock, at once betook him to his corner, offered him the hand of fellowship, and throughout the remainder of the fight stood by him to afford him the benefit of that experience and advice which he is so capable of imparting.

ROUND 1.—Both came grinning to the scratch, and manœuvred
for a brief space for an opening. Paddock looked, as usual, big and
burly, but it was evident he was no longer the active, fresh man we
had before seen. His mug was more marked with age, and there was
a dulness about his eye we never remember in former days. His condition was good and he was in good health, but still he looked only
Tom Paddock in name. Sayers was more fleshy than he should have
been, but this was the only fault to be found with him. His eye
was as bright and clear as a hawk's, and the ease of his movements
was a picture to behold. His attitude was, as usual, all readiness
for a shoot or a jump. Paddock, instead of rushing as had been
expected, steadied himself, and felt with his left for an opening. It
was not long before he attempted it, but Sayers stopped him easily.
He made a second attempt, and Sayers stepped back, shaking his
noddle and laughing. After a little sparring Paddock tried again, and
got on Tom's brow, but not heavily. Again they dodged, and at length
two counter hits were exchanged, each getting on to the proboscis.
After this Paddock again reached Tom's nozzle rather sharply, but
was stopped in another attempt. Another bit of cautious sparring
eventually led to very heavy exchanges, in which Sayers left a mark
on Paddock's left cheek, and napped a warm one over the right
peeper, slightly removing the bark, and giving Paddock the first
event. Several rapid passes were now made on both sides, but they
were evidently mere trials to find out what each intended. After a
pause Sayers tried his favourite double, which he succeeded in landing on Paddock's cheek, but not very heavily. More sharp exchanges
followed, the advantage being with Sayers, until they both retreated
and stood to cool themselves, the heat being intense. After a few seconds thus employed, they again approached one another smiling, and
after a dodge or two they exchanged slight reminders on the side of
the nut, broke away, and then got at it again, when heavy counter
hits were exchanged, but Sayers was first, and inflicted a cut on Paddock's left brow, calling forth the juice in abundance. Paddock landed
on the cheek, but not heavily. After this slight exchanges with the
left took place, and they again stood, Sayers awaited the onslaught,
and Paddock puzzled. At last the latter dashed in, and was easily
stopped twice in succession. He rushed after Sayers, who ducked
under his arm, and, as Paddock turned round again, nailed him very
heavily over the left peeper, renewed the supply of carmine, and then
got out of harm's way. Paddock, nothing daunted, dashed in, but
Sayers stopped him most beautifully, and then putting in his double
got well on the old spot. Paddock once more bored in, and was
neatly stopped, but, persevering with his usual gameness, heavy exchanges ensued all in favour of Sayers, who was as straight as a die,
and got heavily on the left cheek and brow. Paddock, wild, rushed
after him ; Sayers ducked, and then planted his left on the left cheek,

another hot one, and then on the snout, renewing the ruby. As Paddock bored in, he made a cannon off the cushion by putting his double heavily on the mark and nose without a return, and Paddock then, rushing after him, bored him down. This round lasted 15 minutes, and at its conclusion the backers of Sayers offered 2 to 1,—an offer not accepted by the Paddock party, who looked indigo. It was patent to all good judges even thus early that Paddock was only Paddock in name, and that all the steel was out of him; and he has since informed us that he felt tired and worn out, and that he had no chance from this time. His gameness, therefore, in persevering so long and so manfully against his own conviction is the more commendable.

2.—Both came up grinning, but while Sayers was almost scathless, Paddock's mug showed that Sayers had been there. Paddock, nothing daunted, rattled in, and got on to the top of Tom's nob. Sayers returned, but not heavily, and sharp counter hits followed, Sayers on the damaged ogle, and Paddock on the left cheek. After this, Sayers got home his dangerous right on the side of Paddock's nob, and the latter fell.

3.—Paddock seemed slow, while Sayers was as fresh as a daisy; Paddock attempted to lead, but was very short. He, however, stopped Tom's return. Heavy exchanges followed, Sayers receiving on the left cheek, and getting heavily on Paddock's damaged squinter. Paddock, nothing daunted, made several desperate efforts, but Sayers got away with the greatest ease, and at length as Paddock persevered, he once more countered him on the old spot, drawing more of the red port, and stopped Paddock's return. Twice again did Sayers repeat this visitation, and get away from Paddock's kindly intentions. Sayers then tried to lead off, but was well stopped. He made another attempt, and lodged his favourite double on the mark and nose, and then stopped Paddock's return. Paddock now endeavoured to force the fighting, but Sayers danced away under his arm, came again, and, as Paddock rushed in, delivered a tremendous left-hander on the cheek, by the side of the smeller, drawing more home-brewed from the fresh cut. Paddock, angry, made several desperate efforts, but was well stopped. At length they got close, and in the heavy exchanges, Sayers got his right heavily on the side of the nut, and received on the mouth. Paddock now dashed in, and although Sayers pinked him on the nose and eye, he persevered until he forced Sayers down.

4.—Paddock's nob seemed a good deal out of the perpendicular, while Sayers had scarcely a mark. Paddock still smiled, and attempted to lead, but the dash and vigour we remember of yore was all gone; his blows seemed but half-arm hits, and did not get near their destination. Almost every time Sayers stopped him with ease, and at last, as Paddock came boring in, he met him heavily on the cheek producing another supply of cochineal. Still did Paddock persevere, but only to be nailed again, and to have the Red Republican once more called forth. After this he got home on Tom's chest and then on the cheek, but the blows lacked vigour. Exchanges ensued, in which Paddock removed the bark from Tom's sniffer, and turned on the main, but it was not a material damage. After a rest, in which both piped for wind, they again got at it and a tremendous rally took place, in which Sayers was straightest and heaviest; he, however, got a hot-un on the mouth, which drew the Badminton. This was a tremendous give-and-take round, and Paddock got it heavily on the left side of his nob, while Sayers received it chiefly on the hardest parts of his cast-iron canister. In the end Paddock was down, amidst the vociferous cheers of the Sayers party.

5.—Paddock made two ineffectual attempts to deliver, each being short, after which Sayers missed his favourite double. He then stopped Paddock's one, two, and exchanges followed, in which Paddock reached Tom's chin, and received with interest on the damaged cheek. Again did they deliver, left and right, and Paddock drew more gravy from Tom's sucker. Paddock rattled to it, but Sayers countered heavily on the snorer, again calling forth the ruby; he, however, napped one on the kisser, which must have shaken his false ivories. After this they piped for wind, the perspiration oozed from every pore, and they were evidently both tired. Paddock retired for a wipe, and after a pause Sayers went to him, and Paddock, seeing this, rushed in, but Tom danced away, followed by Paddock, who eventually got a reminder on the cheek, and Sayers, in getting away from the return, fell.

6.—Sayers feinted and dodged until Paddock came to him, when Tom got home a very hot one on the snuff-box, turning on the vermillion galore. Paddock, wild, dashed at him to deliver the right, but Sayers getting quickly out of mischief, the blow fell on the stake, and evidently caused the poor fellow intense pain. He was not cowed, however, but followed Sayers, who fell, and Paddock's umpire appealing, the referee desired Sayers to be cautious.

7.—Paddock, slow, came up cautiously, and after a few dodges, led off, but was short, and received a reminder on the beak from Tom's left. Sayers then got heavily on the mark with the left, and stopped the return. This led to heavy exchanges, in which Paddock received on the nose, and lost more juice, while Sayers only got it on the brow. Paddock tried again and again to lead off, but Sayers danced away, or ducked under his arm, and each time nailed him heavily on the nose, or left cheek, and, finally, Paddock fell weak.

8.—Paddock's left peeper was now completely closed, and the left side of his knowledge-box much swollen. He was sent up very clean, however, and again tried to lead off, but Sayers was too quick for him, and got away. Still did the gallant Paddock persevere, but Sayers stopped him with ease, and returned on the damaged visual organ very heavily. Paddock again dashed in, but was short, his blows lacking vigour; and Sayers returned on the mark. Again and again did Paddock make an onslaught, but there was none of the vigour of the Paddock of former days; he was repeatedly stopped with ease, and Sayers caught him again and again on the mark and damaged chop. At last they got close together, and Paddock succeeded in knocking Sayers off his pins by a heavy right-hander on the whistler, which inflicted a severe cut, and drew the carmine (loud cheers for Paddock, who had thus won the two first events).

9.—The blow in the last round had evidently shaken Sayers, who was slow to the call of time, and came up with a suspicious mark on his potato-trap. Paddock tried to follow up his advantage, and incautiously went in, when Sayers met him with a beautiful left-hander on the snout, which sent him staggering, and put an end to his rushing for the time. This enabled Sayers to recover a little, and then, as Paddock afterwards came in, he made another call on the cheek, and got cleverly away from the return. Paddock followed him up, and heavy left-handed exchanges took place in favour of Sayers, who afterwards stopped Paddock's right twice in succession. Good exchanges ensued to a close, and Paddock got down, just escaping Tom's right.

10.—After slight harmless exchanges, they stood piping, until Paddock took the initiative, but Sayers danced under his arm, and, as he turned round, pinked him on the blind goggle, and then, putting in his double, renewed the home-brewed from the cheek. Paddock tried a return, but was stopped twice in succession, and then got another little-un on the cut-water. After some neat stopping on both sides, Sayers made another call on the cheek, then on the chest, and after sharp exchanges, as Paddock rushed after him, he slipped and fell, but obviously from accident.

11.—Paddock at once rushed to close quarters, but found Sayers nothing loth; they struggled for a brief period, and in the end both fell, it being obvious that Sayers was the stronger man.

12.—Paddock, who was piping, and evidently fatigued, tried to lead off, but was miserably short. After a slight exchange they again closed, and, after a short struggle, Sayers threw and fell on his man, amidst the cheers of his admirers. One hour and two minutes had now elapsed.

13.—Paddock, whose mug was all shapes but the right, and whose remaining goggle glared most ferociously, rushed in and missed. Sayers, in getting back, fell, and there was a claim of foul; Massey and Macdonald, according to the custom of modern seconds, neglecting their man, and rushing to the referee. There was not the slightest ground for the claim, Sayers evidently having fallen from pure accident ; but the usual complimentary remarks were offered by the card-sharpers and other blackguards, whose only interest was, perhaps, the value of a pot of beer depending on the result, and who were proportionately anxious to win, tie, or wrangle rather than loose their valuable (?) investments. After some time the ring-keepers succeeded in clearing these gentry away, and inducing Macdonald and Massey to return to their duty ; and the referee having said "Fight on," the battle proceeded.

14.—Paddock, to whom the delay had afforded a short respite, dashed in, caught Sayers on the cheek, closed, and both fell.

15.—Sayers feinted, and got on to Tom's nozzle, drawing more claret, and, in getting away from a rush, crossed his legs near the stakes and fell.

16.—Paddock, who was evidently fast getting worn out, at the instigation of his seconds dashed in, as if to make a final effort to turn the scale ; he let go both hands, but was short, and Sayers once more pinked him on the swollen smeller. Paddock still persevered, and more exchanges, but not of a severe description, took place ; followed by a breakway and a pause. Again did they get at it, and some heavy counter-hitting took place ; Sayers well on the mouth and nose, and Paddock on the brow and forehead. Paddock then rushed in and bored Sayers down at the ropes. (Another claim of foul disallowed.)

17.—Paddock, desperate, rushed at once to work ; and they pegged away with a will, but the punishment was all one way. At last they closed and rolled over, Sayers being top-sawyer. In the struggle and fall the spikes in Sayers's boot in some way inflicted two severe wounds in Paddock's leg, and Massey declared that the injury had been committed on purpose ; but this every one who saw the fight was convinced was preposterous. Even supposing it was Sayers's spikes, it was evidently accidental, but so clumsily did they roll over that it is not impossible that it was done by the spikes in the heel of Paddock's other boot, which spikes were much longer and sharper than those of Sayers. The idea of Sayers doing such a thing deliberately when he actually had the battle in hand is too ridiculous to admit of a question.

18.—Paddock rushed in and caught Sayers on the side of the head with his right, and they closed and pegged away at close quarters until Sayers got down.

19.—The in-fighting in the last round had told a tale on Paddock's nob, which was much swollen, and the left cheek was now beginning to follow suit with the right. At last they got close, and both fell, Paddock under. Massey made another claim that Sayers fell with his knees on Paddock, but it was evidently an attempt to snatch a verdict.

20.—Paddock tried to make an expiring effort, but was wofully short, and Sayers countered heavily with the left on the damaged cheek, and then repeated the dose with great severity, staggering the gallant Tom, who, however, soon collected himself, and once more led off, but out of distance. He then stood, until Sayers went to him, popped a heavy one on the nose, and then the right on the cheek, and closed at the ropes, where he fibbed Paddock very heavily, and both fell, Paddock under.

21 and last.—Paddock came very slowly to the scratch, evidently without the ghost of a shadow of a chance. He was groggy, and could scarcely see; the close quarters in the last round had done their work, and any odds might have been had on Sayers. Paddock tried a rush, but, of course, Sayers was nowhere near him, and as he came again Sayers met him full on the right cheek, a very heavy hit with his left. It staggered poor Tom, who was evidently all abroad, and all but fell. He put out his hands, as if to catch hold of Sayers to support himself, and the latter, who had drawn back his right hand to deliver the coup de grace, seeing how matters stood, at once restrained himself, and seizing Paddock's outstretched hand shook it warmly, and conducted him to his corner, where his seconds, seeing it was all over, at once threw up the sponge, and Sayers was proclaimed the victor in one hour and twenty minutes. Paddock was much exhausted, and it was some time before he was sufficiently himself to realize the fact that he had been defeated, when he shed bitter tears of mortification. That he had any cause for grief beyond the fact that he was defeated no one could say, for if ever man persevered against nature to make a turn it was he, for notwithstanding the constant severe props he got whenever he attempted to lead, he tried it on again and again, and, to his praise be it said, took his gruel with a good temper exceeding anything we have ever witnessed on his behalf during the whole of his career. As soon as possible after the event was over, the men were dressed and conveyed on board the vessel, where Paddock received every attention his state required; but it was long before he recovered from the mortification he felt at his unexpected defeat. Sayers in the meantime went round among the spectators, and made a collection for him amounting to £30.

REMARKS.—Although the above battle tells its own tale, our account would not be complete unless we appended a few remarks, not only upon the contest itself, but also upon the general management and the other concomitants. From the very commencement it was obvious to us that all the fight was out of Tom Paddock. All the devil and determination for which he had been so famous had completely left him, and he was almost as slow and ineffective as

the old Tipton. True, he left no stone unturned, and never once
flinched from the severity of the punishment administered to him.
He took all that Sayers gave with apparent indifference, and although
it was obvious his powers of delivering had departed, his extraordinary gifts as a receiver of punishment were fully equal to his
olden reputation; and, as we have before remarked, his good temper
exceeded anything we have ever witnessed on his part. It was
supposed by many that had he not injured his right hand by the
blow delivered upon the stake he would have done better; but, as he
used that mawley afterwards so effectually as to floor the Champion,
and as he admitted to us that he felt his cause to be hopeless previous to that accident, such speculations go for nought. That both
his daddles eventually became much swollen and innocuous is true,
but that he could have turned the tide in his favour, had this not been
the case, we do not believe. It was not the mere hardness of the
hammer that was wanting, but the steam for wielding the hammer
was entirely absent. The principal cause of regret was that he
should have been induced, after his severe illness, to try conclusions
with one so much fresher, and, as it turned out, stronger than himself; but, however much his physical powers had declined, it was all
along evident that his old spirit of daring everything was as strong in
him as ever. From the first moment he entered the ring he did all,
and more than all, that could be required of him to make a turn in
his favour, but in vain. As may be gathered from our account,
he once or twice seemed to gain a slight advantage, but it was very
short lived. Enough, however, was done by him to convince us that
had he been the Paddock of five years ago, the chance of Tom Sayers
retaining his proud position would have been anything but "rosy."
The collection made for Paddock proved the estimation in which his
gallantry was held by the spectators, and we do hope that, as it will
in all probability be his last encounter, his friends and the public
will testify their admiration of such a brave fellow by contributing
liberally towards establishing him in a position to earn his own live-
lihood. Many gentlemen have already paid him for his colours, and
this example cannot be too widely followed. His backers inform us
that it is intended to give him a benefit within a week or ten days;
but they have as yet been unable to secure an arena. Full particulars, however, will be announced in our next. On this occasion,
we are sure we shall be stating no more than the truth in saying that
his gallant opponent will be present to lend a helping hand to his
fallen adversary, and that no exertions will be spared on his part to
secure him such a bumper as he so richly deserves.

Tom Sayers, throughout the contest, fought with that extraordinary
judgment of time and distance which has so much distinguished him
during the last few years of his career; and from the first it was
apparent that any diffidence he might have displayed in his mill with

the Slasher had completely disappeared. He abstained, to a considerable extent, from the harlequinade which he displayed in that encounter, and often stood and fought with his ponderous opponent with steadiness and precision. He fell down, it is true, three times without a blow, but only on one of these occasions could it be fairly said that it was not accidental, and even then we do not believe that it was a wilful act, especially as it was clear that the tumbling system was farthest from his thoughts, and his great desire was to keep Paddock on his legs. Tom had now reached the very pinnacle of his fame, for among the not very extensive range of big ones then in the field—Harry Poulson, Aaron Jones, the Tipton Slasher, and Tom Paddock had fallen beneath his punishing arm, while Harry Broome, having struck his flag to Tom Paddock, and Harry Orme (who had also retired) surrendered to Harry Broome, there was a clear title made for the Little Wonder, Tom Sayers, the first ten-stone Champion !

This state of things seemed likely to leave Tom to enjoy in *otium cum dignitate* the laurels of his many hard-fought days. The year 1858 grew old, when once more "an Unknown" was talked of, who would be backed to try conclusions for the £400 and belt against the redoubted Tom. Again these rumours came from the head-quarters of the erewhile champion, Harry Broome, in the Haymarket ; and, to the astonishment of every one who recollected the "lame and impotent conclusion" which, sixteen months before, marked what was supposed to be the first and last appearance within any ring of Mr. Bill Bainge (Benjamin), that worthy was named as the man for the coming fight.

It was urged by himself and his friends, that he did not have fair play in his training for his former battle ; that he was very far from well on the day of fighting ; that these drawbacks, coupled with the novelty of his position in entering the ring for the first time, and going through the ceremony of peeling, &c., before the assembled throng, had quite unnerved him, and rendered him almost

oblivious as to what had actually taken place. The
weather, too (it was January, and bitterly cold), had a
great effect on him, his frame not being accustomed
to the exposure in a "state of buff;" and besides all
this, he himself asserted that the suddenness and severity
of the punishment he received was something that
had more paralysed than hurt him. He had felt ever
since that a stigma attached to his name, which he felt
sure was not deserved. He believed himself at heart to
be no coward, and being anxious to vindicate himself he
had begged his backer to give him an opportunity of
clearing his character, and that gentleman, believing his
version of the case to be true, had kindly granted him a
new trial. Of course, when Sayers heard of the challenge
he was nothing loth, feeling, as he did, conscious of victory,
and imagining that what he considered such an easy job
would bring him six months nearer to the retention of
the belt as his own private property, he threw not the
slightest difficulty in the way of settling preliminaries,
and articles were signed and delivered at once.

The men did not go into training immediately, as they
had nearly six months before them, but Benjamin took
every opportunity of gaining such knowledge as might
assist him in his undertaking, and acting under the advice
of an old ring-goer, he lost no time in securing the services
of ould Nat Langham, whose judgment and generalship
could not but prove of the greatest assistance. Liberal
offers were made to Nat to go down to Shirenewton, where
Benjamin was resident, to take the entire management of
him, but Nat rightly judged that his own business was
such as to require his presence; and, therefore, contented
himself with an occasional run down for a couple of days,

when he enforced upon his pupil some of his own peculiar
style of practice in many a heavy bout with the mufflers.
As he could not undertake the whole training, however,
Nat recommended Bill's backer to send a retaining fee to
the bold Bendigo, whose country habits, sobriety, vigilance,
and judgment he knew could be depended upon, and the
appearance of his *protégé* on the day of battle proved that
his confidence had not been misplaced, for his whole
bearing was the very perfection of condition. Bendy,
however, had a corporation of most Daniel Lambert-like
proportions, no doubt much increased by good living, in
which he had indulged while superintending his new
pupil, and was therefore a curious choice for the trainer
to a candidate for the championship.

As to the gallant Tom, he occupied the next four
months after the articles were signed in starring it about
the country, and exhibiting himself, his cups and his belts,
to hosts of admiring friends. He took a benefit here, a
benefit there, and a couple of benefits in one week somewhere else, and so on, and was everywhere so well received
that he must have returned to town, prior to his going
into work, with a perfect sack full of "shiners," and these
we trust he had the good sense to deposit in some safe
place where they may be comeatable on his final retirement
from the Ring, which he had already considered as fixed
for June 1860, when the belt would become his private property. From the very first he had held this match extremely light, and had expressed the most overweening
confidence, a confidence which at one time during the
fight now under description we thought was very near
proving his downfal, from the fact of his having split on
the same rock which has proved fatal to many a good man

8

and true under similar circumstances. We allude to
neglect of training. The first portion of Tom's exercise,
which did not extend over more than seven weeks, was
taken, as on former occasions, in the neighbourhood of
Tunbridge Wells, but about a month later he removed to
Rottingdean, another favourite locality of his, for the purpose of sea bathing, and it was during his stay at this
place that his practices were anything but conducive to
high condition. During his so-called training, Tom, instead
of the usual walking, running, &c., was repeatedly seen on
horseback in full career after the harriers which meet in
the neighbourhood, and during these gallops his falls were
anything but few and far between. Had the champion,
by an unlucky purl, dislocated a limb or sprained an ankle
or a wrist, what a pretty pickle his backers would have
been in, and how he would have cursed his own folly !
His backers' money would have been thrown away, his
belt would have been forfeited, and he would have had to
recommence his career of three years as its holder, in addition to losing the confidence of those who were behind
him. As it was, on entering the ring, the general remark
was that he was too fleshy, and there were signs of a pro-
tuberance in the neighbourhood of his bread-basket which
told an unmistakeable tale. Many a brave fellow has
suffered severely for this reckless despising of an adversary,
and has thereby lost a position which he has never been
able to regain.

The rumours and speculations anent this match were of
the most extraordinary character. Tales of deep-laid con-
spiracies to rob the public, such as it has never been our ill
fortune to see put into practice during our career as chroni-
clers of this truly British sport, were rife. The croakers,

who always look at the dark side of the picture, and by listen-
ing to the statements of those who attempt to decry the ring
by blackening the characters of its members, are always ready
to see "a barney" in every match, could not be persuaded
to believe that Tom Sayers had far too high a notion of
himself to listen to any suggestions on such a subject;
and that, even admitting, for the sake of argument, that
his principles might give way (which we were confident
they would not), his pride and vanity were such as to
forbid the supposition. While on the subject of "barneys"
we may be permitted to remark that such occurrences are
much more common in the imaginations of some would-be
knowing ones, who are literally know-nothings, than in
the actual practice of the P.R.; and that we firmly believe,
and we state it earnestly and seriously, that there is far
less of this kind of thing in the doings of the members of
the Prize Ring than in almost any other sport. Besides
these rumours about "Mr. Barney," there were whisper-
ings that Benjamin was in reality an extraordinary good
man, and that the winning of the former fight by Sayers
was purely a piece of accidental good fortune. How these
various "shaves" were received by the general public and
by the *cognoscenti* may be best gathered from the fact that
as the day approached no one would take less than 4 to 1
about Benjamin winning, and that many persons laid
5 to 2 that Sayers would win in a quarter of an hour.
The betting on the whole, however, was small in amount,
the cause no doubt being the preposterous odds demanded,
which, as the backers of Sayers said, was actually buying
money.

Shortly after eleven o'clock Tom Sayers modestly
dropped his castor over the ropes, and then as modestly

crept under them himself. He was attended by Jerry Noon
and Harry Brunton, and was received with enthusiastic
cheers. He had wisely donned his milling boots and
drawers, and had therefore only to remove his outer shell.
After an interval of five minutes he was followed by Benjamin, who made his *entrée* in an equally unpretending
way. He also was well received. He was waited on
by the Bold Bendigo and Jack Macdonald. At this time
there were several offers to bet £20 to £5 on Sayers, but
there were no takers. Despatch being the order of the
day, no time was lost by the men in preparing for action.
Benjamin, like Sayers, had taken the precaution to make
ready beforehand, so that a very few minutes sufficed to
strip and tie the colours in their appropriate places.
Sayers sported a pink and white striped brocaded silk of
the richest description, while Benjamin adhered to the
old-fashioned blue and white spot. By twenty-three
minutes past eleven o'clock, under a burning sun, the men
were delivered at the scratch and stood ready for hostilities
amidst the most profound silence. Benjamin appeared in
perfect health and condition; he had a smile of confidence
on his mug, and he stood well up in a fearless manner,
presenting a wide contrast to his *début* on the former occasion. He stood well over Sayers, whose height is only
5 feet 8½ inches, and struck us as decidedly the more powerful man. Although Tom was evidently too fleshy, there
was a dash and calm self-possession about him which
denoted the more accustomed boxer. He moved about in
a business-like way, and evidently had no fears for the
result.

THE FIGHT.

Round 1.—Benjamin stood well on the defensive, and there was much in his position to remind us of his Mentor, Nat Langham. He fixed his eye on Tom, and sparred for a short time to see what could be done. His whole bearing, indeed, was such as to call forth a general remark that he was a different man. Tom dodged in and out in his usual style, evidently trying for his favourite double, but Benjamin was ready. At length Tom dashed in, and delivered his left on the cheek, but was beautifully countered on the smelling bottle, and Benjamin had the honour of gaining "first blood" from that organ, a success which was hailed with much cheering from the Taffies. Sayers seemed pricked at this, and making his favourite dodge, he popped the left on the body and then on the left cheek, knocking Benjamin off his pins, thus gaining the second event, and equalizing matters.

2.—Benjamin, nothing daunted, came steadily to the scratch, and, after a feint, let go his left, which was well stopped. He got away from the return, and after some sparring got home the left on the chest, and they got to close quarters, when the in-fighting was of a heavy description. Each got pepper on the nozzle and whistler, and Sayers also planted heavily on the side of Bill's nob. In the close at the ropes Benjamin was forced down.

3.—Both came up a good deal flushed, and each seemed blowing. Benjamin looked serious, and was rather cautious. Sayers, anxious to be at work, dashed in, and got home a very straight one on the proboscis, but Benjamin, with great quickness, countered him on the left cheek, just under the eye. This led to desperate exchanges, in which there appeared to be no best. At length Sayers caught his man round his neck, and holding him tight, pegged away with a will on his dial, and finally threw him heavily, his nob coming with some force against the stake.

4.—Benjamin, desperate, at once rushed to work, and after some tremendous exchanges, each getting it on the left eye, Benjamin fell.

5.—Sayers tried to lead off, but Benjy walked away, in obedience to his seconds. Sayers followed until they got close together, and a magnificent rally followed, in which Sayers drew the claret from Bill's right brow, and also paid a heavy visit to the conk. Bill got on Tom's left cheek, but his blows had not the precision and weight visible on the part of Sayers.

6.—Benjamin was evidently shaken by the punishment he had received, which even at this early hour was very severe. He sparred, and was evidently in no hurry. Sayers seeing this went to him, but was exceedingly wild in his deliveries. At last he got home on the bread-basket, but without effect, and Benjamin missed his return. Tom now feinted, and just reached Bill's smeller, but it was a mere

flyblow. He tried a body blow, and was well countered on the cheek
and mouth. A close and in-fighting followed, in which both were
very wild, but in which Tom again turned on the main from Benjamin's nose. After a struggle both fell through the ropes.

7.—Benjamin looked savage. He lost no time in dashing at his
man, and a tremendous round followed. Sayers let go the left at the
nose, but Benjy countered him straight and well with the same hand,
opening up a fresh bottle. Several tremendous counters with the
left followed, Benjamin astonishing every one by his calmness, and
by the precision with which he timed his hits. Each got pepper on
the nose and eyes, and Sayers napped a nasty one on the middle of
the forehead. Sayers now missed his left, and Bill returned well on
the cheek. They broke 'away, and after surveying one another
again went to it, and more heavy exchanges took place, in which
Tom again turned on the main from Bill's nasal fountain. Benjamin
persevered, and again did they dispute the ground inch by inch.
Both were blowing, and the confidence of Bill's friends was looking
up. It was plain both men meant to do all they knew in this bout,
and that each felt that it was to be the turning point, one way or the
other. Sayers now got heavily on the left eye, which began to close,
while Bill caught him on the mouth. The fighting was tremendous,
and the way Benjamin stood to his man was beyond all praise.
Sayers now and then was extremely wild, and had Benjamin possessed more knowledge of the art the result might have been serious,
for Tom was evidently tiring fast, but still the greater force of his
hitting was evidently telling a tale. As hit succeeded hit Bill's dial
grew more slantindicular; but he was undaunted, and evidently
had made up his mind to do or die. At length they got to close
quarters, when some heavy fibbing took place, and both fell; Benjamin under.

8.—Bill's left eye was all but closed, the bump at the side telling
of Tom's powers of delivery. Sayers was much flushed, and puffing
like a grampus; he lost no time, however, in going to work, evidently
hoping to frighten his man. Benjamin was ready, and after some
sharp exchanges in his favour, he retreated. Tom followed, and as
Benjamin attempted to plant his left, Tom cross-countered him
heavily with his right on the jaw, and knocked him off his pins. He
was almost out of time, and it required all the exertions of his
seconds to get him round.

9.—Benjamin shook himself, and came up resolutely, but evidently
much shaken. He sparred a little, and on Tom going in, he timed
him neatly on the middle of the dial, but without much force. Again
did Sayers try it with a like result, and Benjamin then dashed in,
but was short. Sayers returned with great quickness on the bad eye,
and poor Benjamin was again floored.

10.—Benjamin struggled up gamely, although requested to give in: he held up his hands, and tried to counter with his man, but Tom with great neatness got well home on the good eye, avoiding the return, and Benjamin once more dropped. His seconds threw up the sponge, but the poor fellow broke from them, with an intimation that he was not licked, and wanted to prove he was no cur, and commenced

11 and last.—Benjamin tried to lead off, but it was evidently a mere flash in the pan; he missed and stumbled forward, when Tom gave him a slight tap on the nose, which sent him for the last time to grass. He was conveyed to his corner, and his seconds then declared he should fight no longer. Sayers went to him to shake hands, but Benjamin, who was all but blind, wished to commence another round. This, of course, could not be listened to, and the poor fellow was forced from the ring against his will, Sayers being proclaimed the winner in 22 minutes, amidst the enthusiastic cheers of his friends. Benjamin was much exhausted, and his punishment was as heavy as one generally sees in double the time. He took it, however, unflinchingly, never complaining from first to last; and on this occasion, although defeated, his most determined enemy (if he has one) cannot say he was dishonoured. Sayers also was much exhausted, but this arose not so much from his punishment, although in this respect he did not come off scatheless, as from his want of condition telling upon him in a battle which was disputed for some rounds with unwonted quickness and desperation.

REMARKS.—Having commented upon the want of condition of Tom Sayers, and having gone at some length into a description of this short but merry fight, it is unnecessary to trouble our readers with many remarks thereupon. That Benjamin succeeded in redeeming his character, and proving that he can receive punishment and struggle hard for victory when properly looked after, is not for a moment to be denied, but that he will ever make a star in the pugilistic horizon we do not for a moment believe. He is, at 34, too old to learn the rudiments of the business; at that age even the limbs of a practised boxer begin to get stiff, and it is therefore extremely improbable that those of a man trained to other pursuits can acquire that quickness and readiness so necessary to a finished pugilist. Had he begun many years ago, we think it not improbable, with such strength and activity as he possesses, he might have hoped to rank in the first division. The desperation with which he contested the seventh round—which was one of the sharpest and severest we ever saw—evidently showed what he might have done; but as it is we think, having fulfilled his mission and proved to his friends that he is composed of more sterling metal than they gave him credit for, the best advice we can give him is to shun for the future the attractions of the P.R., and devote himself to the duties of his station in his own country. We are glad for his own credit sake that he determined to undergo this second ordeal, and equally glad that he came out of it so successfully. It also gives us pleasure to know that he has good and staunch friends at his back, who having witnessed his performance on Tuesday, are perfectly satisfied with him, and possess both the will and the means to help him in his future career. Of Tom Sayers we have but little to say. He did not fight so well on Tuesday as we have seen him on former occasions ; and, as we think this was entirely owing to want of condition, we feel we are only doing him a favour in impressing upon him the necessity in future of leaving no stone unturned to retain that confidence which has been so implicitly placed in him.

Thus ended the second attempt of the Broomes (Harry and Frederick) to wrest the belt from the hero of these pages, but there were other "Richmonds" now in the field. Bob Brettle of Birmingham could not persuade himself that he could not interpose a check to the victorious career of the little champion. Bob had his own reasons, too, for believing he had a chance. He had tried conclusions with the champion with the gloves, and believed in his heart he had the best of it ; and in this, perhaps, he was not far wrong, for it was pretty generally known that Tom was much more at home with his digits in nature's habiliments, and in a four-and-twenty feet ring, than when they were muffled up in horsehair in the sparring school. The backers of Tom at first laughed at Bob's propositions, but he declared he was in earnest, and went so far as to say they would wish they had let him alone before they had done with him. After much palaver Sayers offered to stake £400 to £200, but Brettle then required the belt to be thrown in. This, of course, was rejected, Tom considering that as holder of that trophy he was only bound to defend it on even terms. Brettle was extremely loth to give up his chance for the belt, but still he did not think it equivalent to the extra £200 which Sayers had offered to stake, and eventually he waived all pretensions to the "ornamental," and closed the bargain on the chance of obtaining the "useful," which would have sufficed to purchase a belt of double the value.

At the meeting at Owen Swift's, where the articles were finally ratified, a friend of the champion's treated the match with such ridicule that he ventured to suggest the probability of Bob being licked in *ten minutes*, whereupon Brettle, in the heat of the moment, offered to bet £100 to £10 against such a contingency. "Make it £200 to £20," said Tom's friend, "and it's a bet." "Done," said Bob, and the money was staked in the hands of Alec Keene. All these preliminaries were adjusted before the second fight for the championship in April, between Tom Sayers and Bill Benjamin, it being stipulated that Tom should name a day after that event was decided.

At Tattersall's on the previous Monday, September 18th, the event seemed to attract as much attention as the speculations on either of the great handicaps, and in the yard a regular ring was formed, where betting or offers to bet went on very briskly. The backers of Tom commenced by offering 5 to 2, at which some few investments were made, but the Brums soon opened their mouths for longer odds, and would take no less than 3 to 1, and at this price again money was laid until the Sayersites in their turn held back, and speculation left off at offers of 5 to 2. In the evening at the sporting houses 3 to 1 might have been got in some few instances, and a sanguine admirer of Tom's actually laid 4 to 1, but we believe he was a solitary specimen.

For at least a month, Mr. Gideon, one of the most earnest backers of Sayers, had been on the look-out for a

scene of action which might be reached with ease and
comfort, and which at the same time should be so situated
as to be beyond the reach of the rough and ready attendants at boxing matches, whose presence is anything but
desirable, and also tolerably safe from the too-prying eyes
of the powers that be, who do not love a mill, and who
will in the most unaccountable manner interfere with the
pleasures of the Fancy, on the ground that a friendly
boxing match is a breach of the peace. A few consulta-
tions with other managers of excursions, and a considerable expenditure of time and trouble, ended in the perfect
success of Mr. Gideon's arrangements, and not only did he
carry the expedition to a triumphant *dénouement*, but in-
sured the utmost comfort to all the travellers. Of course
the profits of the expedition were equally divided between
the backers of both men, and the figure being tolerably
high, and the company unusually numerous, there is no
doubt each realised a handsome sum. Owing to the distance to be travelled, a very early start was found absolutely necessary, and seven o'clock being the hour named,
the "lads wot loves a mill" had to be early afoot; and
many there were who having, as usual, devoted the first
two or three hours of the morning of the 20th of September to "seeing life," found some difficulty in opening
their eyes in their very first sleep to enable them to get
to the starting post in time. Many a one started
breakfastless, and many were the wistful glances cast at
the victualling department under the able charge of Mr.
Dan Pinkstone, an old and well-known caterer, long before the end of the journey was attained; but as the train
could not be stopped there was of course no chance of an
issue of stores from the commissariat until the goal was

reached—a field near Ashford, in Kent, being the *champ clos* for the combat.

The train comprised thirty-six carriages, every one of which had at least its full complement of travellers and many were over-full. The start was effected by a quarter before eight, and with the aid of two powerful engines a rapid and pleasant journey was effected to the scene of action, on entirely maiden ground, some sixty miles from the metropolis, which was reached shortly after ten o'clock. The vast multitude lost no time in clearing out from the carriages, and a pioneer, who had gone on ahead the previous evening, placing himself at the head of the army, proceeded, closely followed by the veteran commissary and his *posse comitatus*, to the proposed scene of action. No time was out to waste in preparing the lists, which were in readiness before eleven o'clock. While these preliminaries were being arranged, a brisk business was carried on in the sale of inner ring tickets, and our readers may judge of the class of spectators and their number when we tell them that the sale realised a sum of £54 10s. for the benefit of the P.B.A. This done, Billy Duncan and his constables proceeded to clear out the ring, and experienced the usual difficulty in persuading the company to seat themselves at a sufficient distance from the enclosure. All were naturally anxious to be as close as possible, and accordingly had seated themselves in compact rows, those in front close to the ropes. The consequence was, that all were crowded together, and many were scarcely able to get a glimpse of the ring. And now as we have brought the men *en face*, we will say a few words concerning Tom's present antagonist.

Bob BRETTLE was born at Portobello, near Edinburgh,

in January, 1832, and was, therefore, six years younger than Tom Sayers. On the present occasion he just turned the scale at 10st. 4lb., and did not appear in any way too fleshy. By calling he was a glassblower, and it was while engaged in one of the larger establishments in the hardware districts that he first became connected with the P.R. His first essay of which we have any record was with Malpas of Birmingham, whom he fought, for £50 a side, on the 14th of February, 1854. There were 80 rounds, principally in favour of Bob, but eventually there was a claim of foul on his part. A wrangle took place; the referee gave two decisions, and ultimately the stakes were drawn. Brettle's next encounter was with old Jack Jones of Portsmouth, for £100 a side, on the 21st of November, 1854. Jack had only been out of the hospital a few weeks, and was in anything but condition; but still he had all the best of the mill, Brettle resorting to the dropping system. Forty-nine rounds were fought in 105 minutes, when darkness came on, and as neither man was much punished, the referee ordered them to fight again on the following Saturday. On that day Jones was at the appointed place, but Brettle did not show, and it being discovered subsequently that he had been apprehended, either through the kind offices of his friends or by his own negligence, the stakes were awarded to Jones. After this Bob was idle until the 20th of November, 1855, when he defeated Roger Coyne of Birmingham, for £25 a side, in 49 rounds and 48 minutes. Then came his match with Sam Simmonds, for £200 a side, which took place near Didcot, June 3, 1856, and was won by Bob very easily in 13 rounds and 16 minutes.

Another year, or rather more, elapsed before Bob made

another essay, his next opponent being Job Cobley, whom
he fought for £100 a side, August 4, 1857. Here Bob's
greater weight and superior strength enabled him to take
a decided lead, and Job, finding it too hot to be pleasant,
resorted to dropping, and finally lost the battle by falling
without a blow in the 47th round, at the expiration of
90 minutes.

On the 26th of January following, Brettle met Bob
Travers for £100 a side at Appledore, when, after fighting
42 rounds in 65 minutes, the police interfered. An adjournment took place to the following day, when they
met again at Shell Haven, and after fighting 100 rounds
iu two hours and five minutes, Bob Travers, who had, like
the Enthusiastic Potboy, found the earth the safest place,
was decided to have lost the battle by falling without a
blow.

Bob's only subsequent encounter was with Jem Mace
of Norwich, who, it may be remembered, met him for
£100 a side on the 21st of September, 1858, and at the
end of two rounds and three minutes, although with none
the worst of it, hid his diminished head, and declined to
have any more. This was Bob's last appearance prior to
the present, and it was imagined by most people that he
would retire from the ring, but the temptation of a turn
at the Champion was too great for him, and induced him
to try a flight at the top of the tree. It is difficult to
understand whence he got the confidence to match himself
against Sayers, unless it was from his supposed superiority
with the gloves; in the case of Tom Sayers an unusually
delusive test. This brings us to the eventful 20th of
September, 1858, and the ring at Ashford.

So soon as all were seated a cap was seen to fly over the

heads of the dense mass, and in a second Bob Brettle,
aided by his seconds, Alec Keene and Jem Hodgkiss of
Birmingham, was seen elbowing his way through the
crowd. He was vociferously cheered on all hands, and his
good-humoured mug brightened up with a broad grin of
delight at the hearty welcome.   Tom Sayers was not long
behind him, and as he entered on the scene, attended by
Jack Macdonald and Harry Brunton, he too was greeted
with a tremendous ovation, which he acknowledged in a
becoming manner, and then shook hands good-humouredly
with his opponent.   The spectators now began to make
their final investments, and several bets of 3 to 1 were
made and staked to considerable amounts. The last, however, that we heard was £25 to £10 on Sayers. After
the lads had completed their toilettes Brettle came
forward and offered to take £150 to £50 from Tom, but
the Champion declined, as his money was all on.   Bob
then held up the note and offered to take the same
odds from any spectator, but silence was the only
reply, and he had to return the flimsy to his "cly."
Tom's colour was a very handsome blue and white stripe,
with blue border; and Bob's a dark blue, with a white star.
Brettle's boots having been examined by Tom's seconds,
it was found that the spikes were beyond the regulation
length, and had to be filed, but this was so inefficiently
done that they were far too sharp and long for the purpose for which they were intended.   Had Sayers' seconds
done their duty resolutely they would have shown them
to the referee, who doubtless would have ordered a still
further curtailment, but Tom personally requested them
to make no bother about it, as, in his own words, he
"could give all that in."

THE FIGHT.

ROUND 1.—On throwing off their blankets there was a great disparity in the appearance of the men, much greater indeed than would have been expected from the slight difference in weight. Tom, whose condition was superb, was broad-shouldered, thick-loined, and muscular, the weight being just where it ought to be; while Brettle looked narrow and round on the shoulders, and had not the upright, firm bearing of the Champion. In height, too, there appeared more than the actual difference of a bare inch. Tom's mug, of the two, was fleshier than his opponent's, but it looked hard as nails. In point of age it was evident there was a considerable difference in favour of the Brum, whose fresh complexion and healthful country appearance contrasted strongly with the Champion's bronzed but somewhat stale complexion. The wear and tear of fifteen contests, and the gay life he has led, have evidently left their mark, and we should imagine that if Tom is fortunate enough to retain the belt the stipulated time, he will be only too glad to retire upon his laurels. Each had a pleasant, good-humoured smile on his phiz, but the Champion seemed to be more at home than his adversary. Bob looked leary, and walked round his man with a kind of crab-like, sideway movement, and leering out of the corner of his eye, was evidently on the look-out to catch the Champion tripping, and make a dash at him with his right. Tom was awake, however, and though not moving far from the scratch, stepped with his adversary and contrived to keep him continually facing him. At length Bob finding his man so "fly" to his "little game," dashed straight at him, and let go the left, which caught Tom very slightly on the nose. Tom nodded and smiled as much as to say, "Wait a minute;" and Bob renewed his journey round his man, who remained in the middle of the ring. At length Brettle again dashed in, and exchanges took place, in which Tom left his mark on Bob's forehead, the bump being of considerable size. Brettle retreated, came again, and lunging out his left was prettily countered on the mouth, from which "first blood" was instantly visible, the blow being a hot 'un. Some neat exchanges followed on the side of the head; they then broke away, and, as Sayers followed his man, Bob ducked his head, but Sayers caught him a sharp spank on the proboscis, which led to counter-hitting, when Tom got well on the forehead, and Bob fell. A claim of first knock-down for Tom was made but disallowed, as Bob was evidently getting down when the blow reached him.

2.—Bob's nose and mouth showed that Tom had been there; he, however, dashed in, and heavy exchanges took place, Tom getting on to the left peeper and Brettle the body. Brettle now broke away, and resorted to his cunning peripatetic dodge, but Tom only grinned and waited for him. At length Bob dashed in, and got on the chest very slightly, Sayers returning well on the kisser. Brettle, after another pedestrian excursion, came again and let go the left, which was stopped, and he again "walked round and showed his muscle." Tom stepped with him, and each tried to draw the other, until Brettle at last let go his left, and sharp exchanges followed on the cheek with the left, and Sayers fell. A claim of knock-down for Brettle not allowed, Tom being on the hop, and partially slipping down.

3.—Sayers, on coming up, had a slight mark on the left cheek, which caused the Brums to cheer vociferously. Brettle seeing it, made a dash to force the fighting, but Tom stopped him by a straight one on the whistler, and then closed. This led to some sharp but very wild in-fighting in Tom's corner, and at last Brettle was down on his knees with all the worst of it.

4.—The Brum came up blinking with his left eye, which had evidently got pepper in the last wild rally, and seemed as if about to close. It was now discovered that the ten minutes had just expired, and that his bet of £200 was saved. He lost no time in getting to work, but giving one or two sideway steps he dashed in, planted his right on the ribs, and then one or two sharp counter-hits were exchanged. While dodging and stepping in and out, Brettle's spikes came into dangerous collision with Tom's shin, and inflicted a serious wound; Tom pointed to the injured spot and shook his head, whereupon Bob apologised, assured him that it was unintentional, and promised to be more careful for the future. The wound was excessively deep, and only shows the extreme danger of using such absurd spikes, which are utterly useless to a man who intends really to keep on his legs. Tom, after a little dodging, got heavily on the nose, and counter-hits were exchanged, Tom getting very heavily on the left peeper, and receiving a hot one on the jaw which knocked him clean off his legs. "First knock down" for Brettle, who was enthusiastically cheered as he went to his corner.

5.—On coming up there was no mark of Bob's visitation on Tom's jaw, but the effect of Tom's blows on Brettle's mouth and eye was very visible. His nose and left eye were swollen, and the claret was still visible from his mouth. The backers of Tom offered 4 to 1, but in only one instance was it taken—viz., by Bob Travers, who invested "a tenner" on the pet. Brettle, after a little queer manœuvring, rushed in left and right, and got the latter on the body, but not heavily. He looked serious, and walked round and round, but finding Tom ready he tried a dash, succeeding in landing the right on the body. Tom got heavily on the forehead and then counter-hits being exchanged, Brettle got slightly on the neck, and Tom with his right caught Brettle very heavily on the left shoulder, and Bob went down in Tom's corner. Sayers ran after Brettle as he was being carried to his corner with a curious look of anxiety and alarm on his countenance, evidently thinking that he had inflicted some dangerous injury. Finding, however, that the blow had not had the serious effect he feared, he walked smiling to his corner.

6.—Brettle came up looking very serious, and several times led off left and right but quite out of distance. Tom then stepped in and tried his left, which Brettle cleverly avoided, and then returned on the chest. They quickly got to close quarters, and after a sharp exchange on the neck, Brettle fell forward on his hands in Sayers' corner, Tom missing a terrific upper-cut with his right as he fell.

7 and last.—Brettle missed several well-intended lunges with the right, and then walked round the ring; he came again, and tried the left with a similar result. He kept hitting out of distance, as if afraid of Tom's right, which had already missed him so narrowly. Again and again did he step in and out, and as Sayers tried to catch him on the hop he would point and grin; at last he got slightly on the chest, receiving a little one on the cheek. Brettle retreated, and then hit out with his left most furiously, but missed, and Tom countered him heavily on the shoulder; Brettle immediately put his right hand to his shoulder as if in pain; he, however, shook himself together, and tried to stand and prop his man with his right, but from the expression of his countenance something evidently was amiss, and on Tom's approaching him he got down in his own corner, apparently suffering considerable pain. Solid Coates, his umpire, at once went to his corner, and on inquiry found that he had dislocated his shoulder, either by the force of his own blow, or from the effect of Tom's heavy counter; and this being the case, of course he had no option but to resign the victory to Tom Sayers, who was hailed the conqueror in *fifteen minutes*. Tom at once went to shake hands with his fallen foe, and then resuming his clothes, quickly reappeared among his friends without a mark to show that he had been fighting. A medical friend who was on the ground quickly attended upon poor Brettle, and lost no time in restoring his arm to its position, and the poor fellow, more injured in mind than body, was soon sufficiently recovered to enter freely into conversation with his friends, many of whom believed, and, we hear, still believe, that he had to the full as good a chance as Tom Sayers at the time so disastrous a termination to the battle occurred. That this was so is, of course, but a matter of opinion; our ideas on the subject will be found in the remarks appended below. That Bob's own opinion did not coincide with that of his friends may be gathered from the fact that he has since called upon us to state his intention of retiring from the ring. He says he knows of no man of his weight who is likely to try conclusions with him; he has no intention of again overmatching himself as on the present occasion, and as he has a good business in Birmingham he thinks he can well afford to leave fighting alone, at any rate as an active professor of the art. In this resolve we think he is perfectly right, and as he is a thoroughly honest, upright young fellow, and of

9   4

an excellent temper, we do not doubt of his success. He already
numbers troops of friends, and we sincerely hope that his uniform
civility and obliging disposition will have the effect of doubling his
connection, and quickly placing him in a position to render him as
independent as his most sincere friends could desire.

Before closing this part of our account we should not be rendering
justice where it is due did we not mention that Jack Macdonald, one
of Tom Sayers' seconds, on finding the nature of Bob's injuries
rushed to his corner, and rendered very material assistance to the
surgeon in attendance in restoring the dislocated arm to its socket.

REMARKS.—Where the battle was of such short duration, it is, of
course, difficult to find much to say in the shape of remarks. To every
judge of milling who was on the ground, not excluding some of
Brettle's own friends, it was obvious from the very first round that,
bar an accident, the victory must lie with the favourite. In fact, in
our own hearing, at the conclusion of the first round, where Tom
drew the crimson from Brettle's mouth, and set his sign manual on
his forehead, one of the backers of the latter said, "It's all over ;
we shan't win." It had been anticipated that the Champion, in his
anxiety to win the bet of £200 to £20, would at once take the initiative, and that thereby he would throw himself open to the dangerous
right-handed counters of Bob ; but those who knew Tom Sayers were
too well acquainted with his judgment and tact to believe in any such
thing, hence their confidence and the great odds they so freely laid.
From the very commencement it was obvious Tom saw the game he
had to play, and the calm way in which he shifted his position so as
always to present a square front to the enemy delighted every one.
He was, of course, taken by surprise at Bob's getting home first,
but this only rendered him steadier, and convinced him that he must
act in a cautious manner. We do not believe he for a moment contemplated going for the bet, although we feel convinced that had one
vicious upper-cut got home he must have won it to the greatest certainty. In all his recent fights he has been the one that has fought
in the jump-about, dancing-master style, but here he was the steady
old stager, quietly biding his time and seldom throwing away a hit.
The knock-down blow in the fourth round was indubitably a fair
knock-down, but it must not be forgotten that although matters
thereby looked favourable for Brettle, the real fact was that Tom
in his counter got home much heavier than his opponent, and that
had he been stepping in instead of back at the moment he would not
have been floored. The proof of the effectiveness of the blow was
seen on the men again appearing at the scratch, when Tom showed
no mark, while the evidence of his visitation to Bob's eye was unmistakable. That the battle terminated as it did we cannot help
feeling was fortunate for Brettle. Tom's dangerous right—never
brought into play until he has his man "safe," as he says—was

already busy; true, he missed once or twice, but he is not the man to do this often, and had it got home effectively there is no telling what injury he might have inflicted. The actual cause of Bob's accident it is impossible to fathom. Some aver that it was partly caused by the heavy blow in the fifth round, others that the shoulder was injured by the fall on his hands, but, as he was able to use it so vigorously in the last round, we believe both these suppositions to be wrong. Possibly they may have rendered the muscles weaker than usual, and predisposed the arm for such a *contretemps*, but our own idea is that Bob, swinging his arm out so very viciously at a distance from his man, and receiving a tap on the collar-bone at the same moment, the joint was jerked out entirely in that manner. That his arm was dislocated there was not the slightest doubt, for we have the evidence not only of the surgeon himself, but also of Jack Macdonald, as to the dislocation being reduced; and even if we had not, the expression of poor Brettle's countenance and his contortions when in his corner were far too natural to have been put on for the occasion. We should not have thought it necessary to make these observations had we not heard it whispered that a set of idiots, who think everything connected with the ring is "a barney," or something tantamount to it, have been going about saying that there was no accident at all, and that the statement as to Brettle's accident was all moonshine. The gentry who make these remarks should look at home, and before throwing mud at persons in different walks of life to themselves, should consider whether in the event of a similar compliment being paid to themselves there would not be a much larger portion of the sticking part attached to themselves, and whether they could be as easily whitewashed as their humbler, though perhaps honester brethren of the P.R. Of Brettle's performances we need say but little. He evidently found himself outgeneraled from the first: and this being the case, all that remained for him to do was to make the best of a bad bargain, and this we are bound to say he did to the utmost of his ability. Our own opinion was, before the battle, that he had not the ghost of a chance, and that opinion was borne out by that result. We are sorry that he was disappointed in his expectations, which were entirely raised by his underrating his man; but as we do not believe he will be a loser by his defeat, he is, perhaps, not to be so much pitied as some of his less fortunate compeers. He has been always a general favourite, and so long as he perseveres in his present straightforward course he must retain the good wishes of all parties. As we have stated above, we think he has taken a wise resolution in retiring from the Ring, and we hope that no vain flattery on the part of any interested admirers will induce him to change his resolution.

These excellent remarks of the writer on the readiness

of silly persons to impute dishonesty to the losing pugilist
are as laudable as they are just and honest.

With this easy defeat of Brettle we shall close the third
chapter of our history, reserving for the fourth and concluding one a glance at the History of the Championship,
and the interesting events of the great though undecided
international conflict at Farnborough.

CHAPTER IV.

The Championship, brief history of—Challenges to Sayers, Aaron Jones and Heenan—Overtures from the New World—Matched with "the Benicia Boy"—Sketch of John Camel Heenan—The fight at Farnborough—Reflections—Testimonials to Sayers—He retires—His last Ring appearance—The Wadhurst fight—Subsequent life, last illness, and death.

BEFORE narrating the particulars of Sayers' last, and, if not most gallant, at least most talked of battle, it may be interesting to many to whom the history of the Ring is unknown, and a refresher to those whose reading has included the text-books of pugilism, to give a succinct narrative of the Championship of England and of the holders of the belt.

A SUCCINCT HISTORY OF THE CHAMPIONSHIP.

Though there can be no reasonable doubt that the earliest weapons of defence and offence were those which Nature has provided, the inquiry into the methods used by the ancients to render blows with the fist more fatal and effective, would be beside the object we have in view[*]

[*] It is nowhere recorded that in public fights of Greeks or Romans the pugilists contended with naked hands and arms. The *cæstus*, was composed of strong interlaced leather straps, embracing the clenched fist and part of the wrist, these, winding up the forearm, were fixed at the elbow. They appear to have been often armed with knobs of brass, iron, &c. There is a full description of the *cæstus* worn by Erix in the fifth book of the *Æneid*. The *chirotheca* were boxing-gloves stuffed with lead. These barbarous weapons

in this brief sketch of our English championship. Waiving, then, all questions of the antiquity of what Britons understand as the art pugilistic, we proceed at once to notice the progress of boxing in England in its present form.

James Figg, a native of Thame, Oxfordshire, of whose portrait, name, and fame we owe the preservation to two great men—the first, William Hogarth, Nature's painter and the satirist of vice, the second, Captain Godfrey, a man whose spirited little quarto, "A Treatise on the Useful Science of Defence," contains inherent proof of his own modesty, manliness, and bravery—is the first recorded champion. In 1719, we find incidentally, from the pages of Captain Godfrey, that professors of gymnastics and boxing were numerous, but foremost of these stood Figg, who in that year had an "Academy" in Tottenham-court-road, then a great centre of attraction.* Figg's placards profess to teach "defence scientifically," and his fame for "stops and parries" was so great that we find him mentioned in the *Tatler*, *Guardian*, and *Craftsman*, the foremost literary miscellanies of the time. We find in some lists of "champions" the names of "Pipes and Gretting." They neither of them had any claim to the title farther than the then common use of the word "champion" by every public boxer.

GEORGE TAYLOR was the successor of Figg, who died in 1740, having retired in 1734. He was also proprietor

were neutralized in their fatal effects by the *amphotides*, a defensive helmet of thongs and stiff leather covering the temporal bones and arteries, encompassing the ears, and buckling under the chin or at back of the neck.

* A curious facsimile of Figg's card, from an etching by Hogarth, is given in "Pugilistica," by the author of this little volume.

of "the Great Booth in Tottenham-court-road." Before this date, however, he had been defeated by Jack Broughton, the waterman.*

JACK BROUGHTON, the father of the English P.R., having defeated Pipes, George Stevenson, Jack James, the Soldier, and other "champions" of George Taylor's Great Booth, including George Taylor himself, seceded in 1742 from that establishment, and under "royal, noble, and distinguished patronage," opened "Broughton's New Amphitheatre," "at the back of the late Mr. Figg's," on the 10th March, 1743. Here was first promulgated a "Code," called "Mr. Broughton's Rules," seven in number, and these served as the statutes of the Ring until 1838 (nearly one hundred years), when they were superseded by the "New rules of the Ring," which, with some modifications in 1843, 1853, and 1864, still regulate pugilistic encounters. After eighteen years' championship, in April, 1750, Broughton succumbed to Jack Slack, who by a chance blow blinded the mighty Broughton, and in fourteen minutes the champion fell from his high estate. The Duke of Cumberland, who had been Broughton's constant patron, lost £10,000. Broughton retired, and Slack held his style and title. Pierce Egan tells us that he was ruined, and that Duke William left him to "whistle down the wind, a prey to fortune." If Pierce had met with the following in the Annual Register for 1789, he would have amended his statement.

"January.—Died at his house at Walcot-place, Lambeth, in his 85th year, the celebrated John Broughton, whose skill in boxing is well known, and will be ever recorded in the annals of that science. He was originally

* For further details see "Pugilistica," vol. i. chaps. ii. and iii.

bred a waterman. His patron, the late Duke of Cumberland, got him appointed one of the yeomen of the guard, which place he enjoyed till his death. He was buried in Lambeth Church on the 21st inst., and his funeral procession was adorned with the presence of the several capital professors of boxing. He is supposed to have died worth £7000."

Slack, whose height was the same as that of the gallant Tom Sayers, was nearly 14 stone in weight, so that he must have been either a prodigy of strength, or he must have entered the ring more in the form of a prize ox than that of a pugilist. This boxer was only twice called upon to defend his title after his defeat of Broughton until the year 1760, being ten years after that event. In that year the Duke of Cumberland brought out Bill Stevens (the Nailer), who, being a man of great strength and skill, and being also much younger than Slack, easily upset his pretensions to high rank. Bill Stevens, although a promising miller, appears to have formed a very early acquaintance with "Mr. Barney," a gentleman whose interference at prize battles has of late years been, we are glad to say, extremely unfrequent. We find that only three months after the fight with Slack, Stevens met George Meggs, a collier, of Bristol, for 200 guineas. The mill, if such it can be called, came off at the Tennis Court, and from the very commencement it was apparent what was intended. Stevens had made up his mind to lose the fight, but how to do so and still make the semblance of a struggle, was his difficulty. Meggs could do nothing with him, and was what Tom Sayers would call a perfect "chunck;" at last in 17 minutes, Stevens, with the greatest effrontery, declared that he would fight no more, and Meggs was proclaimed the Champion. Stevens quickly sunk to the lowest depths of degradation. He fought one or two other battles, but they were with men of no repute, and are not worthy of record. Meggs quickly lost his position, being defeated easily by one Millsom, who, in turn, handed the name of champion to Tom Juchau (the Paviour). Tom had to defend it against Bill Darts, whom he fought for 1000 guineas. Long and desperately did he struggle, and the odds varied almost every round. Tom's hour at length arrived, however, and Darts bore off the belt. Darts defeated Dogget (a bargee), and Swansey (the butcher), and at the end of a five years' reign was deposed by Lyons (the waterman of Kingston-on-Thames), after a slashing fight of 45 minutes, in June, 1769. How or by whom Lyons was overthrown, we know not, as we have no record of any further performances on his part. Two years afterwards, however, we find one Peter Corcoran, a native of the Emerald Isle, claiming the championship, and defending his rights against Bill Darts, who striving to regain his ancient position, fought him May 10, 1771, for £200. The battle was won in a single round by Corcoran, and was alleged to be anything but square. His next encounter was with Harry Sellers, and here there appears to be no doubt that the friends of Sellers were the *buyers*, while Corcoran was the seller, as after 23 minutes Corcoran gave in without the semblance of a struggle, and without having any punishment whatever. This was the finish of his career, and he sunk into oblivion. Sellers lost his title to one Harris, who in turn was succeeded by the celebrated Tom Johnson, who appears to have been an enormously powerful man, standing about 5ft. 9in., and weighing

14 stone. His courage was extraordinary, but his knowledge of the art of self-defence does not seem to have been of first-class order. Johnson defeated Bill Warr, who fought on the dropping system, and next vanquished Mike Ryan twice in succession; but there seems not much doubt that had Ryan kept his temper he might have turned the tables.

Johnson's next match was with the gigantic Perrins, a man of 17 stone weight, and standing over 6ft. 2in. This was somewhat of the Caunt and Bendigo style, and was only won by Johnson through his adopting the go-down game to avoid the terrific hugs of his antagonist. The adoption of these shifty tactics, causing then, as it does now, the disgust of all lovers of fair play and stand-up fighting, seems to have lost Johnson many staunch friends. His hour of retribution soon after arrived. A man named Brain (alias Big Ben) who on a former occasion had had to forfeit to Johnson from illness, issued a fresh challenge, which was at once accepted, and a match was made for 500 guineas, which took place Jan. 17, 1791, when Johnson was forty-one years of age, his opponent being four years younger. Brain was as powerful a man as Johnson, and a harder hitter. The battle was a tremendous hand-to-hand encounter. Each scorned to stop or shift, but they stood and hit away round after round, each being in turn floored by terrific blows. At last Johnson got tired, and in the concluding few rounds fell very weak. The battle was concluded by his being hit out of time by a blow on the mouth. This was Johnson's last battle, and he died six years afterwards in Cork. Brain, like Johnson, never again entered the P. R. He was matched in 1794, with one Wood, a coachman; but before the fight could come off he was seized with an illness from which he never recovered, and he died on the 8th of April in the same year.

On the death of Brain the renowned Dan Mendoza at once laid claim to the title of Champion. Mendoza had twice defeated Gentleman Humphries, and had also overturned Bill Warr, a quondam opponent of Johnson. Warr, on his conqueror taking unto himself the pride of place, appears to have obtained fresh courage, and moved for a new trial, which Dan most graciously accorded him. The court sat on Bexley Heath, November 12, 1794, but the arguments of Warr were of so paltry a character that in the short space of 15 minutes Mendoza was allowed to have shown sufficient cause for retaining his place, and Bill Warr was mulcted in all the costs of the trial. On the 15th of April, 1795, Dan Mendoza had to resign in favour of the greatest boxer of the age (the late Mr. John Jackson). They fought for 200 guineas a side, and poor Dan was overthrown in nine rounds, occupying the short space of ten and a half minutes. Dan fought twice after his defeat by Jackson, viz.—with Harry Lee, whom he defeated in 1806, and with Tom Owen, to whom he succumbed in 1820, Mendoza being then 57 years of age and Owen 52. Mendoza died, aged 73, September 3, 1836. Mr. Jackson (Gentleman Jackson, as he was deservedly called) found no one possessing sufficient hardihood to dispute his right to the Championship, and in a few years quietly retired from the Ring. For a long period he carried on his rooms in Bond-street, where he had the honour of instructing members of the royal family and the nobility and gentry in the science of self-defence, many of whom afterwards rose to high stations either as

statesmen, warriors, or literary men. Mr. Jackson accu-
mulated a considerable fortune, and on retiring into
private life enjoyed the intimacy and gained the respect
and affection of many of his former pupils. He was
always a welcome guest at their houses, and at his death
in 1845, he was much lamented. He was in his 76th
year. Mr. Jackson had the honour of being selected as
one of the pages at the coronation of George the Fourth.

On Mr. Jackson's retirement, Jem Belcher, who seems
in size and daring to have been a prototype of Tom Sayers,
appeared upon the scene, and Dan Mendoza, who was
supposed to be next to Mr. Jackson, not feeling disposed
to dispute his pretensions, Joe Berks, a butcher, attempted
to pull him from the seat of honour. They fought twice,
but with the same result, each battle resulting in the easy
defeat of Berks, who, although taller and two stone
heavier than Jem, had not the ghost of a chance against
his superior skill and quickness. Jem then defeated Jack
Fearby, a 15-stone man, six feet in height, who scarcely
touched him, while Fearby was fearfully punished in the
short space of 20 minutes. This was in April, 1803.
On the 24th July following, Jem had the misfortune to
lose his eye in playing rackets, and having gone into
business as a publican, it was thought he would not re-
enter the ring. Jem, who was a native of Bristol, now
brought into notice his fellow-townsman, Harry Pearce
(the Game Chicken), whom he matched against his former
opponent Berks, and Pearce twice defeated that hero with
as great ease as Jem himself. Pearce was hailed as Champion at this time, and Belcher offered no opposition. In
October 1805, Pearce had to defend his newly acquired
honours against Mr. Gully, staking 600 guineas to 400

guineas. The fight lasted 77 minutes, during which 64 rounds were fought at Hailsham, and Pearce was the winner.

Jem Belcher, who seems to have been brooding over his own misfortunes, now allowed jealousy of his own pupil to get the better of him, and in an unlucky moment he challenged him. Pearce, although reluctant to encounter his old and tried friend, could not of course decline to defend his title, and a match was made for 500 guineas, which came off Dec. 6, 1806. Belcher was still only 26 years of age; but the loss of his eye, and the dissipated life he had led told a tale, and he had not a chance against the superior strength and vigour of Pearce, who defeated him in 18 rounds and 35 minutes. Pearce never again entered the ring. He was consumptive by nature, and, being rather partial to gay life, quickly added to the seeds of disease already sown in him, and retiring to Bristol in 1807, died in 1809. In 1808 the title of Champion was by acclamation awarded to Mr. Gully, who after his defeat by Pearce had twice conquered Gregson, and who at the time was certainly the fittest man for the post. Mr. Gully, however, declined to defend the office, having retired into private life ; and the renowned Tom Cribb, who had also defeated Gregson, and that too with consummate ease, and moreover in 1807 vanquished Jem Belcher, although not without difficulty, was pitched upon as eligible.

Cribb was by no means unwilling to undertake the responsibility of office. No sooner, however, did Jem Belcher hear of this than the old leaven commenced working again, and he could not rest satisfied until he had had another trial with his conqueror. The fight came off Feb. 1, 1809, on Epsom Race Course (what a contrast to modern times!), and was won by Tom in 31 rounds and 40 minutes. Notwithstanding the shortness of this battle, it showed that had Belcher possessed his original stamina, Tom Cribb, although so much bigger and heavier, would have stood a poor chance against his superior skill and activity. It was Belcher's last appearance in the P. R., and he died in 1811, at the early age of 30. Tom Cribb, who was a 14-stone man, and rather a slow hitter, was one of the gamest of the game, and possessed of prodigious strength. He was not destined to hold his laurels without some desperate struggles, and his two heavy battles with Molineaux are even now the constant theme of conversation, and the subject of admiration to the few Ring-goers of the Old School who remember them. The first fight took place for 200 guineas a side, at Copthall Common, Dec. 10, 1810; 35 rounds were fought in 55 minutes, and for real milling never was such a battle seen. Both fought with a spirit and determination which electrified the spectators, and several times during the fight it was trick and tie. Strong as Tom Cribb was, the gallant black was stronger, and it was the superior skill and determination alone of the former that in the end gained him the victory. Indeed, at one time, in the nineteenth round, Molineaux had Cribb in such a ticklish position on the ropes, and held him so tight while he fibbed him, that many persons were of opinion he would have won had not the ring been broken in. At the conclusion, Cribb was almost as much exhausted as his opponent, and it was some time before he recovered himself.

The public were so satisfied with the performance of

Molineaux, that they resolved to give him another chance, and these heroes met again on the 28th of September, 1811, at Thistleton Gap, for £300 a-side. On this occasion Tom Cribb was taken in hand by Captain Barclay, who trained him on his own system at Ury, and reduced his weight to 13 st. 6 lb. Tom never looked better than on this occasion. The Captain's system had done wonders, and so confident were his friends that they laid 3 to 1 on him. The fight took place on a stage, and there were some 20,000 persons present. This battle was far different from the first. Cribb at once took a decided lead: Molineaux appeared no longer the same man, and was defeated in 11 rounds, occupying less than 20 minutes. In the ninth, his jaw was fractured by a terrible right-hander from the champion.

Tom Cribb never again entered the P. R., although he held the Championship for many years, no one having the hardihood to dispute his right. He was the first champion on record to whom a belt was presented as a badge of office. That belt, which is made of lion's skin, and ornamented with large silver claws, was, with Tom's presentation-cup, last in the possession of Tom Sayers. In the latter part of Tom Cribb's reign many pugilists arrogated to themselves the title of Champion, but not one of them had the hardihood to beard the hero himself. Among those who set up on their own hook, were Hickman (the Gas Man), Jack Carter, and Bill Neat. Hickman was defeated by Neat, while Neat and Jack Carter were both conquered without much trouble by Tom Spring. It was this latter boxer who was brought into notice by Tom Cribb, and was always looked upon by him as "his boy," who was destined, on the retirement of Cribb, to succeed him in his honours.

Tom Spring, who was born in 1795, and was about
13st. 2lb., defeated Ned Painter, and was in turn beaten
by that boxer, who however retired from the ring without giving Tom a chance of playing out the rubber.
Spring then defeated Jack Carter in May, 1819, on
Crawley Downs, after a long scientific encounter, in
which Carter never got the lead, and, indeed, never had
a chance, although the public at the commencement laid
3 to 1 on him. His next opponents were Ben Burn, Bob
Burn, Josh. Hudson, Tom Oliver, and Bill Neat; and it
was after his fight with the latter that Tom Cribb re-
signed the Championship into his keeping. Spring had
not long to wait before he was called on to uphold his
new-born honours, and twice in the year 1824 did he
have to defend himself against the onslaughts of Jack
Langan (the Irish Champion). Long and desperately did
Langan struggle, but in vain, against the superior science
of Spring; each battle ended in his downfall, the first in
140 minutes, and the second in 108; in each encounter
there were 77 rounds. Spring was never a severe hitter;
his hands were so soft that he never polished off his men
with the quickness perceptible with some of his predecessors. Such was his science, however, and the excellence
of his guard, that it was with the greatest difficulty he
could be got at. After his second defeat of Langan, Tom
Spring announced his retirement from the ring, and
again was there an interregnum before it could be decided who should reign in his stead. Langan refused to
re-enter the P. R., and. Josh Hudson, who had defeated
Jem Ward in 1823, was the first man selected; but a
fortnight after Spring's retirement he was defeated with
ease by Tom Cannon, and on his making a second attempt
suffered a like fate.

Cannon, having arrogated to himself the Champion's seat, was at once challenged by Jem Ward, who had much improved since his defeat by Hudson, and a match for £500 a-side was won by Jem in 10 minutes, in July, 1825. Jem on this victory was encircled with a Champion's belt, which he retained undisturbed until January 2, 1827, when he was defeated by Peter Crawley in 11 rounds, occupying 26 minutes.

Crawley was now of course proclaimed the Champion, but at a benefit at the Tennis Court, two days after the fight, on Ward's friends offering to make a fresh match, Peter Crawley announced that he had done with the Ring for ever as a principal, and that Ward was welcome to resume the position he had lost in their recent fight. Jem was only twice more called upon to protect his honours, viz., with old Jack Carter, whom he defeated May 27, 1828, and Simon Byrne, for whom he performed a similar office in July, 1831. In 1832 Jem went into business at Liverpool, and announced that he had retired from the Ring, and would present a belt to the first man who proved worthy of it. The first claimant was the well-known Deaf Burke, who, in May, 1832, defeated old Jack Carter, and in January following polished off in style one Macone, who stood 6 feet 2 in height and weighed 15 stone, the Deaf-un being only 5 feet 8 inches, and 13 stone. The Deaf-un's claims were disputed by Simon Byrne, who, as will be remembered, was Ward's last opponent, and he and Burke were matched to fight for £100 a-side in May, 1833. This desperate encounter, it is well known, ended fatally to Byrne.

Burke now challenged Jem Ward for £100 a-side, but Ward declined to come out for that amount, and

there was much talk in fancy circles about an unknown
being found to fight the Deaf-un. That worthy, whose
cly was never too well supplied, offered to fight any one
for £100, which was the extent of his tether, but no one
fancied him at that price, and at length, in 1837, he went
to the United States, where he fought and beat O'Rourke
the Irish Champion, but had to cut and run from the
friends of the latter, who threatened to convert him into
sausages with their bowie-knives. After defeating
another Paddy, named O'Conner, in the States, he returned to England in 1838, and once more proclaimed
himself Champion, He quickly found, however, that
·during his absence circumstances had altered cases. There
had arisen upon the pugilistic horizon sundry big men and
true, every one of whom was an ugly customer. There
was Ben Caunt, there was bold Bendigo, and there was
Brassey of Bradford, each of whom was more than a
match for the Deaf-un. During his absence Caunt and
Bendigo had fought twice, the second battle being lost by
Bendy, who fell without a blow, and upon the Deaf-un's
arriving and claiming the belt, the first who disputed his
right, was Bendigo, with whom, after much chaff on both
sides, Burke was matched, and staked £120 to £100.
The fight came off February 12, 1839, Burke weighing
12st. 6lb., and Bendigo about 12st. Burke was the
favourite, but he never had a chance, and in the end he
lost the battle by butting his opponent with his nob,
which was at once proclaimed foul. The fight occupied 24
minutes, during which ten rounds were fought.

Jem Ward now girded the promised belt upon the loins
of Bendigo, it having taken seven years before he could
make up his mind who should wear it. A fresh match

was shortly afterwards talked of between Caunt and Bendigo, but Caunt, from some cause unknown, did not come to the fore, and Bendy proclaimed himself ready to meet any one in the world. His career was shortly afterwards stopped, for on the 23rd of March, 1840, while turning somersaults, he had the misfortune to break his kneecap, which for several years rendered him incapable of violent exertion, and he had to retire. Immediately this was announced the Deaf-un once more laid claim to the Championship, whereupon Nick Ward, brother to Jem, denied his right, and they were matched forthwith for £50 a-side. They fought September 22, 1840, and Burke was defeated in 17 rounds.

Nick Ward now considered himself Champion, and, like his predecessors, threw down the gauntlet, which was not long allowed to remain, for Ben Caunt, who, after a desperate combat, had conquered Brassey on the 27th of October, 1840, also put in his claims to the belt, and after a little discussion a match was made for £100 a-side, which came off on the 2nd of February, 1841. From the beginning Ward adopted the dropping system, which, by-the-by, was by no means necessary, for he was far the better fighter and tactician, and there is little doubt that he could always have defeated Caunt had it not been for a want of something within his mind to give him the required confidence. On the present occasion he was destined to be successful, for Big Ben, losing his temper at being baulked by Nick's dropping in the seventh round, lent him such a pair of cracks on the side of his nob when down on both knees that the referee had no option but to decide against him. Caunt, of course, was deeply mortified at this, and a fresh match was at once made for

£100 a-side, which came off on the 11th of May, 1840, on which occasion a transferable belt was added to the stakes. In this mill the verdict on the former occasion was reversed, and at the end of the thirty-fifth round Ward, although by no means heavily punished, declined to have any more. The belt, therefore, became the property of Ben, who now, finding no one sufficiently venturous to dispute his rights, paid a visit to the United States, whence he returned in March, 1842, bringing with him Charley Freeman (the American giant), whose brief career in this country is alluded to *ante*, pp. 68, 69.

For some time after Ben's return he was allowed to rest upon his laurels; but early in 1845, Johnny Broome having offered to produce a man to fight Caunt, the latter came out once more, and on inquiry it transpired, to the surprise of all, that Bendigo was to be the Simon Pure. Caunt was nothing loth, and the fight came off September 9, 1845, for £200 a-side. How that fight was decided against Caunt is well known.

Caunt several times attempted to make a fresh match, but in vain—Bendy was not to be had; and in 1846 both Caunt and Bendigo announced their retirement from the Ring, and Bendy intimated that he would hand the belt to the worthiest candidate. In 1850, however, he seems to have changed his mind, and, there being no one on the cards fit to hold the proud position, Bendy called at our office and announced that, as no one seemed inclined to do battle for the trophy, he would again come out and try whether any young one could be tempted to try his mettle against such an old 'un. The only man who had the hardihood to take up this challenge was Tom Paddock, who, beyond his two defeats of Nobby Clarke, had hitherto done nothing worthy of notice. Tom, however, was then a fine, fresh young fellow, full of pluck and strength, although destitute of knowledge of the art. They were matched for £200 a-side, and fought June 5, 1850, at Mildenhall. It was a gallant and determined battle, and the youthful vigour of Paddock, evinced by his continued desperate rushes, had well nigh proved too much for his staler opponent. Towards the conclusion, however, Paddock lost his temper completely, and Bendy having resorted to his usual dropping game, Tom so far allowed his passion to get the better of him, that, in the 49th round, he struck Bendy while on his knees, and the referee was constrained to decide against him.

On the stakes for this match being handed to Bendigo a fortnight after the fight, that eccentric individual for the last time announced that, feeling satisfied with his performances, he now really intended to retire from the Ring; and once more did the title of champion go begging. Not long did it remain in abeyance, for the Tipton Slasher, who had for some time had his eye upon the proud position, shortly announced that he was ready and willing to uphold his right to it against all comers. He said he would fight any man breathing for £200 or £300 a-side, or he would stake £350 to £300, and fight Tom Paddock. A meeting took place soon after, at which he and Paddock were matched on these terms, but the match ended in smoke. Shortly after they were again matched for £150 a-side, but this ended in a draw. The Fancy were in despair, but had not long to brood over their disappointment, for, in a very brief period, another engagement was entered into between them, for £100 a-side, and this engagement really ended in a mill, which came off, December 17th,

1851, at Woking, after several ineffectual attempts to
bring it off in other localities. *Bell's Life* of the period
speaks in anything but terms of praise of this encounter,
which is there denominated a mere scramble, unworthy
of the name of a fight, and still less of a fight for the
Championship. The result was apparent from the second
round. Paddock displayed no points sufficient to bring
out the qualities which the Slasher was alleged to possess.
From the very commencement the Slasher had a strong
lead, and, at last, in the 27th and last round, at the expiration of 42 minutes, Paddock, after falling in his own
corner, jumped up, and running after the Slasher as he was
retiring to his corner, dealt him a blow behind the ear,
which floored the Tipton close to his second's knee. A
claim of foul was at once made, and the *fiat* of the referee
was, of course, in favour of Perry. The Slasher claimed
from Bendy the belt he had obtained from Caunt, which
the latter refused to deliver up, declaring it was his own
property ; but he offered to fight Perry for £500 a-side.

On the Tipton accepting his terms, however, the bold
Bendy backed out, and from that time remained a quiet
spectator of fistic doings. What has become of the belt,
which, by every rule of fair play, should have been given
to Perry, is not known. The Slasher, unwilling to remain
idle, declared his readiness to meet any one who fancied
him, for £200 a-side, whereupon Harry Broome, in May,
1851, declared his readiness to back an Unknown against
him. This Unknown, as our readers are aware, eventually turned out to be the bold Harry himself, and he
and the Tipton met on the 29th of September, 1851, at
Mildenhall. Neither man appeared in first-rate trim, the
Slasher looking old and stale, and Broome far too fleshy

for such an encounter. The science of Broome enabled him to make some severe lodgments upon the old one, but it was evident the strength and weight were too much for him, unless some accident should give him a turn in his favour. At length, in the 15th round, Broome fell on his knees, and the Slasher, letting go his right at the same moment, caught him a hot one just as he reached the ground. An appeal was instantly made to Peter Crawley, the referee, who ruled it a decided foul, and Broome was declared the winner. Peter came in for a good share of abuse for his decision on this occasion, and was even threatened by the Slasher, whereupon the burly veteran commenced peeling, in order to have a round with Perry to justify his own decision, and hostilities were only prevented by the Slasher being forced away by his friends. An attempt was afterwards made to upset the decision, and Perry talked of taking legal proceedings, but fortunately he thought better of it, and Broome received the stakes. Although there was much talk about a fresh match, none was ever made, and Broome enjoyed his honours unmolested until 1852, when he was challenged by Harry Orme, who, having twice defeated Aaron Jones, was looked upon as a likely one to take the shine out of Master Harry. They fought for £250 a-side, on the 18th April, 1853, just seven years ago, at Brandon, in Norfolk. The mill was won by Broome in 31 rounds, occupying 2 hours 18 minutes, but not without receiving a very considerable amount of punishment. Both, indeed, were severely mauled, and the mill was the nearest approach to the affairs of olden days that had been seen for some time, and was the first Champion fight of a great number that had not ended in a foul of one kind or another. There was an excellent ring throughout, thanks to the constables of the Association, and altogether matters passed off in the most satisfactory manner to all except the losers. After receiving the money for this affair, Broome was again matched with the Tipton Slasher for £200 a-side, but, after two deposits had been made, Harry forfeited, and publicly intimated that he would not again tempt fortune in the P. R., having a more profitable game to play. Orme also retired, his friends being so well pleased with his performances that they installed him as a boniface at the "Jane Shore," Shoreditch. The Slasher was therefore again dubbed Champion, and beyond some talk about a fresh match between himself and Paddock, which ended in the latter backing out, had the course all to himself, until he was called upon to defend his title to the new belt against the claim of the gallant Tom Sayers. This brings our hero again upon the scene. How Tom disposed of the gigantic Tipton, and subsequently of Bill Benjamin, Tom Paddock, and George Brettle, is told in the third chapter of this biography; and how he maintained the honour of the title, and the character of his country against his Transatlantic challengers, it shall be the business of this fourth chapter to narrate.

Origin of the Match.—Not long after the defeat of Aaron Jones by Sayers, the former, seeing no immediate prospect of making a fortune in this country, and having small inclination to tempt the blind goddess again with the gallant Tom, resolved to seek in other lands that success which seemed denied to him in his own. He selected the United States as the best field, and thither accordingly he betook himself. Being a fine-looking young fellow, of good address, and remarkably quiet deportment, he instantly found favour among our cousins, and, making good use of his advantages, rapidly rose in their estimation. His anecdotes of British sporting, and particularly of the doings of himself and his brother pugs, delighted the young bloods of the City of New York, and the subject of pugilism, which had usually only been rife among a chosen few, rapidly became the general theme of conversation. It was soon after his arrival that John Heenan was selected by certain parties in New York as the proper man to " whip " John Morrissey, who, for some reason, had become obnoxious to them. Morrissey, having taken up the gauntlet, had picked out Sheppard, alias Jack Hamilton, an old friend of Tom Sayers, as his trainer, and Heenan's friends, hearing of this, thought their best trump would be Aaron Jones, and Jones accordingly was fixed upon to train the Benicia Boy. This was another excellent chance for Aaron, who took every advantage of it, and did all in his power to get the " Boy " fit for his task. The account of the fight represented, however, that Aaron was not very successful in his efforts, Heenan during the last weeks of his training being attacked by an old ailment, which effectually stopped his work, and consequently forced him to go into the ring with at least a stone of superabundant flesh, and to this his defeat was attributed. About the close of 1858, distance having lent enchantment to the view, it seems to have occurred to Aaron that Tom Sayers was not such a very formidable customer after all, and it began to be rumoured that he was coming home to have a shy for the belt. It was at the same time, too, that rumours reached this country

that Uncle Sam was about to send over one of his champions to see what he could do towards humbling the
pride of little Tom.   Early in 1849 rumour ripened into
certainty, and a letter reached *Bell's Life* office from Mr.
Wilkes, enquiring, on what terms Heenan could be placed
on the rota to have his turn against Sayers.   A good
deal of astonishment was created at the time by the fact
that the defeated man, and not the winner of the American fight for the championship, had been selected; but
when it came to be remembered that Morrissey, the
winner, was an Irishman by birth; and not a native
American, the wonderment ceased, and Heenan was
recognised as the proper representative of America.
The Editor of *Bell's Life* replied to Mr. Wilkes's letter
intimating immediately on the receipt of a deposit from
Heenan he could be placed on the list.   He further
stated, however, that in the event of his winning he would
not be permitted to take the belt back to America, without leaving its equivalent in value or remaining here
three years to contest its possession against all comers on
the usual terms.   By the next mail, after Mr. Wilkes's
first letter, came a second, dated New York, March 29,
1859, which was as follows :—

> "Office *Wilkes's Spirit of the Times*, New York,
> " March 29, 1859.

"DEAR SIR,—Enclosed please find a draft for £200 sterling, drawn
in your favour on the Bank of Liverpool, which I have been requested
to forward to you, on the part of Aaron Jones, in order that you may
deposit for him the necessary sum for a meeting with the Champion
of England within six months of the date of the battle of the 5th
April, between Sayers and Benjamin ; and in case the winner of
that fight do not accept, you will please hold the money subject to
my order.   The language with which Jones accompanies this draft
is as follows :—'I, Aaron Jones, hereby challenge the winner of the

coming fight for the championship, to fight me in six months from that time for two hundred pounds and the Champion's bell. The fight to take place near London, and to be governed by the rules of the London Prize Ring.' Jones also requests me to say to you for him that 'he would prefer having the forfeit or first deposit to be as much as *fifty pounds*, as he does not wish to be at the trouble of crossing the Atlantic for nothing, though he is willing to pay his own expenses over and back to get the fight.' He also hopes that Sayers will, for old acquaintance sake, give him the first chance; but this is a consideration which I have no right to press, after having previously consented to lay before you the wishes or the claims of Heenan. Your sense of propriety will find a law for the matter, and will, I hope, likewise permit me to remain,

" Yours, very truly at command,
"GEO. WILKES.

" P.S.—I am also desired by the backers of Jones to say that the stakes will be increased to *five hundred pounds* a side, if the Champion wishes it. " G. W."

To this letter Sayers at once replied, closing with the proposition of Jones, and thus placing that hero first on the list of candidates after his second battle with Benjamin. Hardly had the missive of the gallant Tom been despatched when another letter arrived from Mr. Wilkes— who throughout acted as the adviser and amanuensis of both Jones and Heenan—enclosing a sum of £50, which he had been directed by his friends to stake with us on the part of Heenan. In that letter he requested the stakeholder, if not contrary to rule, to give Heenan's claim the preference, as that aspiring youth had been the first to challenge Sayers, and was fearful that if he was not at once placed on the list of candidates, his chance of encountering Sayers might be entirely lost by some unforeseen accident. Inasmuch, however, as Jones, with prudent foresight, had been the first to post the coal, the stakeholder felt bound, according to practice, to give him the priority, and Heenan was compelled reluctantly to moderate his impatience ; Heenan, like Jones, offered, if Sayers wished, to increase the stakes to £500 a side.

Shortly after the second defeat of Bill Benjamin, Tom Sayers was called upon to meet Jack Macdonald, who had been delegated by Aaron Jones to act the part of plenipotentiary on his behalf. Another conference was held, and after many *pros* and *cons*, articles were signed, sealed, and delivered, under which Jones was bound to fight the Champion early in the current year, a margin of one month being allowed on either side as to the actual day of battle. For this match £50 a side was deposited. It was not long after this that a further communication was received from Mr. Wilkes, requesting the stakeholder to return him £50 out of the £200 he had sent for Jones, to pay the passage of Aaron to Europe, and to transfer the remaining £100 to the account of the match between Heenan and Sayers. . He added, that if Jones intended to go on with his match he would have to find the remainder of his money himself, his American friends having some reason to be dissatisfied with him, and being desirous of transferring all their interest to the Benicia Boy. By the very next mail came another letter intimating that Jones would be able to find all his money himself, and therefore the match was still to be considered "on," and so for several months the matter rested.

In the following October the public were startled at reading the following letter from Mr. Wilkes to the Editor of *Bell's Life in London :—*

" Office *Wilkes's Spirit of the Times,* New York,
" October 7, 1859.

"MY DEAR SIR,—I take pleasure of informing you that Aaron Jones, conceding to the common desire on this side of the Atlantic to see Heenan have the first chance at Sayers for the Championship (after the Unknown), has desired me to have forfeited the £50 which now remain staked for him in your hands against Sayers. Enclosed I send you Jones's letter authorizing me to take this course; and as I represent the money of his backers, your authority for declaring the match "off" will, I suppose, be considered complete. I forget, as I write, whether Sayers has already covered a deposit of Heenan's for the Championship; if not, please let the same deposit be made and covered in his case (£50) as was made and covered in the case of Aaron Jones. I am very solicitous about this point as, for special reasons, I want Heenan regularly upon the record at as early a moment as possible. I send with this a note to Sayers, directed to your care, in which I apprise him of Jones's forfeit. Please preserve the note of Jones to me, and believe me to be yours, ever truly, at command,

"GEO. WILKES,
"Editor Wilkes's Spirit of the Times."

This communication was of course made known to Sayers without loss of time, and having now no business on hand, the way was clear for the Benicia Boy, and Tom's backers being anxious that he should finish his career as quickly as possible, and get into business, at once covered the £50 of Heenan, and signed articles for Tom to fight him on or about the day originally fixed for the fight with Jones, supposing it was the wish of Heenan to step into Jones's shoes. In this, however, the English managers of the affair had mistaken the meaning of Mr. Wilkes's letter, for on their writing to him, with details of what had been done, the following reply was forwarded:—

"Office, Wilkes's Spirit,
"New York, Nov. 23, 1859.

"MY DEAR SIR,—Your letter of 3rd inst., enclosing copy of articles for a fight between Heenan and Sayers, and signed by the latter, for our acceptance, reached me yesterday, and have been communicated to Heenan. We are all, however, taken by surprise at the proposal that the fight should come off in February next, instead of at the expiration of the regular six months, as was stipulated in the original proposition, and I am requested on Heenan's part to say, that he expects the usual preparatory term will be granted to him. By reference to his cartel you will find he challenged Sayers to fight him near London for £200 and the Champion's Belt, in six months from the date of his (Sayers) reception of that challenge, or the date of the first deposit under it. This challenge having reached England during the pendency of the engagement between Sayers and the Unknown, was kept in abeyance in your hands, and having been further kept back by the next succeeding engagement of Sayers with Jones, was not recognised or received by Sayers until after he had accepted forfeit from Aaron Jones. Being thus left free of all engagements, he responded to the challenge of Heenan, and on the 26th Oct. (I believe) covered the £50 deposit, which you had for months held in Heenan's name. The articles for this *new match*, however, were not signed by Sayers until the 3rd Nov. inst., and consequently Heenan claims that he is entitled to six months' preliminary time from either one or the other of those dates. He, however, desires me to say that if there be anything in the rules of the P. R. Benevolent Association which entitles the Champion to reduce the term for meeting on his acceptance of a regular six months' challenge, he will conform to those rules, and fight Sayers at the indicated time, even though it will leave him deficient of the due preparation ; but he utterly repudiates the idea (which the selection of February by Sayers perhaps infers) that his match with Sayers is a continuation of the match with Jones. With this explanation he desires to state that he will be ready to put up his second deposit of £50 at Owen Swift's in London, on the 15th December next, and if he be not represented at that time by any agent from this country, he begs you will continue your past kindness and again put up the money for him. Waiving no right, but conceding to all rules, he remains your obedient servant, through very respectfully yours,

"GEORGE WILKES."

At first it was feared this would occasion a hitch in the match, but it was not the case. Tom was nothing loth to let the affair take its course. He had promised to give Heenan a chance, and would not disappoint him. He proposed, therefore, to extend the time to the end of March, and a missive with this proposition was despatched across the Atlantic, together with a proposition from Tom that the stakes should be £500 a side, or as much more as Heenan could get. Before, however, it could reach its destination, a Mr. Falkland had left that country as the representative and forerunner of Heenan, prepared, immediately on his arrival, to do the needful on his behalf. Early in December, Mr. Falkland presented himself at the stakeholder's, where he was met by some of the friends of Sayers, but as Tom was not present it was agreed that the evening of Dec. 15, which was set apart for staking a further sum of £50 a side at Owen Swift's, should be selected for coming to terms. At Owen's, on the night in question, Tom made his appearance, and quickly fraternising with the ambassador of his foe, found not the slightest difficulty in arranging everything on the satisfactory footing upon which the match has since stood. Mr. Falkland had instructions not to make the match for more than £200, as Heenan could lay out the remainder of his money to more advantage in bets, the odds being against him. The following day articles were drawn in the approved form, and information was forthwith despatched to Heenan that his presence in the Old Country was at once required.

In the meantime, on the other side of the Atlantic, things had well nigh tended to prevent the consummation of the wishes of the Fancy. John Heenan and his quondam opponent Morrissey had got to loggerheads, and Heenan proposed to fight Morrissey a second time before fighting Sayers. Through the timely diplomacy of Mr. Wilkes, however, the difficulty was solved, by Morrissey promising to give Heenan another chance, in either England or America, for his own sum, should he prove fortunate enough to defeat our champion. With this promise the "Boy" was forced to be content, and after innumerable hair-breadth escapes from warrants 'ont against him for an alleged breach of the peace, he succeeded (again thanks to the good management of Mr. Wilkes) in getting on board the *Asia*, which brought him to this country, landing at Liverpool on the 16th of January, 1860; and now, having landed him on the shores of Old England, the present seems a fit place for a few lines on the "Benicia Boy."

JOHN CAMEL HEENAN was born in the year 1834, in the Naval Arsenal at Troy, United States, where his father was employed in the laboratory department of the gun factory as a charger of shells, &c. His father and mother, as we have already stated, are Irish. Whether Heenan ever assisted his dad in his work we have not inquired; but he seems at an early age to have become forgeman at Benicia, whence he takes his nickname; and it was while working here that he from time to time displayed fistic powers of no ordinary quality. No doubt that the Hibernian blood in his veins added not a little to his inclination for a turn-up with any one who fancied him, and that his coat was often trailed through the fair in the hope that some one might tread on it. Be this as it may, he acquired experience in the use of his digits, which an occasional turn-up at the diggings in California, whither he subsequently betook himself, doubtless tended to improve. On his arrival in New York he seems to have obtained for himself at once a position as one of the leading pugilists of the city, and this, too, without once entering the ring. This being the case, he had no difficulty in obtaining office under Government, and was soon appointed an Inspector of Customs, for, be it known to our unsophisticated readers, the leader of such a class as the race of pugilists in the States is no mean man; and his influence for good, if properly directed, is of great use to the Government. Heenan, being thus rendered comparatively independent, appears to have had no intention of tempting fortune in the P.R. until persuaded by interested people, who desired the downfall of John Morrissey, to throw up his situation, and enter the lists against that worthy, at whose hands he suffered defeat. After this event, Morrissey, at one time, we are told, actually proposed to find money to back Heenan against Sayers, but subsequently a quarrel arose between them, which resulted in another challenge from Heenan to Morrissey; the present trial for the English championship, however, put this aside. Not long after Heenan was picked out as fittest to contend with our little champion, and the history of the negotiations to this match has been already detailed.

Subsequently to the fight we are about to detail, Heenan returned to America, where he was the lion of the day for a brief period, the deliberate and elaborate falsehoods and exaggerations of the American press, in respect to his battle with Sayers, and his treatment on that occasion, awaking general sympathy. Like most American mob heroes, he soon found his popularity on the wane, and returned, at the opening of the late civil war, to the land and people where his pretended friends asserted he had been so foully treated. Heenan, it must be in justice stated, had no part or blame in these misrepresentations and libels on Englishmen and fair play. Heenan returned to this country with a declaration that he did not intend to fight again. Shortly afterwards Tom King, having defeated Jem Mace (who by

the defeat of Sam Hurst, the Staleybridge Infant, had
become champion), declared his retirement from the ring
and his candidature for another ring of the dimensions
of a lady's third finger. In the course of 1863, it was
whispered among some Corinthians of the turf, with
whom Heenan had become a great favourite by his uniform civility and good conduct, that the Benicia Boy
would do battle with anyone who might fancy a bout
with him for not less a sum than £1000; Heenan decidedly objecting to any publication of a challenge in the
newspapers, the propositions, the carrying out of which
was entrusted to Owen Swift, caused Tom King to prick
up his ears. Could it be that there was a Yankee with
1000 sovereigns behind him and no one to put in a claim ?
King, urged by his friends, took up the gauntlet, and the
£2000 were posted. As the day of battle, fixed for the 10th
of December, 1863, approached, all fears as to the match
not being genuine subsided, and in racing circles the match
created much interest, numerous bets of 6 to 4 being laid
on the Benicia Boy, whose appearance at Newmarket
during the October meetings fully justified the confidence
reposed in him. Heenan took his breathings almost entirely at Newmarket in company with his own brother
and Macdonald, but required very little, if any, looking
after. His feats as a pedestrian during his work were
something extraordinary; six miles and a "bittock"
did he generally turn in ordinary walking, and many a
spin and a tie-up did he give to some of our crack jocks,
among whom are to be found no mean specimens of fair
toe-and-heel walkers. Heenan's spins at the top of his
speed, too, not a little "astonished the Browns ;" he could
on a pinch do his quarter in 56 seconds—not bad for a

fourteen stone man, standing nearly 6ft. 2in. When
stripped his frame was a perfect model for a sculptor.
Every muscle was swollen out to a gigantic size, and
every tendon and sinew was distinctly visible; taken altogether, such a specimen of a Herculean frame had not
been seen in the British P.R. for very many years. King's
weight on the occasion of the fight, which took place at
Wadhurst, Sussex, on the 10th December, 1863, was
thirteen stone. It will be in the recollection of all how
after a brave, but by no means a clever battle, of twenty-
four rounds, occupying but thirty-five minutes, the gallant
Tom thoroughly extinguished Heenan's pretensions to the
laurels of the championship. From this period, with
the exception of an appearance before the quarter sessions
at Colchester, with King and others, on a charge of breach
of the peace at Wadhurst on the day aforesaid, which
ended in an acquittal, Heenan's career—he is still in
England—has not belonged to public life. We may also
note that this was Tom Sayers' last appearance in the
roped ring, he acting in the capacity of second to his
former adversary, the Benicia Boy.

We will now hark back to London and the doings of
the day previous to the eventful 17th of April, 1860.

Though it was made known to those who invested their
gold in the tickets for the journey " to and from London "
that the start would be as early as four o'clock, this
seemed to have no effect in deterring those who had
resolved to be " thar," as our Yankee visitors expressed it.

The scene at Owen Swift's and at Harry Brunton's,
where tickets were obtainable on Monday night, beggars
description ; the crush was terrific ; and many were

entirely unsuccessful in getting tickets at all. Nat Langham's, Alec Keene's, and other sporting houses, were also
crammed, but there was not the same difficulty in carrying on the business of the landlords as at the first houses
named, where at one time trade was at a stand-still.
Many of the frequenters of the sporting hostelries evidently determined to make a night of it in order to make
a certainty of being up betimes in the morning, and that
they carried their intentions fully into effect was plainly
visible in their countenances on their emerging into daylight. The more prudent ring-goers, however, took time
by the forelook, and early ensconced themselves in their
beds until the summons to be up and doing should arouse
them.

The scene at London Bridge station was one of continual bustle for an least an hour before the time appointed
for the start, and, judging from the early arrivals, all
seemed impressed with the necessity of taking time by the
forelook. The precincts of the station reminded us of
the crush on the Derby day, but the effect was far more
striking from the circumstance of its being a "midnight
flitting." The company's arrangements, however, were
such as to meet the pressing requirements, and the travellers by the late trains from the provinces, and those who
had postponed the purchase of their tickets until the last
moment were enabled to provide themselves with the
necessary passport at the last moment. Two monster
trains were prepared, and as early as half-past three the
first, which consisted of thirty-three carriages, was so full
that the non-arrival of the men, both of whom were
accommodated at private lodgings close by, alone delayed
its departure. The champion arrived first, and his fresh,

stylish appearance indicated a good night's rest, and especial pains with his *toilette*. He was soon followed by Heenan, who seemed to wish to avoid recognition, and instantly proceeded to a compartment reserved for him and his seconds. The tickets were then collected, and at twenty minutes past four they started on their journey. By this time night had cast off her sable mantle, and day dawned with that peculiar tint which foretold the brilliant sunny weather with which that expedition was favoured., Throughout the whole of the metropolitan districts, which extends for sixteen miles from London, the police, both mounted and on foot, and all armed with cutlasses, were on the look out on each side of the line even at this early hour; but the speed at which the train proceeded at once satisfied those watchful guardians that the mill was never intended to take place within their bailiwick, after leaving which scarcely a soul was to be seen beyond husbandmen proceeding to their daily avocations.

Great preparations were made to " stop the mill" further down, both on the Dover and Brighton lines; but they were unnecessary, as the travellers turned off at Reigate Junction on to the Guildford line, along which the train rattled at a good pace—we may say, " in peaceful serenity" —until within a short distance of the latter old-fashioned country town, where the first stoppage was made for water. In due course the journey was resumed, and in a short time the travellers entered the wild district where the military town of Aldershott is situated, the deserted appearance of which satisfied all that the " pilot" to whom the selection of the *locale* had been entrusted had made a " happy choice." It was near seven o'clock when the first train discharged its. living burthen at Farnborough station,

after a most pleasant journey through one of the prettiest
countries in England, which, illumined by a glorious sun,
and shooting forth in vernal beauty, must have inspired
all with feelings of intense gratification; whilst the
Benicia Boy and the numerous Americans present must
have been struck with the highly favourable contrast to
the miserable pilgrimage which from all accounts preceded their representative's last appearance in the ring,
when he fought Morrissey in America. No time was
lost in choosing the spot for the ring, which was quickly
and well formed by the veteran Tom Oliver and his son,
in a meadow adjoining the railway, situate on the borders
of Hampshire and Surrey, and within half-a-mile of the
Farnborough station on the South Western line. By
this time the second train had reached its destination,
and the crowd could not have numbered fewer than
twelve hundred persons, both of high and low degree,
though compared with former mills the present " con-
gregation" must unhesitatingly be pronounced the most
aristocratic ever assembled at the ring side. It included
the bearers of names highly distinguished in the pages of
Burke and Debrett; officers of the army and navy,
members of Parliament, justices of the peace, and even
brethren of the cloth; whilst the muster of literati on
behalf of the leading metropolitan journals and the most
popular periodicals and miscellanies—to say nothing of
the editorial and pictorial staffs of our American con-
temporaries, *Wilkes's Spirit of the Times* and *Leslie's
Illustrated News*—gave quite a new feature to the gather-
ing, and evinced at the same time the overwhelming
interest and excitement this great national event has
created throughout both hemispheres. The sale of inner-

ring tickets (raised to 10s. each on this occasion) produced
a large revenue to the Pugilistic Benevolent Association,
and Duncan's speculation in chairs must have been a
most successful one, judging from the demand for those
conveniences, by means of which the spectators were
enabled to "see the fight" with comparative comfort.

APPEARANCE OF THE MEN.—All being in readiness,
and the immense crowd disposed in tolerable order by
the exertions of those of the ring-keepers who chose
to do their duty, Tom Sayers appeared at the ring side,
and having deposited his hat within the ropes, quickly
followed it himself, attended by his old pal, Harry
Brunton, and the accomplished Jemmy Welsh, as seconds.
The Benicia Boy was not long in following his example,
attended by Jack Macdonald and his trainer, Cusick.
Tom looked as dapper and well set up as ever, and was
full of smiles. The Boy, whose attire was not quite so
fashionable, was also all on the broad grin. They eyed one
another curiously for a few seconds, this being, it must
be recollected, their first meeting, and then advancing,
shook hands most cordially together, each regarding the
other with evident friendly feeling. The warmth of the
greeting appeared to give great satisfaction to the surrounding multitude, who cheered vociferously. The
men conversed for a few minutes, but of course the subject of their interview did not transpire. Umpires and
a referee having now been appointed, the signal was
given to prepare for the combat. The first ceremony,
that of tying the colours to the stakes, was then proceeded with, and no time was out to waste in doffing
their upper toggery. Each had taken the precaution to
put on his boots and drawers previous to entering the

ring, so that the usual tedious process of lacing the men's
boots was dispensed with. In Heenan's case, however, there
would have been no necessity for this, as his boots were
of fashionable make, with elastic sides. He was the first
to appear in buff, and a single glance was sufficient to
show that his condition was all that could be required
by the most fastidious. Tom's mahogany bust was
quickly after bared to the gaze of the multitude, and
here, too, was evidence of strict attention to his work.
They had a final rub from their seconds, and now
advanced to give the final friendly shake. This was the
time to get a fair idea of their respective proportions, and
in size it really looked a horse to a hen. Heenan stood
full 4½ inches over Tom, and had an immense advantage
in length. Every muscle on his broad back, his shoulders,
and arms, was well developed, and gave evidence of
enormous power. His legs are rather light, but still
there is no lack here of wire and activity. His skin
was exceedingly fair and transparent, and shone like
that of a thorough bred. His mug was hard, and looked
older than we expected, his cheek-bones being very pro-
minent, and now that they had been denuded of much
that was superfluous, his *tout ensemble* was far more like
that of his brother professional than his first interview
with us. Tom looked brown and hard as nails : his
well-knit frame seemed fitter than we have seen it for
years. He looked visibly older even than when he
fought Brettle, but considering what he has gone through,
this is not to be wondered at. The only points in which
there appeared any advantage on his side were in his
loins and his legs, which were cast in a decidedly stronger
mould than those of his towering opponent. The con-

trast between them was far greater than between Tom
and the Tipton Slasher, and taking into consideration the
fact that the advantage in age on this occasion was
t'other way, Tom's work seemed indeed cut out. That
he had the remotest doubt as to the result we do not for
an instant believe. He smiled confidently, and had evidently made up his mind to do or die. Heenan seemed
to have an equally decided opinion as to the termination
of the battle, and, to use an expression of his own
countrymen, he was "all thar." He won the toss for
corners, and, of course, placed himself with his back to
the sun ; and, in addition to this, he had the advantage
of being on slightly rising ground, so that Tom had all
the way through to fight up hill. The usual ceremony
was now gone through by the seconds and men. Time
was called at twenty-nine minutes past seven, and they
commenced

THE FIGHT.

ROUND I.—Heenan at once threw himself into very fair position,
his left well balanced ready for a shoot, and the right across the
body. Tom's position was the same as ever, lightly but firmly
planted on his pins. He smiled and nodded, and on Heenan trying
to lead off his left got well back. Heenan tried again, his reach
being tremendous, but again did Tom get well away. Tom now
essayed a draw, but the Boy was awake. Each feinted and dodged
to find out a weak point, but for a short time each fortress was too
well guarded. At last Tom let go his left and right, but out of distance. Heenan shook his nob and grinned, then again tried a lead,
but was short. They got gradually to Heenan's corner, who appeared disposed to fight on the defensive, and the sun being in
Tom's eyes seemed to bother him not a little. At length they
came together, and sharp left-handers were exchanged, Tom getting
on the "Boy's" nose, drawing first blood, and Heenan leaving his
sign manual on Tom's frontispiece. Heavy counter-hits followed.
Tom again getting on the nose, and receiving on the nob. More
sparring ensued to a close, when Heenan seized Tom round the

neck, but Tom pegged away at the back of his head until he made him leave that, and Tom fell, laughing.

2.—Heenan showed marks of Tom's handiwork on the back of his neck, and Tom's forehead was flushed. Heenan kept to his corner, whither Tom went to draw him out ; when he thought Tom was near enough, the Boy lunged out his left, but Tom stopped him and got back. The Boy tried again, and just reached Tom's nose. After one or two feints a pretty counter took place, Tom getting on the nose, and receiving a sharp one over the right eye. Heenan then closed, got well hold of him, and threw the Champion, falling heavily on him. Offers to take 2 to 1.

3.—After a little lively fiddling, Tom got too near to the big-un, who instantly slung out his left straight and full on the bridge of Tom's beak, knocking him clean off his pins. ["First knock down" for Heenan.]

4.—Tom, on coming up, looked rather astonished, and his eyes blinked in the sun like a dissipated owl. Heenan went at once to him at the scratch, dodged him, and once more planted a heavy spank with his left. This time on the jaw, and down went Tom again, amidst the shouts of the Yankees, who now offered 6 to 4 on Heenan. The Sayers party looked excessively blue.

5.—Tom's mug showed visible marks of the Boy's powers of hitting. He was cautious and kept away from his man ; Jack followed, and letting go his left on the mouth, was well countered by Tom on the proboscis. Heenan now bored in, and after dodging Tom, got again heavily on the sneezer, and Tom fell.

6.—Tom's countenance, though not swelled, was much flushed, while the boy was almost scatheless. He was somewhat wild, and tried both hands, but missed. Counter-hits ensued, in which Tom received the full weight of Heenan's ponderous fist on his right arm, which was driven back against his face. Tom reached Heenan's left cheek, leaving his mark. Heenan retaliated on the right brow, and Tom fell.

7.—Tom's right peeper displayed marks of pepper, and it was perceptible that he had sustained severe injury to his right arm, which was beginning to swell, and which he now kept close to his body, as if to support it. Still he went to Heenan in his corner, and that hero delivered his left, but not effectively on the chest. Tom danced away, and as he turned round napped a little one from the right on his back. He was quicky out of harm's way, and, coming again, dodged his man until he let fly, when Tom countered him heavily on the right cheek, drawing the claret and raising a considerable bump. The blow staggered Heenan, who stood all of a heap for a moment. Soon did he collect himself, and as Tom came again, lodged a little one on the nose, but was once more countered very heavily on the right cheek, the cut being increased and the bump enlarged. Slight exchanges followed, in which Tom received on the right eye and Heenan on the right cheek, whereupon Heenan went to his corner for a sponge. He seemed in no hurry to come away, and Tom stood in the middle of the ring until the Boy went slowly to him, and tried his left, but it was no go. He tried again, but only just reached Tom's brow. Tom now feinted and got home on the right peeper, Heenan missing an upper-cut. Tom danced away, came again on another tack, and bang went his left on the sore spot, a heavy spank, and he was instantly out of danger, laughing; Heenan rushed after him, but was well stopped, thrice in succession. Again and again Tom went to him, and baulked his efforts to effect a lodgment, and then Heenan napped another slashing crack on the right cheek, which had the effect of at once closing his dexter goggle. He retreated for a wipe, and was followed by Tom, and some mutual cautious dodging and feinting took place. At last Heenan got on the top of Tom's smeller, but not heavily, and Tom then avoided another attempt. Once more did Heenan retire to Jack Macdonald for consolation and advice; Tom walking round and eyeing him in an inquisitive manner, as if admiring his handiwork. Tom, after satisfying his curiosity, went close, and slight exchanges followed, without mischief. Heenan tried his left and was stopped. Both very cautious, and neither disposed to go within gun-shot. Heenan now led off and got slightly on the mouth with his left, Tom retaliating on the closed peeper. Mutual taps and stops, and then Tom got his left heavily on the old spot another cracker, whereupon Jack once more retired into the privacy of his corner, amidst cries of 2 to 1 on Sayers. Tom, after a few turns and a touch of the sponge, went to him, but Heenan shook his nob and seemed disinclined for work. Tom finding he could not draw him, retreated, whereupon the Boy came out, and let go his left viciously, which was beautifully stopped. He then feinted, and got well on the bridge of Tom's snorer as he was retreating, and again knocked him off his pins. Tom rolled over, laughing, and was carried to his corner. This round lasted 13 minutes, and was a fine specimen of stratagem and skill, especially on the part of Tom. His right arm now was much swollen, and so painful, that he could make little or no use of it.

8.—Tom slowest to the call of time, but directly he was at the scratch the Boy retired to his corner, whither Tom had to follow him. Heenan at once let go his left, but Tom laughed and jumped back. A slight exchange followed, and Tom napped a straight one on the sniffer. Heenan now missed a couple of well-meant shots, and Tom jumped away from a third, and as he turned his back upon Heenan got a right-hander on the back of the neck. Heenan followed him up, but Tom grinned and jumped nimbly away. His activity on his pins was as remarkable as ever. Heenan pursued him, and at last lodged his left slightly on the nozzle, and once more turned on the tap. Tom, however, countered him on the damaged

cheek, which caused the Boy to retire for the kind offices of Jack
Macdonald. On Tom's going to him he let go his left on the kisser,
drawing the carmine, and this led to pretty exchanges at long shots
on the cheek. Heenan at this time appeared weak, and the hopes
of the Sayers party were greatly in the ascendant. Heenan preferred his corner to the scratch, and Tom had some difficulty in persuading him to leave. This he at last accomplished, and some
beautiful stops were made on both sides. Another break away
ensued, after which they countered effectively, but Tom was heaviest
on the right cheek which was now swelled as big as two. Heenan's
blow alighted on Tom's oration trap, and drew more of the ruby.
On his trying to repeat this lodgment Tom stopped him cleverly.
Capital exchanges followed, in which Tom was again at home on
the cheek very heavily. Heenan rushed at him, but Tom was away,
and after once or twice being baulked Heenan again retired to his
corner. After Tom had scrutinized him carefully, he rubbed his
hands and went to him, whereupon Heenan let fly his left, but Tom
got well away laughing ; Heenan shook his head and also laughed
good-humouredly. Tom now crept in, and pop went his left on the
plague spot, and off went the Champion laughing. More dodging
and stopping on both sides, until Tom was once more on the cheek
a slogger. Heenan retaliated sharply on the bridge of the snout, and
was stopped in a second attempt, and Tom nailed him on the right
cheek very heavily and got away. Heenan tried to take the lead,
but Tom jumped back. The Boy persevering, got well on the forehead, but was unsuccessful in a second essay. The first was sufficient to leave a bump on the gallant Tom. More sparring until a
severe counter exchange took place, in which Tom got a hot un on the
whistler, which shook his ivories, and turned on a fresh tap. It was
a staggerer, but Tom recovered and went to his man, when more
severe counters were interchanged, Heenan getting another rum one
on the cheek, and dropping his left with effect on Tom's smeller.
Both now indulged in a wipe and washed their mouths out. They
came again now like giants refreshed, and each in turn tried a lead,
but each was well stopped. Tom's right arm, from the continual
stopping such a heavy cannonade as Heenan's, was now much discoloured and swollen, and utterly useless for all purposes of hitting, and he was thus deprived of his principal weapon. After a
good deal of this another heavy exchange followed, in which Tom
was at home on the old spot, and Heenan on the jaw heavily, knocking Tom once more off his pins. This round lasted 20 minutes, and
was a splendid specimen of milling on both sides. Tom's nose and
mouth were bleeding, but both his eyes were well open. His arm
was his chief drawback. Heenan's right eye had been long closed,
his cheek was fearfully swollen, and his mouth was also somewhat
out of straight.

    9.— Heenan came up as if he intended to force the fighting. He led off viciously, but Tom got well away. The Boy followed him closely, and at last got on Tom's mouth, drawing more of the juice. He followed suit on the snuffer-tray with a like result, and counter-hits ensued, in which each did mischief. Heenan continued to bore in, and at last Tom, after getting a little one on the back, dropped laughing.

10.—Tom was very slow to the call of time, and appeared to want nursing. It was evidently heavy work struggling against such superior metal. He stood in the middle of the ring until Heenan went to him, when slight counter hits were exchanged ; after which they closed. Heenan lifted Tom from the ground and threw him heavily with the greatest ease.

11.—Tom, again very much behindhand in coming to time, [and the friends of Heenan did not appear to be in much hurry. When they did come up Tom had to go into Heenan's corner. After a dodge or two Tom got his right on the good eye rather heavily, but it was not such a right-hander as of yore, and evidently gave him pain. Heenan returned on the chest, and Tom fell.

12.—" Time, time," neither too ready. On Sayers at last facing his man, Heenan caught him, but not very heavily, on the jaw, and dropped on the saving suit.

13.—Heenan, first to leave his second's knee, now went to Tom, and after a dodge or two popped the left very straight on Tom's nose, once more knocking him clean off his legs. He turned round on returning to his corner, and looking to Mr. Falkland, his umpire, exclaimed, "That's one for you, Fred." Offers were now made to lay 5 to 4 on Heenan, but the takers seemed scarce.

14.—Tom, very weak, came up cautiously and slowly, his nose being large enough for two. Heenan, seeing Tom's state, tried to force the fighting, but Tom got cleverly out of difficulty. Heenan followed him up, and popped a rattler on the throat, without a return. He paused, and then sent in a little one on the scent-bottle, but Tom countered him well and straight on the nose, drawing the crimson in profusion. Heenan, nothing daunted, let go his left, and was stopped. He then swung round his right heavily on the jaw. They got to close quarters, and some heavy in-fighting took place, in which Tom was very busy. At length both were down heavily, Heenan under.

15.—Neither seemed in a hurry to leave his second's knee, but Tom was slowest in answering the call. Heenan at once went to him, got the left well on the proboscis and his right on the jaw, and down again fell the Champion in a heap.

16.—Tom shook himself together, but was very cautious. He sparred as if requiring rest, until Heenan came in, when slight exchanges took place, Tom getting it on the nose, and Heenan on the whistler, but neither very heavy. Heenan then made a sudden dart,

and planting heavily on Tom's mouth, once more knocked him off
his legs. [Loud cheers for Heenan.]

17.—Tom did not display many marks from his repeated knock-
down blows, but came up smiling, although somewhat tired.
Heenan's mug was decidedly the most disfigured, being so much
swelled. Heenan took the lead, but did not get heavily on. He
tried again with his right, but the blow passed over Tom's nob.
Counter hits followed on the nose, in which Tom's delivery was most
effective, but Tom was down.

18.—Very slight exchanges, followed by a heavy counter, in which
Heenan's mouth came in for pepper, and Tom got it slightly on the
nose, and fell.

19.—Tom slow to time; Heenan not in a hurry. At last, on
facing one another, Heenan went in to a close, and throwing Tom,
fell on him.

20.—Heenan followed Sayers, who was on the retreat, and after
one or two dodges, caught him on the jaw heavily with his right.
He tried again, but Tom jumped back. Still he persevered, and
heavy exchanges followed at close quarters, and both were in the end
down at the ropes.

21.—Sayers very slow, which Heenan seeing, dashed at him,
slung out the left on the nose, and again floored the Champion.

22.—Tom seemed none the worse for this floorer; it rather seemed
to do him good, for he came fresher, which Heenan seeing, he retired to his corner. Tom followed and tried to deliver, but missed,
and the Benicia Boy dropped him with another straight one on the
jaw. Heenan's left hand was now much puffed, and did not seem
to leave such impressions as formerly.

23.—The time was very badly kept on both sides, and there were
now complaints that the Benicia Boy was allowed a stool in the
ring. An appeal was made to the referee, who at once ordered its
removal, as contrary to the laws. Heenan rushed at Tom, who
retreated, and got one on the back. Tom then turned round and
missed his right. They closed, and Tom pegged away merrily on
the nose and left cheek, and in the end both down, Tom under.
One hour and eleven minutes had now elapsed.

24.—The Benicia Boy, first up, tried his left by a sudden dart, but
was stopped. An attempt with the right just landed on the side of
Tom's nut, and he fell. [5 to 4 on Heenan still offered.]

25.—Tom, weak, came up slow, but cheerful. He waited the
attack, which was not long in coming, and after getting a little one
on the side of his head, Tom popped his left very heavily on the
snout, drawing more home-brewed. Heenan, wild, rushed in and
bored Tom down.

26.—Tom, fresher, came up gaily, and tried to lead off with his
left, but the Boy stopped him prettily. Another effort landed on

Heenan's good eye. Heenan in return planted a rattler on Tom's jaw with his right, which staggered him, and was all but a knock down. Tom soon shook himself together, whereupon the Boy let fly his left, but Tom was well away. Following up, the Boy got on Tom's chest, but not heavily. Exchanges; Heenan on the tato-trap, and Tom on the nose, a smasher, each drawing the cork. Heavy counters followed with the left, and they broke away. The Boy came again, and got on Tom's snorer heavily with his left, once more staggering him. Twice after this did Tom stop Heenan's right, and they closed. After some slight fibbing Tom fell, Heenan hitting him when down. An appeal of foul was overruled, the blow being obviously accidental.

27.—The Boy came up determined, and led off, but Tom was away. A second attempt was equally unsuccessful, and as Tom turned his back to dash away, the Boy caught him on the neck, but not heavily. Sharp exchanges followed, Tom on the left cheek and nose, and the Boy on the mouth. Heenan then went in and tried his left, but was short, whereupon he retired to his corner, had a wipe, and wetted his whistle, and then went to the middle of the ring. Tom joined issue at once, and some heavy exchanges took place, each on the nose, and Heenan now tried to close, reaching after Tom to catch him round the neck. Tom kept out of harm's way, but at length the Boy bored him down at the ropes.

28.—Both much fatigued, wanted all the time they could get. After some sparring Heenan ran at Tom, who darted away. The Boy rapidly pursued, and they got together, and in the fibbing Tom was busy on Heenan's good cheek, while he caught it on the mouth. In the end Tom was down.

29.—Tom still slow to time. The Boy at once went to him, and got heavily on the top of his nut. Tom countered with effect with his right on the left cheek, and then popped his left on the proboscis. Heavy exchanges followed in Tom's favour, who met the Boy very straight and effectively on the nozzle, opening a fresh bin. A break away, followed by slight exchanges, led to a harmless close, and Tom slipped down.

30.—Heenan's other eye was now quickly closing, and he had evidently no time to lose. He was strongest on his legs, but his punishment was far more visible than Tom's. He tried to lead off, but Tom met him neatly on the nose, turning on the red port. The Boy rushed at Tom, and literally ran over and fell on him.

31.—After standing some time in his corner, Heenan was fetched out by Tom, who had now recovered a little. A short spar was followed by another retreat, after which Tom went in and got a little un on the left cheek, but it lacked steam. More sparring, and Heenan again retired. Tom stood and examined him with the eye of a connoisseur until he came out, when good exchanges took place, Tom getting heavily on the mouth, and Heenan on the nose. A break away; more sparring for wind; Heenan again to his corner. On Tom going at him he slung out his left heavily on the nose, and prone once more fell the brave Champion.

32.—Tom all alive, dodged, and caught the Boy on the chin. He turned to retreat, and the boy nailed him on the body, but not heavily. Heenan then tried repeatedly to draw Tom, but the latter would not go into Heenan's corner. The Boy, therefore, had to go out, and some rapid hits and stops followed, without any apparent damage; each, however, got a small tap on the mouth. Heenan having taken another rest in his corner, came out and got a hot one on the left cheek for his pains, which all but shut up the other eye. This brought on exchanges, each on the mazzard, and then Heenan reached Tom's nose. Heavy, determined counter-deliveries on the nose ensued, after which Heenan floored Tom by a right-hander on the cheek. The betting was now even, Sayers for choice. It was obvious that, strong as Heenan was, unless he could make a decided change, he must in a very few minutes be blind.

33.—The Benicia Boy, feeling he had no time to lose, rushed in, but only just reached Tom's chest. Both seemed fagged, and they stood a few seconds, and then went to close quarters, where Tom, as usual, was busy on the Boy's frontispiece, until he let him slip through his arms on to the ground.

34.—The Boy again tried to force the fighting, but Tom got away. They then stood and sparred until Heenan let fly his left, which did not reach its destination. He retired for counsel, and then came at Tom and tried his right at the body, but without success. Steady exchanges led to close and rapid in-fighting, and both fell, Tom under. Heenan's eye all but closed up.

35.—The Benicia Boy dashed viciously in, and caught Tom on the snout, but the blow was without powder. Tom retreated from the vigorous onslaught; Heenan followed and got home on the jaw with the right, still with no effect. Tom now turned and ran, Heenan after him, when, on turning round, Tom napped one on the nose. He, however, landed another little pop on the good eye. Sharp exchanges at close quarters ended in the downfall of Tom. Two hours had now elapsed.

36.—The Benicia Boy's face was a spectacle to behold, while Tom was very weak. The Boy rushed to a close, and caught Tom round the neck, dragging him to the ropes. At this time, the police, who had been gradually making their way to the ring, began a violent struggle to get close and put a stop to hostilities. The Boy tried to hold Tom, but the latter slipped through his arms and fell.

37th and last.—Tom was first up, and seemed the better man; he made his left twice on Heenan's eye, and the latter at length caught

him round the neck at the ropes and there held him. Tom's efforts
to extricate himself were vain, but he administered severe punishment to the Boy's face. The police at this time got closer, there was
a rush to the ropes from all sides, and we, in company with others,
including the referee, were completely shut out from the view. We
are informed that the round ended in both going to grass at the expiration of *two hours and six minutes.* We had hoped that the men
would now have been withdrawn, as the referee had been forced
from his post, and the police were close by. The battle, so far as it
may be called a battle, was for the time over, and the men should at
once have been taken away. We are informed, however, that
although the referee sent orders for a cessation of hostilities, five more
so-called rounds were fought with pretty equal advantage. The ring
was half full of people, however, and neither man had a fair chance.
Much do we regret the unpleasant duty that now is imposed upon
us, of finding fault with the Benicia Boy for conduct which was not
only unmanly, but quite against the rules of the Ring, and had the
referee been present, would inevitably have lost him the battle.
A gentleman connected with the *Bell's Life,* who was present, and
who had endeavoured to stop hostilities, informs us that at the end
of the fourth of these supplementary rounds, while Sayers was on
his second's knee, Heenan rushed at him in a very excited state, let
fly left and right at Tom's seconds, floored them, and kicked them
when on the ground in desperate style, after which he closed with
Sayers, and, after a wild rally, they fell together. The final round
was merely a wild scramble, in which both fell. The referee by
this time was able to get near, and ordered the men to desist from
fighting. Immediately after this Heenan rushed away from the
ring, and ran some distance with the activity of a deer, proving
that, as far as strength was concerned, he was as fit as ever;
but he had not been away from the ring many minutes before
he was totally blind. Tom Sayers, although a little tired, and
suffering from his arm and the desperate hug in the 37th round,
was also strong on his pins, and could have fought some time
longer. The blues being now in force, there was, of course,
no chance of the men again meeting, and an adjournment
was necessary. It was found that the authorities were up in arms
in all directions, so that it would be idle waste of time to go elsewhere. Backward home was therefore the word, and the men and
their friends returned to the metropolis shortly after three o'clock.
The whole time occupied, up to the men's leaving the ring, was two
hours and twenty minutes.

REMARKS.—Up to the unfortunate termination this was decidedly
the very best Championship Fight we ever witnessed. It was to the
time aforesaid fought out with a manliness, a fairness, and a determination on both sides worthy of the highest commendation. Without

any attempt at shifting, each scorned to take a mean advantage,
and loudly and repeatedly was each of them cheered. The game
displayed on both sides was remarkable. The gluttony and bottom
of Tom Sayers are too proverbial to need further comment at our
hand ; but as certain rumours have been flying about to the effect
that Heenan was destitute of these qualities, we deem it right to express our belief that a gamer, more determined fellow, never pulled
a shirt off. His punishment was terrible, and yet he took it, round
after round, without flinching, and almost invariably with a smile
on his face. We are bound to own that in this, as in his talent, he
has very agreeably disappointed us ; and had we not known his
career, we certainly should never have set him down for a novice.
He has an excellent delivery with his left, which was as straight as
a dart, and early in the fight was very heavy. It appears to us,
however, that his hands are not strong, for before half the battle was
got through his left hand was so much swelled as to be almost useless ; and this, doubtless, was fortunate for Tom, who, with his right
arm gone, could have made but a poor stand against such a weapon
had it retained its original hardness. Of his right Heenan makes
but little use, but this is a quality he may yet learn. Of his conduct
at the conclusion of the battle we cannot speak in too strong terms.
We trust it was occasioned by the state of excitement in which he
was owing to the ring being broken, and by the fact that, being
almost blind, he took the unoffending seconds of his opponent for
some other persons. We assure him that such conduct is not calculated to gain him friends in this country, and that if he allows his
temper to get the better of his judgment again in a similar way it
may cost him dear. Of Tom Sayers we need not say more than that
he fought the battle throughout with consummate tact and judgment, and, considering that his right arm (his principal weapon)
was rendered almost useless from the commencement, too much
praise cannot be awarded to him for his courage and coolness. We
are of opinion, even without that arm, that he would eventually
have pulled through, had the fight been finished on the day ; but it
is useless speculating on cases which may yet again be brought on
for trial, and we shall therefore leave the public to form their own
opinions. On the question of nationality, the only point that has
been decided, and the only point in our opinion requiring decision, is
that both England and America possess brave sons, and each country
has reason to be proud of the champion she has selected. Both
were, doubtless, anxious to have it settled ; but for ourselves, were
we asked, we should say each is so good that he is deserving a belt,
and we would call on our countrymen to subscribe for such a trophy
as a reward for Heenan's enterprise and boldness in coming, as he
has done, to beard the British champion on his own ground.

The writer of these lines having been one of the less than half-dozen sporting writers and reporters who remained among the driving crowd which swayed hither and thither in the broken ring after the departure of the referee, and of several who wrote their published accounts from hearsay, feels himself freely entitled to express his unbiassed opinion on the probable result of the battle, and to describe "the occurrents of the hardy fight," in its last struggles, from the avouchment of his own eyesight.

The fight, which began at twenty-four minutes past seven, was over at a quarter to ten, lasting two hours and twenty minutes.

When the ring was broken in, in the thirty-seventh round, and the referee shut out from view, Heenan, who was fast becoming blind, hugged Sayers on the ropes. The ropes were lowered by Tom's friends, doubtless, not cut; but had the referee been there, he would unquestionably have ordered the round to have been closed. Rule 28 of the Ring Code was as follows, *before* the Farnborough fight. It has since been enlarged in its scope to prevent similar dangerous practices more effectually :—"28. Where a man shall have his antagonist across the ropes in such a position as to be helpless, and to endanger his life by strangulation or apoplexy, it shall be in the power of the referee to direct the seconds to take their man away, and thus conclude the round; and that the man or his seconds refusing to obey the direction of the referee shall be deemed the loser." Of this the Yankee scribes chose to be utterly oblivious, though the articles specified the battle to be under the New Rules of the Ring—*i.e.*, those of 1853. The referee, however, so say the American party, sent an order for the cessation of hostilities. This, though since confirmed, was not believed by Sayers' friends, who, seeing victory within his grasp, thought it a mere *ruse* to obtain a drawn battle.

Five rounds were fought, Heenan's sight being so defective that, in the fourth of these, the forty-first, Heenan rushed from his corner while Sayers was on his second's knee, and, letting fly at Jemmy Welsh, knocked him nearly over, and kicked at Harry Brunton, if he did not strike him, of which we are not certain. He then hugged Sayers, and they both fell; Tom hitting up in Heenan's battered frontispiece. A cry was raised that the referee had declared the fight over, whereon Heenan rushed from the ring with great activity, followed by his clamorous friends. We stayed, and found Sayers strong, with his sight good, and in all respects but his injured dexter arm—of little use since the fourth round—able, as he said, " to fight an hour."

Leaving Tom, we hurried to the carriages, the train standing on the Farnborough embankment, where we saw Heenan, already blind as a bat, lifted into his compartment. Arrived at the Bricklayers' Arms Station, we accompanied the gallant champion to the hostelrie of his old friend, Ned Elgee, the Swan, Old Kent-road. Here no sooner was the hero seated, for he refused to go to bed, than he inquired after his opponent. His friend and backer (Mr. John Gideon) suggested that the heroes should meet and shake hands, and the writer hastened across the road to invite the Benicia Boy and his friends. He was in a close cab, wrapped in blankets—blind, unpresentable, and seemingly unconscious. Tom was soon cheerful, and over a little tea regretted that the doctor's veto prevented his partaking of the champagne creaming around him to his health and success, amid plaudits to his bravery. Sayers was next morning at Norfolk-street, at the stakeholder and referee's office, and a photograph has fixed beyond dispute his condition, which, save his right arm already spoken of, was nothing beyond a tumefied mouth and a few bumps on his hard forehead. Heenan, on the contrary, despite the absurd declarations of his American letter-writer, was not in a condition to see or be seen. For fully forty-eight hours he was in "darkness," and for more than that time in a critical condition, as we know from unimpugnable proof. The friends of Heenan pretended to base their great grievance on the fact that, as the contest was not finished on the day, it ought to have been resumed during the week. The answer to this is—First, that this was mere bounce, as Heenan was in no condition to resume hostilities ; secondly, that in the condition of Sayers's right arm he was entitled, by ring precedents (the fight having been once interrupted), to a reasonable period to recover its use ; thirdly, that it would have been contrary to all dictates of humanity—and fairness, which includes humanity, is a prized attribute of British boxing ; fourthly, that public opinion was opposed in the strongest manner to the two brave fellows who had so heroically contended, and had been baulked of a result by no fault or shortcoming of either, after such punishment as they had undergone, renewing their interrupted struggle. For these and other cogent reasons, it was proposed by the referee and stakeholder, and—after the subsidence of the American mortification to a better state of feeling—agreed to by both men, that two similar belts should be made, one to be presented to each champion. We shall not record the ceremonial of this presentation, which was performed on the part of England by Frank Dowling, Esq., editor of *Bell's Life*, and on that of America by G. Wilkes, Esq., editor of the *New York Spirit of the Times*, as the whole affair, speeches and all, savour too strongly of the circus style of bunkum and bombast. The modest paragraph in the *Times* of May 30th, 1860, though written as an *avant courrier*, is more to our taste :—

"THE CHAMPIONSHIP BELTS.—America and England shake hands cordially to-day. What our greatest diplomatists and engineers have failed to achieve has been accomplished by the Benicia Boy and Tom Sayers, whose fame will descend to future generations, and whose posterity will each be enabled to show a *fac simile* of that much desired "belt," so boldly challenged, so manfully defended. The Atlantic cable has not linked the two nations together, but the good feeling which has been shown by these two gladiators, who on this day receive at the Alhambra their respective 'belts,' will be responded to by the two nations on either side of the Atlantic. We have been favoured with a view of the old belt, 'the belt' still open to competition, and of the two other belts to be presented to the 'two Champions of England,' for such is the inscription upon the case of each. Both are precisely similar in every respect, and the somewhat clumsy workmanship, in frosted silver, carefully copied from the original, is by Mr. C. F. Hancock, of Bruton-street."

How British admiration of true courage expressed itself in the substantial form of a public subscription, and how members of Parliament, the Stock Exchange, Lloyd's, and Mark Lane clubbed their gold pieces, to enable the champion to pass in peace and competence the remainder of his days, guarded from the stings and sorrows of poverty, have been told in the columns of the sporting press. After Mace's victories over Sam Hurst and Tom King, there was some talk of Sayers coming out from his retirement and having a turn with the Norwich man, but it ended in smoke. As Tom, from

tho universal interest excited by his heroic display, was
an object of interest to the multitude, he received liberal
offers from some Yankee circus proprietors, and by the
aid of the "rhino" thus earned became first a share-
holder, and then proprietor of Howes and Cushing's
Circus, under the management, of Jem Myers. The
speculation, we suspect, carried Tom out of his depth,
and the horses, mules, carriages, &c., were sold off some
year after their purchase. Tom's free living degenerated
into excess during this loose and exciting life of a travel-
ling showman and exhibitor, for poor Tom, in his simple
faith, was by no means an Artemus Ward, and no match
for Yankee smartness. There is little doubt that Tom at
this time laid the seeds of the inflammatory disease which
shortened his days, and cut him off at the early age of
thirty-nine.

The kind friends who uncompromisingly stipulated,
when Tom's capital was invested, that he should "fight
no more," did not place any restriction on his reappearance
in the roped arena. When King and Heenan fought, on
December 10, 1863, Sayers conformed to the etiquette of
his profession, and seconded "the American." Heenan's
party evidently believed that Tom's *prestige* would scatter
dismay in the ranks of King's followers, and help to
overwhelm the "young waterman" at the outset. Poor
Sayers' descent had, however, commenced, and when he
stepped into the ring, in Heenan's corner, it was plain he
was there more for dramatic effect than anything else.
Attired in a fur-cap, a yellow flannel jacket, and jack-
boots, he was vociferously applauded when he commenced
his duties in attending to Heenan's toilette. Even then
people said "How are the mighty fallen," for poor Tom

was no more equal to his onerous task than a child.
During the fight at Wadhurst he looked in strange be-
wilderment at King and Heenan, and when the "Benicia
Boy" required assistance, his second was perfectly helpless. Still the gladiator quitted the scene in a graceful
and generous manner, in having stood esquire to the
opponent who was instrumental in bringing out that steel,
courage, and pluck of which the first of English pugilists
was composed.

As it no doubt will prove interesting to all those who
have admired the wonderful pluck and endurance of the
greatest gladiator of modern times to know something of
the progress of that insidious disease which gradually but
surely did its work, we append a few particulars. Since
the memorable battle of Farnborough—when Sayers
appeared in the ring the picture of health, and the result
proved that his *physique* could not have been improved
upon—he now and again showed symptoms of the hectic
flush which is the precursor of an affection of the lungs.
This was brought on by the course of life he subsequently
chose, or rather by the force of circumstances under which
he was placed. Unable to fall back upon those pleasures
of a cultivated mind from his want of education, he became the idol of his fellows ; he cast off all those restraints
which had secured for him health and victory, and plunged
into excesses of living—late hours and dissipation. Nature's
laws were not to be broken with impunity, and in the
beginning of this year he fell into a very low condition,
and betrayed symptoms of consumption, aggravated with
diabetes, and Mr. Adams, F.R.C.S., attended him on
February 20 at his sister's, Mrs. King, 16, Claremont-
square, Pentonville. Upon his robust and healthy frame

a great change had taken place for the worse, and the doctor then feared, from his having wasted away so much, coughing frequently, and losing strength fast, that he was sinking into a decline. He was prone to acknowledge his physical weakness, but when told of the serious nature of the disease then apprehended, he became as docile as a child, and obeyed the injunctions of his medical adviser, who, we may remark in passing, expressed to us the melancholy pleasure which he experienced whilst Tom was under his care. However, the dreaded enemy was stalled-off by careful watching and nursing, and he recovered sufficiently to take a trip to Brighton about the middle of April. When there, he appeared strong and robust, and like his former self. This, however, was not to last long, for at the end of August he returned to his sister's, in Claremont-square, and in a consultation held there between Dr. Adams and Mr. Brown, they came to the conclusion that actual and absolute disease of the lungs had set in, and that he could not survive many weeks. He took a fancy to go to his old friend's, Mr. Mensley, High-street, Camden Town, on October 16, and there he stayed until he died. For the satisfaction of Dr. Adams himself, that gentleman called in Dr. Gull to consult, but they both agreed that nothing more could be done to save him. A reaction took place in his condition after being a fortnight at Mr. Mensley's; he seemed to get fresher and stronger, and for a week remained in a doubtful state, giving hopes to his friends that he would survive the illness. A relapse came on, and with it unconsciousness, and for the last few days he had only a few intervals of consciousness. Mr. Litten, assistant chaplain to St. Pancras Workhouse, attended by desire of Sayers, who administered the consolations of religion. He passed away at six o'clock on Wednesday evening, in the presence of his father, with his two children at hand. During the three weeks of his bedridden illness he occasionally endured great agony, and, as his attendants assured us, sometimes screamed in the night with suffering. For upwards of four-and-twenty hours before his death he was in a state of semi-insensibility, and could only recognise his friends on being aroused and appealed to. But the great change came with comparative peace at last, and when nature compelled him to "throw up the sponge," he left the world, let us hope, without that pain which no man feared less when he stood up in defence of his reputation as the Emperor of British boxers. Many were the inquiries made for the health of poor Tom, and it is satisfactory to know that he was visited by some who had taken a part against him in the battle-field, and that he bid them, each and all, a peaceful farewell.

The amount of money subscribed for Sayers by his personal admirers and the public was £3000, which sum was invested in the names of trustees, Tom to receive the interest during his life, providing he never fought again, and in the event of his fighting again or dying, the interest was to go to the children until of age, when it is to be divided between them. Tom left only two children— young Tom, who has up to the present time been at boarding-school, and is now fourteen years old, and Sarah, who is, we believe, in her seventeenth year. Independent of the interest in this sum, Sayers leaves a considerable amount of property in plate and other valuables. Some of his backers have always treasured up *souvenirs* of him. Mr. John Gideon, Tom's earliest " guide, philosopher, and friend," has the boots in which Sayers fought Heenan, with the Farnborough grass and earth attaching to the spikes, just as the great gladiator left them.

Those who remember the personal appearance of the departed Champion will have his bronzed, square, and good-humoured, lion-like phiz in their mind's eye ; those who did not see him in the flesh must imagine a round, broad, but not particularly thick-set man, standing 5ft. 8½in. in his stocking-feet, with finely-turned hips, and small but powerful and flat loins, remarkably round ribs and girth, and square shoulders. His arms were of medium length, and so round as not to show prominently the biceps, or even the outer muscles of the fore-arm, to the extent often seen in men of far inferior powers of hitting and general strength. Indeed, the bulk of Sayers was so compactly packed that you did not realise his true size and weight at a cursory glance, and it was this close and neat packing of his trunk—excuse the pun—that doubtless was an important ingredient in many a " long day" in which Tom's lasting powers were the admiration of every spectator. Tom's head was certainly of the " bullet" shape, and it was supported by a neck of the sort known as " bull," conveying the idea of enduring strength and determination to back it. We have no phrenological examination of Tom's " bumps" before us, but we doubt not those of combativeness and amativeness were fully developed. Tom's fighting weight began at 10st. 6lb.; in his later battles it was 10st. 10lb. to 10st. 12lb. The photographs which figure in the print-shop windows do not convey a fair idea of Tom's good-tempered and often merry expression : he seems to have been taken when filled with the contemplation of the seriousness of the position of having one's "counterfeit presentment" multiplied and sent forth to the world. From the hips downward Tom was not a "model man." Though round in the calf, his thighs were decidedly deficient in muscular development; yet no man made better use of his pins in getting in and out again, as witness his up-hill performances with the six-foot Slasher, and the ponderous and more active Benicia Boy. It was to Tom's excellent judgment of time and distance that the severity of his hitting was due, and to his mighty heart —a bigger never found place in man's bosom—that his triumphant finish of many a well-fought day is to be attributed. No man ever fought more faithfully to his friends or bravely with his foes in "the battle of life;" and therefore is the tribute of a record of his deeds due to TOM SAYERS.

His remains were consigned to their parent earth, on Wednesday, November 15th, at the Highgate Cemetery, attended by an immense concourse of the sympathizing and curious. A committee of friends, the admirers of true British courage, have resolved to raise a monument over the spot where—

After life's fitful fever he sleeps well.

APPENDIX.

PROSE AND POETRY originated by the Great Battle between Sayers and Heenan, from *The Times*, *All the Year Round*, *The Cornhill Magazine*, *The Saturday Review*, *Punch*, the French press, &c.

IN MEMORIAM: From *The Daily Telegraph*, November 10, 1865; from *The Sporting Life*, November 11, 1865.

FIGHT FOR THE CHAMPIONSHIP.

---◆---

(From *The Times* of April 18th, 1860.)

THERE was when the Championship of England was an office which conferred honour on the highest, when 'Marmion, Lord of Scrivelbaye, of Tamworth tower and town,' held a grant of the lands of the Abbey of Polesworth, on condition of doing battle in single combat against all knightly enemies of his King. The fashion of this office, however, has passed away with the days of chivalry, and lance and battle-axe have been laid aside to become mere things of show, and no more used by men. The Dymocks are still extant, but the modern Champions of England know them not, and the pageant warrior who threw down the gauntlet to some hundred ladies and gentlemen in Court dress at a coronation has been succeeded by a race of brawny and muscular fellows, men who 'mean fighting, and nothing but it,' and who vie with the *athletæ* of old in their rigidity of training and immense powers of endurance. At first there was no lack of Royal patronage for the new race of champions. In Broughton's last prize fight he was backed by the Duke of Cumberland, who almost acted as his second, and few great battles took place at which one or more of the sons of George III. were not present. Sir Thomas Apreece nearly always seconded Gully, until that champion retired from the ring, and having realised a large portion, sat in the House of Commons as member for Pontefract. In those days a noted bruiser was thought good company for any man, and we hear almost without surprise how, about forty years ago, Lord Camelford 'assisted' Belcher when he fought Joe Berks in the Churchyard of St. George's, Hanover Square, in the presence of some 10,000 spectators. Those were the ' good old days,' the ' palmy days ' of the Ring, about which the sporting journals are always so pathetic as having gone by—we are glad to say, never to return. He would be a bold peer, indeed, who would have seconded Sayers yesterday as Lord Deerhurst used to second Spring ; and what would be said now of a cathedral town offering, as of old, 500*l.* to the combatants to beat themselves almost to death within its reverend precincts ? The New Police Act has been the death of pugilism. Its greatest professors now lead a hole-and-corner life while training, or issue forth their challenges in mysterious terms. From this rapid downfall it has been just now for a time arrested by the first attempt to carry off the Champion's belt into another country— and, of course, that country was America. There is no disguising the fact that this challenge has led to an amount of attention being bestowed upon the Prize Ring which it has never received before ; and, much as all decent people disliked the idea of two fine men meeting to beat each other half to death,' it was nevertheless devoutly wished that, as somebody was to be beaten, it might be the American. There is no doubt that Sayers had the good wishes of nine-tenths of the community. There seemed something almost patriotic in its way for a man of his light weight to encounter a brawny giant, who describes himself as being 'half horse, half alligator, and a bit of the snapping turtle,' and who, in addition to all these qualities, has proved himself to be as clever and formidable a prize-fighter as ever entered the Ring. We need scarcely enter on any recapitulation of the events which led to this match, all of which may be summed up in the few words, that Sayers holds 'the belt' as the Champion of England, and in virtue of his office,

while he retains it, is bound for three years to accept
all challenges, no matter from whom. This challenge
accordingly came from America on Heenan's part, and,
in spite of the immense natural advantages of his
challenger, Sayers was bound at once to accept it.
All relating to the day and place fixed for the match
was, of course, kept a profound secret, as the police,
to do them justice, left no means untried to prevent
its taking place. Nevertheless, in spite of all pre-
cautions, a special train was hired, which started from
London Bridge at 4 A.M. yesterday morning. The
train was one of immense length, containing some
thousand persons, all of what are called the upper
classes, though each person was muffled up to the
eyes in shawls and wrappers, so that it was hard to
say whether your *compagnon de voyage* was or was
not the redoubtable Sayers or Heenan himself. All
along the line police were posted, with mounted
patrols at regular distances ; but the train turned off
at Reigate, and after a long run came out in the Farnborough station, close to Aldershott. In an instant
after, all were out in the fields, following the men who
with the ropes and stakes led the way across what
turned out to be a most difficult piece of country.
There seemed a constant succession of double hedges
and ditches, which were crossed at last more or less
successfully, until a rather ·narrow stream, or very
broad muddy ditch (the Blackwater), which divides
Surrey from Hampshire, brought all to a full stop. A
few venturesome spirits essayed to leap this, but their
success was not such as to encourage others, inasmuch
as most contrived to light in the very middle of the
water, and those who did gain the opposite bank had
only to jump back for their pains, as the ring was
formed on the Hampshire side after all.

The instant the enclosure of ropes and stakes, 24
feet square, was formed, Sayers stepped into it, and
was cheered tremendously. Heenan, who followed,
was greeted in the same manner, and the two men,
who there for the first time met, warmly shook hands,

and then stepped back to take a long and careful sur-
vey each of the other. There was a toss for corners,
which Heenan won, and chose that in which he would
have the highest ground, and with his back to the sun,
leaving Sayers the spot where the glare was full in his
face. Umpires for each man were appointed, and a
referee for both, and these preliminaries over, Heenan
proceeded to strip to his waist. It seemed impossible
to restrain a murmur of admiration at the appearance
which he then presented. In height he is about six
feet two, with extraordinarily long arms, deep chest,
and wide and powerful shoulders. His appearance
yesterday was truly formidable. Exercise and long
training had developed the immense muscles of his
arms and shoulders till they appeared like masses of
bone beneath the thin covering of skin. There seemed
not an ounce of superfluous flesh. His ribs showed
like those of a greyhound, save where they were
crossed by powerful thews and sinews, and as he
threw up his long sinewy arms and inflated his huge
chest with the morning air he looked the most formidable of the tribe of gladiators who have ever
entered the arena. Every movement showed the
sinews and muscles working like lithe machinery
beneath their thin fine covering, and every gesture
was made with that natural grace and freedom which
always seem to belong to the highest development of
physical power. Sayers looked at him long and
earnestly, and as one who saw in his every movement
a dangerous customer, and he too stripped in turn.
The contrast between the men was then still more
marked than before. Sayers is only about five feet
eight; his chest is not broad, nor are his arms powerful, and it is only in the strong muscles of the shoulders that one sees anything to account for his tremendous powers of hitting. Sayers, too, looked hard as
flint, but his deficiencies in regard to his antagonist
in height, weight, and strength, and above all, length
of arm, made it almost a matter of surprise how he
could hope to contest with him at all. When to these

disadvantages are added the superior height of the ground on which Heenan stood, and the light of the sun full in Sayers's eyes, it will be seen how tremendous were the obstacles with which he had to contend. As far as training went, however, the utmost had been done for both, and it would not be a lost lesson if some of our young volunteers imitated the boxers in these respects. Their whole system of training may be summed up in two or three words—moderation in eating and drinking, exercise, and constant use of the sponge bath and rough towels. With these aids any man can train; without them he can do nothing. Heenan's skin yesterday was, as we have said, fair and white as marble—Sayers's as dark as that of a mulatto; and the 'fancy' leant strongly to the opinion that the former was too delicate, and would bruise too much—and this was true. As the men stripped the spectators sat down outside the ropes, about six feet distant, in an outer ring, in which were gentlemen of all ranks—members of both Houses in plenty. Authors, poets, painters, soldiers, and even clergymen were present.

There was a minute's pause after the final shaking hands, when the seconds retired and left the antagonists face to face at last. Both instantly put themselves into position—the right hand held close across the body, the left advanced at length, and kept moving gently out as if to feel its way. The immense difference between the height, weight, strength, and length of arm of the men was now more than ever manifest, and the disadvantages under which Sayers laboured appeared to many to be too much for him. The sun shone bright and full in his face, so as almost to blind him; yet Sayers seemed cool and confident, and smiled coolly as he ventured in reach of that tremendous muscular arm. Both seemed very cautious. The feints were quick and constant, and as each avoided the other with more or less agility neither could help laughing. At last Sayers caught a slight blow on the mouth, which he returned heavily, drawing first blood from Heenan, amid shouts of congratulation. Both seemed still more cautious, and after much sparring and warding off an intended blow with the speed of thought, both stopped and looked at each other with hands down. After a little rest, they again sparred and closed, when Sayers gave his adversary some heavy body blows, and got down easily.

Each man was instantly attended by his seconds, who carefully sponged his body and face, and rinsed out his mouth with a little cold water. Again they advanced. Each seemed then to know his antagonist better; the sparring was quicker, and the huge muscular arm of Heenan went backwards and forwards with immense rapidity. Three times he hit at Sayers; but out of distance, and apparently as if to put the Champion off his guard; at last he darted forward like lightning, and dealt Sayers a blow in the mouth which sent him reeling. Tom, however, as if to show how little he cared for it, at once ventured close to his huge antagonist—too close as it proved, for the long arm of Heenan was shot out like a dart, and with a heavy blow on his forehead Tom was knocked almost into his own corner. There were great cheers at this, and though Heenan seemed very pleased, Sayers took it as a matter of course, and went back to his corner, apparently unconcerned. Here he was sponged for a minute, and returned with a deep red lump across his forehead, and his mouth slightly disfigured, though with far less punishment in appearance than could have been expected, owing to his skill in jumping back ere the blow reached, and thus weakening half its force. He was smiling, and seemed quite at ease as he again approached the American in his own corner, who was very careful not to leave it, in order to keep Sayers with the glare of the sun in his face. This seemed to perplex Sayers much, and he again presented an opening, of which the Benicia Boy instantly availed himself and with one blow dashed Sayers to the ground. Again there were tremendous cheers for Heenan, and ironical congratulations to the

Champion in the young novice he had met with. Those who had backed Sayers seemed rather depressed; the betting gradually became even, Heenan being almost as much in favour as the Champion. There were loud cries of 'Time,' at which Heenan advanced to the centre of the ring, and waited for Sayers, retiring as the latter advanced, till the American again had the benefit of the higher ground, and the sun in Tom's eyes. Sayers now found it was useless attempting out-fighting with a man of such enormous strength and length of arm as the American, he therefore tried to dash in, and got a slight blow at Heenan, who returned it with a very heavy one, which sent Tom staggering back, and after some further exchanges, all in favour of the powerful young American, Sayers got down.

Again the men were attended to, and again Sayers came forth, much marked and with a heavy cut over his eyebrow, to cope with Heenan in his own corner. This time the sparring was so long and cautious that at last both men put down their hands and laughed. Again they began, and after a few feints Heenan dashed out his left and for the fourth time fairly struck Sayers to the ground with a very heavy blow. The effect of these repeated blows seemed almost greater on the spectators than on Sayers. The latter tried to treat them lightly, but around the ring a very different opinion was entertained, and Heenan was backed to win, and was cheered and encouraged to the utmost. Both men were duly wiped down, and Sayers's head and face, which were now smeared with blood and heavily bruised and bumped, was held close pressed between two cold sponges to keep down the contusions which had now altered his deep sallow hue.

Shouts now went round the ring that Sayers had virtually already lost, and indeed the punishment he had received was so much more severe than that bestowed upon his tall wiry antagonist, who seemed always smiling and always fresh, that matters really

began to look serious for the Champion, and almost
to warrant the belief that 'the belt was going to
Troy.' Apparently roused by these shouts to stronger
efforts, Sayers came on again, and watching his man
cautiously, stepped back from a dreadful blow aimed
at him, sprang in before the American could recover
himself, and gave Heenan a terrific smash full in the
eye, splitting up the cheek, and sending his huge antagonist reeling like a drunken man back into his
corner. The effect of this blow was so tremendous
that even before half a minute had elapsed Heenan
could scarcely be recognised as the same man, so
swollen, disfigured, and blood-stained were his features. There were loud cheers for Sayers, who went
up to Heenan's corner and peered into his face with
a curious half-puzzled expression, as if he too was as-
tounded by the effects of his own handiwork. Sayers
now let no time slip, but catching a most formidable
blow of Heenan's on his right arm, again dashed in,
and gave in return a still worse blow to the American,
following it up with another, which seemed to smash
his nose, and almost knocked Heenan off his legs in
turn, so that he required the most careful attention
from his seconds to make him fit for the next round.

The betting now changed again, and if Sayers was
not a decided favourite, there at least seemed nothing
to choose between the two. All the rounds had been
long and cautiously fought, but the hitting had been
dreadful, and both men began to show signs of fatigue,
and after long sparring, in the seventh encounter,
both paused, rested, and at last retired to rinse out
their mouths, which were very bloody, with water.
As they came up again Sayers at once dashed in and
gave another terrific blow to Heenan, which sent the
blood pouring down over his broad chest, and seemed
to make his huge form tremble like a child's. Heenan
paused for a moment and then darted in, but Sayers
got under his guard, closed, and, after giving him some
heavy body blows, both fell, Sayers under.

It had been noticed in the last two rounds that

ers made not the least use of his right hand, with
ch in all his previous contests he had admi-
ered such terrific punishment that a full blow
n it may almost bo said to decide the fate of a
:le. The reason of this was now painfully ap-
ent on his again stepping into the ring. In stop-
ӡ one of Heenan's tremendous blows it is supposed
t one of the bones of his right arm was broken.
tain it is that the limb was frightfully swollen,
l so powerless that he could only manage to sup-
t it across his chest. From this time, therefore,
ʒers fought the rest of the battle with his left
ıd, only seeking every opportunity to ease the
dent pain of the injured limb by opening the hand
l resting it on his chest or ribs. He, however,
ʒanced smiling, as did also Heenan, though the
.tures of the latter were so distorted and swollen
ıt it was hard to say what he was doing. Sayers,
twithstanding the loss of his right arm, still pushed
   and gave the American another fearful blow,
ıich sent him staggering back to have the blood
ped from his gashed features, while Sayers as
ual pried in with a curious look to see what mis-
:ief he had done. The blow, however, though
eadful to look at, seemed to have no effect on the
rength of the gaunt iron frame of the American,
ho was quickly out, and after some slight sparring
ʒain launched forth his powerful arm, and striking
ayers on the nose with a blow that was heard all
ʒer the meadow, he felled him like an ox. This
ʒund lasted thirteen minutes, and the men seemed
ɔ distressed at its close that each had to be carried
ɔ his corner. The seconds had much to do with
ponging their faces and washing over the marks of
ɔeir wounds, though some of Heenan's seemed too
eep to be meddled with in this way. Time was
ɔudly called by the umpires, and the American
ɔstantly rose; Sayers was much longer coming up,
hough he seemed almost fresher of the two, but not
ıearly so strong. As soon as Sayers was in reach,

Heenan gave him a heavy blow over the eye, and almost immediately after a still more fierce one on the mouth and nose, which now in poor Sayers seemed all knocked into one. There was slight sparring and both exchanged hits, all the profit in this unpleasant species of barter being on the side of the American. Sayers drew back to spit the blood from his mouth, and was laughed at by some of Heenan's supporters — an imprudent ebullition, inasmuch as Sayers seemed stung by the taunts of the Americans, and again springing in, gave Heenan a blow which sent him tottering back, following it up with another and another, and a fourth tremendous one in the mouth. Heenan seemed staggered by these fearful visitations, and reeled like a drunken man, leaving himself so unguarded, that if Sayers had had the use of his right arm the fight would have ended there and then. As it was, however, Sayers dared not trust himself in the grip of an antagonist so immensely his superior in height, weight, strength, and length of arm, and he could only follow up his advantage by giving another heavy blow with his left in the mouth, and a most tremendous smash into the American's ribs, which sounded all over the meadow as if a box had been smashed in. In a minute after, however, Heenan came up trying to laugh, but only to receive a still worse blow in the face, which covered him with blood, and sent Sayers himself reeling back from the force of his own blow. There was a short pause, during which Tom, as usual, scanned curiously the dreadful effect of his hitting, and both went at it again, each exchanging heavy blows till both were covered with blood—especially the Benicia Boy, who in the end rallied and hit out fiercely, knocking Sayers down with an awful smash. The powerlessness of Sayers' right arm was more than ever manifest in this round, which lasted nearly twenty minutes. He seemed unable even to move it from his side, and it was fortunate indeed for him that Heenan himself made very little use of his

right. Both men now seemed much distressed, and
Heenan presented an awful sight. His face was
gashed with apparently very deep flesh wounds, and
the whole of the right side of his face, eye, nose, and
mouth was simply one huge blue lump. Sayers, too,
was badly punished about the mouth, but his face
and head, though bloody, swollen, and much discoloured, were almost natural when compared to those
of his antagonist. Both were very slow to the call
of time. The Benicia Boy was first out. Sayers
then came out, and Heenan at once, bringing his
gaunt muscular left into play, reached over Tom's
guard like lightning, and knocked him down with a
tremendous blow. Again Sayers was out, though
weak, and Heenan rushed to force the fighting; each
hit the other hard, and after a slight struggle Sayers
got down, laughing. Another round followed with
much the same result as to hitting; but in the close
Heenan lifted Sayers from the ground with ease and
flung him down heavily. Sayers was evidently distressed, and had not the least chance in closing with
his powerful antagonist. Again there was a little
struggle, and Sayers at last got a heavy blow on
Heenan's left eye, the only one with which he could
now see, receiving in return a blow in the chest,
when he managed to get down. Both were very
slow in coming up again, and Sayers being dodged
round as usual, with his face to the sun, seemed
dazzled; again the terrific long arm of the Benicia
Boy came in, and Sayers was knocked down and apparently half stunned. He required much care from
his seconds before he came up again, though when
he did so it at once seemed to revive all his vigour,
for he made straight at Heenan and dealt him a blow
in the face that was heard all over the field. His
antagonist seemed nothing loth to close for all this,
and gave Sayers almost as bad a blow in return, till
they both closed, when Sayers had all the best of
it, and, for the first and only time, threw Heenan
heavily.

In a minute both, though distressed, were at it again, and Heenan, with a fearful blow, knocked Sayers half across the ring. Another round ended, after a few exchanges, with the same result, except that Sayers was even harder hit, and seemed quite stunned.

Strange to say, after these tremendous rounds Sayers still came up fresh, and showed not half the awful marks of punishment visible all over Heenan, who was now a disgusting object. His left hand was much swollen and puffy, and his left eye was fast threatening to close as irremediably as his right had done long before. His friends shouted to him from all parts of the ring to go in and finish Sayers by closing with him, as the latter could now only use one hand ; but Heenan in turn was getting cautious, and did not seem to like the look of running into Sayers, who, always cool and wary, never now threw a chance away. Several rounds were fought after this with success more or less varying, each taking and giving heavy blows, and writhing his battered face into such contortions as might pass for smiles. In all the closes Heenan's immense strength prevailed, and he threw the Champion easily, till in both the 21st and 22nd rounds Sayers was knocked off his legs. Still he came up gaily, though carefully, and generally managed in most of the struggles to give one or more of his heaviest blows on Heenan's left eye, which was now almost gone like the other. The scene gradually became one of the most intense and brutal excitement. There were shouts to Heenan to keep his antagonist in the sun—to close with him and smash him, as he had only one arm, while the friends of Sayers called to him to take his time, as the American was fast blinding and must give in. The bets were even on both men, and then again varied with every round. When Sayers was knocked down almost senseless under a tremendous blow, there were cheers from the Americans till the fields echoed again, which were retorted by the English whenever their Champion sent his huge opponent reeling back from the tremendous blows which were always dealt on the eyes. At this time several policemen came upon the scene, and did their best to force their way into the ring; but the crowd, which now amounted to some 8,000, kept them back by rushing on the ropes, shouting and cheering the combatants to the utmost. During all this time the men fought on with varying success, the heavy 'thuds' upon the face of one or the other being clear above all the din. Sayers seemed getting weaker each time he was knocked off his legs, and Heenan more and more blind. It appeared all a chance whether the English Champion would be struck senseless or Heenan remain sightless, and at his mercy. Sayers now tried getting away, and leading his opponent round the ring. In one of these runs he got a heavy blow on the neck, which enabled his antagonist to overtake him, when they closed, and Sayers fell, Heenan striking him a heavy blow on the head while on the ground. An appeal of foul play was made, but it was overruled, as the blow was supposed to be struck in the heat of fighting, and Heenan, it was truly said, could scarcely see whether his antagonist was up or down. The fighting was still very quick, Heenan almost as strong as ever, and, though apparently much distressed, trying to get it over before he quite lost his sight. In the 38th round Heenan got Sayers's head under his left arm, and, supporting himself by the stake with his right, held his opponent bent down, as if he meant to strangle him. Sayers could no more free himself than if a mountain was on him. At last he got his left arm free, and gave Heenan two dreadful blows on the face, covering them both with the blood; but Heenan, without relaxing his hold, turned himself so as to get his antagonist's neck over the rope, and then leant on it with all his force. Sayers rapidly turned black in the face, and would have been strangled on the spot but that the rules of the ring provide for what would otherwise be fatal contingencies, and both the umpires

called simultaneously to cut the ropes. This was done
at once, and both men fell heavily to the ground,
Sayers nearly half strangled. The police now made
a determined effort to interfere, which those present
seemed equally determined to prevent, and the ropes
of the ring having been cut the enclosure itself was
inundated by a dense crowd, which scarcely left the
combatants six square feet to fight in. Umpires, re-
ferees, and all were overwhelmed, and the whole thing
became a mere close mob round the two men fighting.
After this, four other rounds were fought, in the midst
of this dense mass of partisans of either side, who,
however, allowed the men to fight in the fairest way
they could, consistent with their having hardly any
room to fight at all. This, however, was, on the whole,
unfair to Sayers, whose only chance now lay in avoiding the tremendous blows of his antagonist, against
whom he contended with only one hand, and who,
though now as blind as a bat, was still possessed of
nearly all his immense strength, and, to a little man
like Sayers, very nearly as formidable as ever. In
these rounds sometimes Sayers got awful blows upon
the head and body, and sometimes he managed to
give in return his tremendous lunges full in the disfigured face of his antagonist. At one time caps were
thrown up, and cheers given for Heenan as having
won, when he knocked down Sayers, who would
spring to his feet, and give the American such staggering blows that he in turn was hailed as conqueror.
At length the police forced their way to where they
were fighting, in a space not much larger than an ordinary dining-table, and the referee ordered them at
once to discontinue. To do them justice, both seemed
very willing to leave off, and Heenan was so blind that
in the last round he could not see Sayers, but hit his
unsuspecting second a tremendous blow in the face,
which knocked him head over heels. Both men then
left what had been the ring, Sayers, though much
blown and distressed, walking firmly and coolly away,
with both his eyes open and clear. His right arm,

however, was helpless, his mouth and nose were
dreadfully beaten, and the side of his head and forehead much punished. Heenan was almost unrecog-
nisable as a human being, so dreadful had been his
punishment about the face and neck. Yet he was
still as strong on his legs, apparently, as ever, thanks
to his perfect training, and, after leaving the field of
battle, he ran as nimbly as any of the spectators and
leaped over two small hedges. This, however, was a
final effort, and he almost instantly after became so
utterly blind that he was obliged to be led by the
hand to the train.

How the fight would have terminated but for the
interference of the police it is now literally quite impossible to say or even speculate. At any moment
Sayers 'might have got a blow which would have
struck him almost senseless ; while if Heenan could
have closed with him the Champion's chance would
have been, perhaps, a poor one. On the other hand,
Sayers was carefully avoiding this, and Heenan's sight
was so far gone that in two or three minutes more he
would have lain at the mercy of a child. As matters
now stand, the fight is adjourned *sine die*, and the
only impression left is one of astonishment that Sayers,
with one arm, should have so long contended, with
success, with such a formidable antagonist, and that
Heenan should have borne his terrific punishment
without his strength or courage to fight giving way.

THE FRENCH PRESS ON THE FIGHT AT
FARNBOROUGH.

THE Continental Journals, generally so cynical and
ludicrously ill-informed on English affairs, seem· on
this occasion to have been especially liberal in their
admiration of our insular bravery, and the fortitude of
our Champion in a combat so foreign to French habits
and tastes.

The ' Débats ' devoted four or five of its columns

to a description of the fight. As the narrative is
chiefly taken from the accounts given herein from
the leading English newspapers, it would be superfluous to reproduce it. The conclusions of the writer
of the article, however, are worthy of preservation :—
'This struggle, then, brought face to face the Old
World and the New—Old England and Young
America. The American giant is tall and strong,
like the trees of the New World. His frame is in
proportion to the forests, the lakes, and the rivers, of
America. He reminds us of the primeval nature,
and of the men who measured seven cubits in height,
as in the early ages of the world. Face to face with
him we have seen the Old World, the product of the
ages that have passed away—the highest expression
and product of civilisation—the creature of art. And
yet, after all, these two athletes are of the same
blood, sprung from the same stock. It was England
in its youth and England in its manhood, but the
race was the same. These two men were rivals, but
they could not be enemies. They might accost each
other, as the homeric heroes were wont to accost each
other, and to engage as they did, in single combat.
But woe to the stranger who should meddle with
them, for surely in such a case would their united
strength be turned against the meddler ! The Englishman, looking at the American as he recoiled from
his blows, could not but think with pride—" It is I
who have done this thing ;" and yet he was also
proud of the blows he received from the giant of the
New World, for therein he could not fail to recognise
the vigour of the race. What we wish to point out
is, that the Englishman in this struggle appears as
the faithful type of his nation. What are the attributes of the English race ? What but endurance,
patience, and energy, often latent, but always fierce,
and that never knows defeat—an obstinacy that will
not be conquered, and a secret oath to die rather
than to yield ? Even in the story of this fight
we find one and all those attributes. Even at the

risk of offending the delicate tastes of our readers, we will say that in the sternly obstinate and inflexible resolution with which the Englishman, apparently unconscious of the pain in his right arm, supported with one arm only, and that the left, the shock of the terrific avalanche which fell upon him, is in our eyes a triumph of moral force, and a miraculous exhibition of will. Five-and-twenty times was he flung upon the sward, and five-and-twenty times he rose again, the living image of England on the field of battle. History tells us that Englishmen are always beaten in the first campaign. Like all men of strong character, they gather force from misfortune. It seems that, like Antæus, they must kiss the earth before they know their strength, for after a series of defeats we find them ever masters of the field of battle. If they are not thoroughly beaten at first, their destruction will be a work of time. But there is still another reason which has made us allude to this singular fight. We mean the profound and universal and ardent interest which it has aroused in England, and which seems to us to have a political significance. During the last year and a-half volunteer rifle corps have been formed in England, and the newly-awakened popular interest in the recent fight is intimately connected with the prevalent idea among Englishmen of the necessity of taking measures for the defence of their territory.'

The 'Constitutionnel' follows in the view taken by the 'Débats'; and alludes to a maudlin tirade in the 'Siècle' which spoke of it as 'a barbarous and disgusting exhibition.' The writer thus concludes :—
'We are not living in ordinary times. The prospects of Europe are certainly not pacific. The elements of strife are in secret motion; at what moment a general outbreak may occur it is not in the power of many to predict. But the general arming and cautious preparations for future—it may be proximate —hostilities, combined with other circumstances and experiences too well established, point to a universal

European war with a sure and ominous finger. It
may be that the entire British race all over the globe
may have to defend their rights and liberties as the
only free people on earth, and this at no very distant
period. Several of the French newspapers, in speaking of this fight, have only seen in it a rude and disgusting exhibition. For ourselves, we recognise the
play of animal instinct, but we think there is something else to which attention should be paid. The
first defence of England consists in her wooden walls ;
but her second line of defence consists in the broad
chests and formidable arms which play their part in
contests like that which we have described. England
sees in them a provision for the defence of the country. Such, it seems to us, is the moral of this fight
—such the explanation of the interest it has excited
in every class of English society—and such is our
excuse for having occupied the attention of our
readers with a description of it.'

THE GREAT PUGILISTIC REVIVAL.

(From *All the Year Round*, May 19th, 1860.)

THERE was a period, not more than some six months
ago, when most of us thought we could never publicly state that we had seen a prize fight. We had
some notion that the ' Ring ' was dead ; and that its
ropes and stakes had never been properly disinterred
since their burial, some years back, at Moulsey Hurst.
We had some notion that its exhibitions were illegal,
and that its professors were compelled to live upon
the traditions of the past, and bite their motheaten
boxing-gloves in pugilistic bar-parlours. It is probable that we did not regard these professors as a
downtrodden race, because we considered them at
war with our present civilisation. We looked upon
them as melancholy relics of a departed fashion—as

men who persisted in supplying an article that the
public no longer called for or desired. The present
writer, for one, set them down in his notes for a great
History of England, as having practically gone out
with watchmen, oil-lamps, and stage-coaches.

During the last five years, however, the World
(meaning, of course, the United Kingdom of Great
Britain and Ireland) has witnessed many full-blown
revivals, and, last among them and not least, a
thorough revival of Pugilism. There has seldom been
any demonstration so sudden, so successful, and so
complete. I have seen the late contest between the
immortal Sayers and the immortal Heenan apologeti-
cally described as an 'exceptional event.' The Jour-
nalist was timid, and was feeling his way. I have
also noticed a little shyness on the part of certain
distinguished spectators of the battle, who gave the
Ring the sanction of their presence but not the sanction of their names. A few more of these exceptional
events may dispel all such mock modesty.

From the first moment when the late exceptional
event—the international prize fight—began to assume
the aspect of a great and coming fact, there was the
shallowest possible attempt on all sides to keep up
appearances. People remarked very mildly that such
disgraceful spectacles ought to be stopped, and immediately staked two to one that the Englishman
would beat the American. A member or two in the
House of Commons tamely asked the Home Secretary
what he intended to do, and his reply was generally
to the effect that he would try to keep up appearances.
The powers of the metropolitan police were put in
force, and they kept up appearances by pushing the
training combatants into the country. Local con-
stabulary forces, finding that they also were expected
to behave with superficial decency, hunted the American (not very chivalrously, seeing that they might
have hunted the Englishman), until he was bound
over to keep the peace with two sureties, to the extent of a hundred pounds. That extremely useful end

attained, they retired like good men who had thoroughly done their duty in keeping up appearances.

After conference with my friend the conductor of
this Journal, I received his encouragement personally
to let down these same appearances, and to go to the
fight, and to avow in these pages that I had done so.
This was my commission.

When I went out into the frosty air, instead of
going comfortably to bed about one o'clock, A.M., on
Tuesday morning, April 17, I held a railway ticket in
my hand, that was printed to keep up appearances.
A journey from London Bridge to nowhere and back,
by a special four o'clock train, was all that I was
guaranteed by this slip of cardboard in return for the
sum of three pounds sterling. For all this seeming
mystery, the railway company knew that I knew I
was going to the great prize fight; the policeman
who saw me close my street door at that unseemly
hour knew that I was going to the great prize fight;
the cabman who drove me to my destination was
bursting with intelligence of the great prize fight;
and the crowd who had assembled round the railway
station were either going with me to the great prize
fight, or had come to see me go to the great prize
fight. There was an affectation of secrecy about the
movements of some of the travellers, a reflection of
the many eye-winkings they must have seen for the
last few days; and there was an affectation of caution
on the part of the railway company in dividing the
passengers, and admitting them simultaneously at different entrances. These passengers moved silently
along the passages, and across the platforms, as if
they were trespassers upon the company's property,
who had stolen in while the directors were asleep,
and were about to run away with the rolling stock,
with the connivance of a small number of the railway
officers. The anxious threatening glances that were
cast upon unknown people, and the many whispered
inquiries as to who was, or who was not, a detec-
tive policeman, gave a pretty burglarious tone to

the whole station for at least an hour before daybreak. The farce was extremely well acted, and appearances were carefully kept up to the last.. The
favoured railway had been known for months (it was
the first that was ever mentioned in connection with
the fight); the very spot upon which the battle was
to take place, had been confided to hundreds for
days; and the morning, the hour, and the point of
departure had been openly sold like any commodity
in the market. It was all a preposterous keeping up
of appearances. The fact is, there was no public
desire ever manifested to stop the contest, but a very
strong desire to hear that it had been fairly fought
out. In the face of such a feeling the law was paralysed; its function not being to make a whole people
more virtuous than they really are. The nation has
no logical complaint against the law for standing still
on this occasion, but only for its ridiculous pretence
of being constantly on the alert.

There were never, perhaps, so many passengers
assembled on a railway platform who knew and addressed each other by familiar Christian names. The
whole train might have been taken for a grand village
excursion, but for those unmistakable faces that
rested in the folds of the carriage cushions, under the
dim light of the carriage lamps. The small eyes and
heads, the heavy jaws, and the high cheek bones, were
hung out like candid signboards, to mark the members of the fighting trade. The two or three hundred
Americans, and the small sprinkling of aristocracy
and visitors, were not sufficient to modify in any perceptible degree the thoroughly animal character of
the train.

I obtained a seat in a rather overloaded double
compartment of a second-class carriage. Behind me
were a live lord, a live baronet, a member of Parliament, the very gentlemanly editor of a distinguished
sporting paper which has always done its utmost in
the cause of fair play and honest dealing, an aristocratic Scotchman, a clergyman of the Church of

England, and a renowned poet of the tender passions.
By the side of me was a young, cheerful, round-faced
Australian settler, who had travelled fifteen thousand
miles to see the fight, and to transact a little business
of minor importance. His dress was light, his manner self-reliant, and he looked the kind of man to go
round the world unencumbered with luggage, with a
cigar in his mouth and his hands in his pockets. Opposite this passenger was a mild, long-faced, blinking
gentleman, of Jewish aspect, who talked very fluently,
and seemed to know all the minor deities of the ring.
By his side was a drowsy and ragged member of the
fighting craft, whose prospects seemed blighted, and
whose scalp had been taken by the immortal Sayers
in a battle some eight years before.

The labour of keeping up the conversation in the
carriage rested chiefly upon the Australian settler and
the talkative Jew. The aristocracy seemed shy.
They were diffident, perhaps, of their sporting knowledge, or were sleepy from having been up all night.

'I saw a good fight in Melbourne,' said the Australian, 'about a week afore I left.'

'_Did_ you?' returned the talkative Jew.

'There's a fortune there,' said the Australian, confidently, 'for any man about eight stun nine.'

The drowsy fighting-man, with blighted prospects,
slowly opened one eye.

'There's no good man there,' continued the Australian, 'under nine stun.'

'How about Fibbing Dilly?' asked the talkative
Jew.

'Used up.'

'Joss Humphrey?'

'Bounceable: wants it taken out of him. Fights
at ten stun; gives any man a stun, but won't strip
for less than a thousand pounds.'

'What name?' asked the blighted prize-fighter,
this time opening both eyes, and becoming languidly
interested in the conversation.

'Joss Humphrey,' answered the Australian settler.

'Ah!' returned the blighted prize-fighter, relapsing into drowsiness. Australia seemed a long way off, and capital did not appear to be forthcoming. It was an opening for a smart active young man, but he was not in a position to avail himself of it.

'Nick Muffles could tackle him,' remarked the talkative Jew, addressing himself, almost confidentially, to the blighted prize-fighter.

'Ye-s,' was the drawling answer, finished off with a yawn.

'Nick's clever,' said the Jew.

'Ah!' returned the prize-fighter.

'Ain't he artful?'

'Ah!'

'Don't he get away?'

'And keep away!'

'But ain't it smart?'

'Ah!'

After this favourable review of their absent friends' fighting qualities, the blighted prize-fighter made a few observations in praise of Nature before he again closed his eyes. He seemed to be an admirer of daybreak, and a lover of gardens. The Australian kept up the conversation with the Jew by inquiring after many old prize-fighters whom he had known before he emigrated. Some were dead, some had thrived, some had disappeared. They were all asked after by affectionate Christian names, like many actors and most comic singers. The pugilistic profession seems never to have had more than two 'Misters' in its ranks; the late ex-champion, 'Mr.' Gulley, M.P. for Pontefract; and the late ex-champion, 'Mr.' Jackson, teacher of boxing, and one of the coronation pages to King George the Fourth.

As our journey continued through Kent, and into Surrey, we were amused by seeing many official scarecrows, keeping up appearances by being posted along the line. A few blue-nosed policemen at the stations; four other shivering policemen under a clump of trees; a few galloping police officers, taking equestrian exercise on the coach road below ; represented the winking majesty of the law. Their faces showed the make-believe character of their opposition to the exceptional event.

When after a journey of two hours, we were set down at the Farnborough station, it struck me that no more appropriate fighting-ground could have been chosen throughout England. We were near the great military camp at Aldershot—a place where thirty thousand warriors are always studying how best to kill and to destroy. They belong to a great European prize-fighting association, which boast of some three millions of active members ; by the side of whom the puny company of professed pugilists sink into contempt.

The appearance of our train, and of the passengers who hurriedly alighted from it, was a signal to some of the scared farmers to barricade their dwellings. They knew that fifteen hundred people might prove a dangerous invading army, pushed along as they had been by the strong metropolitan authorities into the feeble arms of the local police.

A muddy tramp over half a mile of marshy meadow land, where we had to jump over small ditches, and struggle through hedges, brought us, at last, to the field selected for the battle. The stakes were driven in with wooden mallets, and the ropes were adjusted by a veteran prize-fighter, about seventy years old— a sage of a hoary and venerable aspect. Around the ring, when formed, we ranged ourselves in a very eager, selfish, noisy, expectant, brutal mob. There was not one man there who could say I am more refined than my neighbour. For the time being we were all equal, and our country was anxiously waiting behind us to read an account of everything we were about to see. There were dukes, lords, marquises, clergymen, actors, singers, managers, authors, reporters, painters, and poets, mixed with plain country gentlemen, military officers, legislators, lawyers, barristers, merchants, card-sharpers, fathers of

families who brought their sons, thieves, fighting-
men, trainers, horse-dealers, doctors, publicans,
contractors, feather-weights, light-weights, middle-
weights, heavy-weights, Americans of all classes,
Irishmen of several classes, and Scotchmen also.
Scarcely an art, a profession, or a class was unre-
presented.   Later in the morning, when the country
was aroused, we had farm labourers, women, country
girls, and little children, a few policemen—still keeping up appearances—and a country idiot, with helpless hands and feeble legs, and gaping mouth, who
was the only innocent, irresponsible spectator of the
fight.   A number of active visitors swarmed up the
slender trees which surrounded the meadow, whence
they looked down upon the ring, like staring and
grinning apes.   There was even a timid old gentleman present who, rather than stay away, had hired
two professional fighting men to protect him.

When the immortal Sayers stepped into the ring,
at about seven o'clock in the morning, he was received,
like a popular performer, with a round of applause.
His immortal face was a deep sallow brown, and
looked like a square block of walnut wood.   His expression was even a little more strongly marked for
pugilism than that of most of his craft.   He was
slightly nervous upon facing the company.

His opponent, the immortal Heenan, next entered
the ring, to be received with quite as much enthusiasm as the English Champion.   He looked much
fairer than Sayers in the face, and was equally
nervous.   His portraits had flattered him in the eyes
of the British public.   There are two styles of nose
which all prize-fighters must be content to select
from—one, presenting a flat, triangular appearance :
the other, indented near the tip, and slightly turned
up, so that you could hang a key upon it.   The immortal Heenan had a moderate nose of the last
pattern.

The two immortal men shook hands, and seemed
to inquire cordially after each other's health, which

was the signal for another round of applause. They
eyed each other curiously and reflectively as they had
never met before.

The ring-keepers—some twenty selected pugilists
with long sticks, of whom some were afterwards disgraced for grossly neglecting their duty—were now
very busy in arranging the visitors, causing those in
front, who had purchased inner-ring tickets at ten
shillings each for the benefit of the P.B.A. (Prize-
fighters' Benevolent Association), to sit down upon
the wet turf, their railway rugs, or camp-stools, that
were selling at a sovereign a piece. One indefati-
gable caterer openly lamented the loss of a ten-pound
note, through his not having brought down a few
boxes for gentlemen to stand upon. The country
people seemed to make little harvest of the general
excitement, except in the sale of oranges. The thieves
were very busy, and the Americans were their greatest
victims. The picking of pockets, however, is no
more peculiar to the Prize Ring than to popular
chapels.

Rounds of applause were very freely bestowed at
every opportunity. There was one when the immortal Sayers took off his coat and shirt; there was
another when the immortal Heenan did the like;
there was a tremendous burst of satisfaction when
the two men, in full fighting order, stripped to the
waist, and advanced towards the 'scratch' in the
centre of the ring. They looked firm, muscular, and
cheerful, the result of their training; but the constitution is not improved by these violent changes from
indulgence and idleness to temperance and enforced
exercise. Consumption and dropsy are common
amongst professional pugilists, and sometimes the
two diseases combine. Everything in training is
sacrificed to showy muscle and wind.

There was a ceremony of tying the combatants'
colours—two gaudy pocket-handkerchiefs—to the
stakes; there was another ceremony of shaking hands
between seconds and champions; there was another

ceremony of tossing for choice of ' corners,' or position
in the ring. There was almost as many ceremonies
as at a Coronation. Everything was conducted according to certain forms and rules, almost super-
stitiously observed.

The choice of the corner was won by the American,
and he took his place. His back was to the sun—a
bright glaring sun—and his ground was slightly
higher than that of his adversary. In stature he is
six feet one and a half inch high; and besides being
five inches taller than Sayers, he is, of course, heavier,
and eight years younger.

The two immortal heroes of the hour stood up
before each other in the most approved attitudes.
Their left sides were advanced; their right arms were
laid across their chest; their left arms were thrown
out and drawn back, like the pawing leg of a horse.
Their visitors watched every movement for the present
in breathless silence, while their seconds peered at
them from opposite corners, like wicket-keepers in a
cricket-field. There was a forced laugh on each
champion's face, that was meant to be agreeable.
Their left feet kept tapping the ground in a kind of
dancing step; their heads were frequently thrown
back, or bobbed down; and they skipped from side to
side after aiming or parrying a blow. At last the
first stage in the fight was reached amidst uproarious
applause; the immortal Sayers had succeeded in drawing ' first blood' from his antagonist.

These movements were repeated with such slight
variation, that pugilism, like most games of skill,
must be pronounced monotonous. It was some little
time before the next great stage in the battle was
reached, and the first knock-down blow was received
by the Englishman.

The excitement round the ring now began to break
out, and hoarse shouts were exchanged from each
side. Enormous sums of money were loudly offered,
by rough and shabby-looking people, upon either
champion, and aristocratic eyes stared intensely

through many eye-glasses. Unruly visitors leaped
up from the grass, and danced wildly near the ropes;
while the ring-keepers applied their sticks, without
stint or favour, to the visitors' heads and shoulders.
The same movements were repeated again and again
by the champions, with pretty nearly the same results.
The immortal Sayers was knocked down at least
twenty times by the immortal Heenan, or fell,
humouring his blows. The turf was soft, and he
had to counterbalance his many disadvantages by
'science,' or careful tactics. He was always picked
up by his seconds in the most affectionate manner,
and carried to his corner, like a Guy Fawkes, to be
sponged.

An hour soon passed in this way, without any
signs of the battle drawing to a conclusion. The
immortal Sayers's face, with the sun full upon it, was
like a battered copper tea-kettle; his right arm was
stiff and helpless; and he was freely spitting blood.
The immortal Heenan's right eye was closed up with
a huge lump of blue flesh, produced by the Englishman's well-directed and determined blows; his upper
lip, too, was puffed out, as if there were six rows of
gums and teeth behind it. When Sayers gave a
telling hit, he stopped and looked inquisitively at his
adversary, to see what damage he had done; and
after Heenan had knocked his opponent down, he
turned to his seconds, threw up both his arms, and
opened his swollen mouth in a gasping manner.

The excitement was now at its height; and a constant roar of voices was kept up round the ring.
People at the back made desperate attempts to mount
the shoulders of those in front. Nervous betting men,
with heavy stakes upon the contest, got out of the
crowd, and walked about the meadow. The wind
hissed through the trees, and the hundreds who clung
to the bending branches shouted loudly for each combatant, according to the tide of battle. A few county
policemen came upon the field to keep up appearances,
and when they timidly ventured to push into the

ng, were quietly hustled on one side by the savage
spectators. A few oaths were heard, but not many;
 he pale faces round the inner circle became paler,
he compressed lips more compressed; bets of various
amounts were still loudly offered and loudly taken;
utsiders leaped up and down with ceaseless activity;
he smacking blows of the combatats were heard, and
heir visible effect was described to excited inquirers,
nd the news passed from mouth to mouth; opinions
luctuated; the Englishman was abused or praised, so
vas the American; the referee was nearly smothered;
nd the only men who really seemed to retain calmness were the two combatants, their seconds, and the
eading prize-fighters present. When, at the end of
wo hours, and in the thirty-seventh round, the
American got the neck of the Englishman across the
ope, it was not the fault of the general multitude
hat murder was not presented to them as a crowning
treat for their money. The American was requested
to 'hold him' by a thousand voices on the ground
and in the trees, but at the height of the uproar the
ring was broken, the referee was forced out of his
place, and all became wild confusion. This is no new
ending to such a contest. The referee was the editor
already referred to, who for years has done as much
as a gentleman in resolute earnest could, to imbue
these men with principles of honour, justice and self-
restraint. Surely there is something wrong, after all,
in the 'Noble Art,' when he is set at nought when
most needed, and when the well-conducted men
among the pugilists cannot rely upon their own
brethren to preserve a clear stage and no favour, but
are forced to the declaration (as they have been in
this case) that even the men of their careful selection
are not to be trusted with the limited responsibility
of keeping the Ring.

This fight has been declared 'a draw,' and a draw
it certainly was in every sense of the word. It drew
hundreds of people from many parts of the globe; it
drew thousands from their beds; it drew four or five

thousand pounds sterling for a special railway train,
one half of which sum will be divided, by arrangement,
between the two men.   It drew all England from its
usual business engagements about mid-day, on the
memorable Tuesday, the 17th of April, 1860.   It drew
thirty-five bales, containing two tons of newspapers
(the largest number ever shipped aboard one ship)
to America at the earliest possible moment.   It drew
several distinguished mercantile bodies into subscrib-
ing testimonials for the English Champion; it drew
uncountable numbers of people into supporting a
great pugilistic revival.

————

ABOUT THE FIGHT FOR THE CHAMPIONSHIP.

(From *The Saturday Review*, April 28th, 1860.)

WE cannot but lament that the great fight has not
been fought out.   Whether the appearance of the
police was the real or the pretended cause of the interruption, we equally regret that the battle was not
continued until one or other of the champions became
the undisputed conqueror.   It is perfectly easy, on
this side of the Atlantic, to rest satisfied with the
accounts which we choose to give and to accept of
the affair.   But we apprehend that in America it will
be stated, and believed, that Heenan, if allowed fair
play, could have won the battle, and that the ring
was wilfully broken up in order to avoid the loss of
British honour and British money involved in the
defeat of Sayers.   Supposing the merits of the trans-
action to be doubtful, we know our acute cousins far
too well not to expect that they will loudly and
steadily repeat that version of it which is most agreeable to their own feelings.   And on this side of the
water, we shall not be wanting in consideration for
the sensitiveness of British vanity.   We fear that the
occurrences of last Tuesday will be the beginning of
a long controversy which is not likely to be set at

st except by a further meeting between the combatants—a step which, however, we must not be understood to advocate.

It is always difficult, even for those who enjoy the best opportunities of observation, and turn them to the best account, to describe exactly what happened at a moment of violent excitement and confusion amid a crowd of men. We could mention celebrated battles as to which nobody agreed in fixing either when they began or when they ended; and, therefore, it need not create surprise that different versions have gained currency of the circumstances under which this fight was prematurely stopped. But we are not without our suspicions that the ring would have been better kept if the English Champion had been fighting a manifestly winning battle. It was said, over and over again, when doubts were hinted, that, whatever happened, the American should have fair play. It is deeply to be regretted if he has not had such a full and undeniable measure of justice dealt to him as would have placed the English national character, in this respect, as high in the estimation of other countries as in our own. It is often alleged, and, we believe, with truth, that one advantage of prize fights, strictly regulated and impartially conducted, is that they tend to cherish a habit of self-restraint and a love of justice which usually make men forbearing and generous even in their angry moments, and, if they, in their passion, infringe the well-known rules of fistic law, insure the interference of the spectators to redress any undue advantage. But, if motives are to be allowed to operate, such as those which we fear did, to some extent, prevail on Tuesday, there is an end to the pretension we have been used to make—to be, in this respect, an example to the world. We would desire all those who were near the ring during the fight between Sayers and Heenan to ask themselves whether they would have acted precisely as they did if they had regarded Sayers throughout as a certain conqueror. We shall not attempt to answer this question for them, and we will only add to it the repeated expression of our regret, that the events of Tuesday do not encourage the expectation that roguery and ruffianism will, in time to come, be banished from the Prize Ring.

But we further have to remark that, if Heenan and his friends complain that the battle was left undecided, the American Champion has chiefly himself to blame for the disappointment which he may think he has sustained. It is certain that he was holding Sayers so that he would have strangled him in another minute, and the ropes enclosing the ring were cut or loosened by some one near at hand, in order to deliver Sayers from what appeared to be the peril of immediate death. When the ropes were once lowered of course the ring was broken, and it is difficult to pronounce whether all the confusion which ensued was, or was not, inevitable. Considering the pressure from without, both from excitement and from the efforts of the police, it was natural to expect that as soon as the barrier of the ropes and stakes had fallen, the small space allotted to the combatants would be inundated by intruders who could not, if they would, have kept outside. It seems to us that Heenan's conduct furnished a pretext which Sayers's friends might, if they chose, lay hold of to break off the battle. We do not say they did, but it is probable that Heenan's friends and countrymen will say so, and it will not be easy to establish, in opposition to their assertions, that the whole of the confusion which followed the lowering of the ropes was accidental and undesigned. But, we must repeat, that for this unsatisfactory conclusion, Heenan has himself to blame. We believe that his treatment of Sayers at the moment when the ropes were loosened, was lawful according to the rules of the Prize Ring. Sayers was not down, and could not get down, because the rope kept him up—and almost any kind of injury may be inflicted so long as the sufferer remains by natural or artificial means upon his legs. We say almost any kind of injury, meaning any that would suggest itself to a combatant trained in the English school of prize-fighters. Such a combatant would know, and, however excited, would probably remember, that if he strangled his opponent, his own life or liberty would be abridged as the penalty of his violence. But Heenan appears to have forgotten this. The life of Sayers was in imminent danger, and it became absolutely necessary to interfere. If the conduct of the bystanders was not within the letter of the laws of the Prize Ring, it was most unquestionably within their spirit. One principal object of those laws is, that fights with fists between healthy and well-trained men may call forth great courage and constancy without any serious risk to life. If American pugilists appear in the English ring, they must be content to fight under such restrictions as our own estimate of the value of human lives and limbs imposes. Suppose some compatriot of Heenan were to introduce gouging in order to hasten the end of an exhausting battle. We believe that gouging as well as strangling is within the written law, but the combatant who practised it would soon be taught that he would not be permitted to Americanise a British Institution. It seems, then, to have been a legitimate interposition which delivered Sayers from the deadly grip of Heenan, but whether all that followed was or was not inevitable cannot be known.

Passing now to the general merits of the battle, we may say at once that the majority of the spectators beheld a sight very different from that for which they bargained. It was not to see the Champion of England knocked clean off his legs some five-and-twenty times that so many hundred Englishmen travelled down to Farnborough. But if they did not witness exactly what most of them expected, they saw even a finer sight. Never in the annals of pugilism were skill, coolness, judgment, variety of resource, pluck, and bottom displayed in such a wonderful degree as by Sayers in this splendid battle. Wherever manly

courage and manly sentiments prevail, his name will
be held in honour. Taking the result as it now
stands, or even supposing a further trial to end in the
defeat of Sayers, we should still say that for spirit,
science, and endurance, his character is unsurpassed
throughout the world. He was pitted against a man
who was his equal in resolution and not very far inferior in skill, while in height, weight and length of
reach he possessed a vast superiority. Heenan, before
this fight, was comparatively an untried man, and it
could not be known beforehand whether, as is so often
found in the noblest specimens of humanity, he had
not a weak point somewhere. There was also the
consideration that he came to us from a land where
nobody's gifts or merits are at all likely to be under-
stated. But the truth now appears to be that Heenan
is five inches taller and two or three stone heavier,
and eight years younger than Sayers, while his length
of arm is extraordinary, even for so tall a man. He
has great natural advantages, and he is quite capable
of turning them to the best account. We all know
that in general a big boy can thrash a small one.
There may be exceptional cases of cowardice, or
awkwardness, or weakness, but the rule is that height
and weight carry the day. Almost every sort of artificial weapon tends more or less to equalise men of
different degrees of stature, but in using the weapons
which nature gave, the advantages usually rest where
instinct teaches us to look for it. Now, the battle between Heenan and Sayers may very fairly be described
as a battle between a big and a little boy. It was
thought that the experience, the quickness, and the
game qualities of Sayers would more than counterbalance the tremendous range and power of his adversary. When Heenan stood forth in the ring, he
was confessed by everybody to be the most magnificent figure seen there within living memory. That
Sayers should have fought so long and so beautifully
as he did is the greatest triumph of the art of which
he has been the worthy chief; and it is a proof, which

is countrymen will not soon forget, that he possesses,
ı the fullest measure, all those qualities which, in
ıore deadly conflicts, have shed imperishable glory
n his country's arms. We might say much, if it
rere necessary, in defence of prize-fighting, but we
rill content ourselves with saying this—that when
British soldiers cease to feel the interest they showed
n this famous battle, they will forfeit, at the same
ime, their character for unrivalled prowess. When
the world has really entered upon a millennium of
peaceful industry, let prize-fighting be abolished, and
let the memory of its heroes pass away. But so long
as restless neighbours will have their Magenta and
Solferino, so long we should like to have occasionally,
on some open unfrequented heath, such a day as has
been seen this week. Let warlike Emperors count
their well-drilled legions. Our own Sovereign may
be content to reckon Sayers among her subjects, and
to say—

> I trust I have within this realm
> Ten thousand good as he.

And an equal tribute of praise and admiration is
surely due to the gallant spirit which brought Heenan
across the ocean, and sustained him until he fully
learned the scope of his own tremendous powers.
But who, let us ask, is Heenan? He was born of
Irish parents in America. The blood which flows in
his veins is that which has been poured so freely on
every battle-field where the armies of the Queen have
triumphed. Indeed, the difference between the rivals
is only this—the parents of both were Irish, but the
one couple migrated to England, and the other to the
United States. Sayers and Heenan in the Prize Ring,
and Marshals M'Mahon and O'Donnell at the head of
armies, appear to have derived their pugnacity from
the same prolific soil. Not that we would attempt to
rob America of any portion of the honour won for
her in this splendid contest. It is enough for us to
know that the stock from which Heenan sprang was

given to the new country by the old, and we believe
there is plenty of it still left at home. In praising
one of these champions we praise the other; and if
we must confess to a slight partiality for Sayers, it is
only the Englishman's inveterate leaning towards a
little fellow fighting an uphill fight against a big one.
Heenan is probably the finest man who ever stepped
into a prize ring. He has shown unflinching courage,
and, as he now knows his own terrific strength,
and may be expected to improve in skill, and to feel
no nervousness, neither England nor America will
soon find a man to beat him. Sayers most amply
justified the confidence which his countrymen reposed in him. A more accomplished, enduring, and
courageous boxer never wore the belt of champion.
We trust the combatants and their friends will feel
that enough has been done and suffered for the honour
of the men and of the countries which gave them
birth.

AN ANECDOTE APROPOS OF TOM SAYERS.

(From *The Cornhill Magazine*, July, 1860.)

In George II.'s time, there was a turbulent navy lieutenant (Handsome Smith he was called—his picture
is at Greenwich now, in brown velvet, and gold and
scarlet; his coat handsome, his waistcoat exceedingly
handsome; but his face by no means the beauty) —
there was, I say, a turbulent young lieutenant who was
broke on a complaint of the French Ambassador, for
obliging a French ship of war to lower her topsails
to his ship at Spithead. But, by the King's orders,
Tom was next day made Captain Smith. Well, if I
were absolute king, I would send Tom Sayers to
the mill for a month, and make him Sir Thomas on
coming out of Clerkenwell. You are a naughty boy,
Tom! but then, you know, we ought to love our
brethren, though ever so naughty. We are moralists,
and reprimand you; and you are hereby reprimanded

accordingly. But in case England should ever have
need of a few score thousand champions, who laugh
at danger; who cope with giants; who, stricken to
the ground, jump up and gaily rally, and fall, and
rise again, and strike, and die rather than yield—in
case the country should need such men, and you
should know them, be pleased to send lists of the
misguided persons to the principal police stations,
where means may some day be found to utilise their
wretched powers, and give their deplorable energies
a right direction. Suppose, Tom, that you and your
friends are pitted against an immense invader—suppose you are bent on holding the ground, and dying
there, if need be—suppose it is life, freedom, honour,
home, you are fighting for, and there is a death-
dealing sword or rifle in your hand, with which you
are going to resist some tremendous enemy who
challenges your championship on your native shore?
Then, Sir Thomas, resist him to the death, and it is
all right: kill him, and heaven bless you. Drive
him into the sea, and there destroy, smash, and drown
him; and let us sing *Laudamus*. In these national
cases, you see, we override the indisputable first laws
of morals. Loving your neighbour is very well, but
suppose your neighbour comes over from Calais and
Boulogne to rob you of your laws, your liberties, your
newspapers, your parliament (all of which *some* dear
neighbours of ours have given up in the most self-
denying manner): suppose any neighbour were to
cross the water and propose this kind of thing to us,
should we not be justified in humbly trying to pitch
him into the water? If it were the King of Belgium
himself we must do so. I mean that fighting, of
course, is wrong; but that there are occasions when,
&c.—I suppose I mean that that one-handed fight of
Sayers is one of the most spirit-stirring little stories
ever told: and, with every love and respect for
Morality—my spirit says to her, ' Do, for goodness'
sake, my dear madam, keep your true, and pure, and
womanly, and gentle remarks for another day. Have

the great kindness to stand a *leetle* aside, and just let
us see one or two more rounds between the men.
That little man with the one hand powerless on his
breast facing yonder giant for hours, and felling him,
too, every now and then! It is the little Java and
the Constitution over again!'   .

THE 'COLLECTIVE WISDOM,' RAILWAY DIRECTORS, AND THE RING.

(Debates of the House of Commons, Tuesday, May 15th,
1860.)

IN Parliament, too, the subject of Tom's fight raised
the question of pugilism upon a collateral issue, and
elicited from the vivacious and genial Prime Minister,
whom England yet mourns, those manly and cosmo-
politan sentiments, which, as Sir Robert Peel gene-
rously said, after a gallantly contested political fight,
'made us all proud of him;' adding, 'and we *are* all
proud of him.' The contemptible figure cut by the
noble lord who raised the 'question,' it would be un-
charitable to dwell on. The report runs as follows:—

Lord LOVAINE rose to ask the question, of which he
had given notice, in reference to the conduct of the
directors of the South-Eastern Railway Company in
running a special train for the conveyance of the
persons who attended the recent prize fight. This
exhibition, he said, had been declared by the Home
Secretary, though rather reluctantly, to be illegal.
It followed, as a consequence, that those who aided
and abetted an illegal act were participators in
it. It was not the first time the South-Eastern
Railway Company had aided and abetted in such
a proceeding. The company had received from the
Legislature almost a monopoly of the traffic of the
counties through which it passed, and its directors
ought not to use their large powers to violate the
law. The company had been warned before, and he

understood the directors had pledged themselves that no such proceeding should again occur. Last year a letter was addressed to them by the bench of magistrates of the county of Surrey on a similar occasion; the answer of the Secretary was, that any arrangements for the conveyance of such excursionists had been made without the knowledge of the directors, and that it should not occur again. But so far was the company from keeping this pledge that it allowed two special trains to be run down the line on the morning of the recent fight. At every station in the county of Surrey these trains were met by the police, but on passing into Hampshire no police were found, the passengers got out at a station in that county, and the fight took place. Nor was this all; with one of these special trains, he was informed, was an officer of the company, a superintendent from the office at London Bridge; the complicity of the directors of the company was thus established; whether it would be possible to bring the law to bear on them was another question. But he thought it incumbent on the House to express a resolution not to allow persons to wield powers granted them by the Legislature in defiance of the law. By such arrangements as the company had made, 2,000 or 3,000 of the greatest ruffians in London could be launched on any quiet neighbourhood to its injury and damage. The South-Western Railway Company had refused to run any special train on its line for the conveyance of these persons. The House knew that the Executive was not very strong when opposed to numbers, as shown by the case of St. George's-in-the-East, where a mob of ruffians had for the last three months been able to keep up a continual disturbance in the church. He thought it right, therefore, to ask whether the Government had in this instance attempted to enforce the law; or whether anything had been done to stop the practice to which he had referred. The noble lord then moved for ‘a copy of all the correspondence between the Home-office and the directors of the South-Eastern

Railway Company, in the years 1859–60, relating to
the conveyance of persons intending to commit a
breach of the law.'

Lord PALMERSTON said—I have no objection to the
noble lord's motion, but I must make a protest against
the sort of exaggerations in which the noble lord has
indulged. He has described the railway launching
2,000 or 3,000 ruffians upon some quiet neighbourhood, in a manner that might lead one to imagine
the train conveyed a set of banditti to plunder, rack,
and ravage the country, murder the people, and commit every sort of atrocity. I am not going to dispute
the point that a fight between two men—not a fight of
enmity, but a trial of strength—is, legally, a breach of
the peace, and an act that renders the parties liable to
prosecution; nor whether the persons who go to witness it are not, technically, involved in the charge.
But as far as they are concerned, they may conceive
it to be a very harmless pursuit: some persons like
what takes place; there may be a difference of opinion,
as a matter of taste, whether it is a spectacle one
would wish to see, or whether it is calculated to ex-
cite disgust. Some people look upon it as an exhibition
of manly courage, characteristic of the people of the
country. I saw the other day a long extract from a
French newspaper, describing this fight as a type of
the national character for endurance, patience under
suffering, of indomitable perseverance, in determined
effort, and holding it up as a specimen of the manly
and admirable qualities of the British race. (Hear,
hear.) All this is, of course, entirely a matter of
opinion, but really setting aside the legal technicalities
of the case, I do not perceive why any number of
persons, say 1,000 if you please, who assemble to witness a prize fight, are in their own persons more
guilty of a breach of the peace than an equal number
of persons who assemble to witness a balloon ascent.
(Laughter.) There they stand, there is no breach
of the peace; they go to see a sight, and when that
sight is over they return, and no injury is done to any

one. They only stand or sit on the grass to witness the performance, and as to the danger to those who perform themselves, I imagine the danger to life in the case of those who go up in balloons is certainly greater (Hear, and laughter) than that of two combatants who merely hit each other as hard as they can, but inflict no permanent injury upon each other. (Hear, hear.) I think there is moderation in all things—moderation in all opinions; and although it may or may not be desirable that the law should be enforced—whatever the law may be—still I do not think any advantage is gained, or good done, either to public morals or public feeling by the sort of exaggerations in which the noble lord has indulged. At the same time the motion is one to which I see no objection, and therefore I do not oppose it.

Lord LOVAINE, in reply, said the noble lord had pleaded the cause of prize-fighting so well that he ought to propose a measure to legalise the practice. He had always thought it was the duty of the Secretary of State to prevent such scenes, and not to excuse them. The noble lord had skilfully defended prize-fighting, about the merits of which he (Lord Lovaine) had not said a word; but he had complained of 2,000 or 3,000 ruffians being taken down to one spot for such a purpose. He granted, however, that all who were present on the occasion in question were not ruffians (a laugh), for some names had been mentioned which were not unknown in that or the other House. (Hear.) But if the noble lord had gone down in the same train with these gentry —(Lord Palmerston made a gesture of surprise). He (Lord Lovaine) could assure the noble lord that he went down only as a casual passenger (loud laughter), and did not find his fellow-travellers the best company in the world. (Continued laughter.) It was not right, however, to call upon the county police to preserve the peace and prevent these fights, while the Government in that House were by their words supporting those who broke the peace. (Hear.)

Mr. Scully said that the noble lord (Lovaine) did not stand alone in his condemnation of such exhibitions. The noble lord, however, should have gone at higher game than the directors of a railway company, who were guided by a desire of profits; but he should have attacked those who were not influenced by such motives, and especially the Minister who gave encouragement to those scenes. (Hear, hear.) It was the duty of the Government to enforce the law, whether they considered it a good law or not. Such used to be the doctrine laid down in his own country, and ought to be applied in this instance. He could only add that his schoolboy experience taught him that those who set others on to fight were generally cowards themselves.

Mr. W. Ewart said he had a few nights since asked the Home Secretary to state what was the law relating to prize fights, but received in reply an indirect defence of the practice. He thought that if the law said one thing the Secretary of State ought not, even by anticipation, to say another. (Hear.) He did not object to fighting with gloves (laughter), as an exercise, nor did he object to the art of self-defence, which was better than the knives or stilettos used in foreign countries. (Hear, hear.) Neither did he object to fencing with foils; but he drew the same distinction between such fencing and a duel with swords as he did between a fight with gloves and a prize fight. The noble lord (Palmerston) had quoted the *Journal des Débats* as eulogising the recent fight, but, in fact, the paper did not justify such proceedings, and only mentioned it as an instance of the pugnacity and vigour of the Anglo-Saxon character. The *Siècle*, however, a paper of great circulation, condemned the proceeding in strong terms. He hoped that the present discussion would terminate, and that they would hear no more in that House about this matter. (Hear, hear.)

Mr. Clive, in justification of the directors of the South-Eastern Railway Company, felt bound to say that he was informed that they did not admit they had forfeited any pledge. Upon a former occasion, a special train was stopped without the directors' knowledge or sanction, at a place intermediate between two stations, where a fight came off, and a promise was given that in future no trains should be allowed to stop anywhere but at stations on the line. Some time after a train stopped at a station, and a fight took place, but the directors maintained that they knew nothing about it, and had not broken their word. They declared, truly or not, that they could not tell the intentions of those who travelled by their trains, and could not assume that any breach of the peace was intended.

Sir W. JOLLIFFE said, admiring as he did the pluck and skill displayed at the recent fight, the question still was whether it did or did not amount to a breach of the peace, and magistrates ought really to know what their position was on such occasions. He lived near the route of the South-Eastern Railway, and was also a magistrate for the county of Surrey. Several prize-fights had taken place in that county, and some of his neighbours who were magistrates had run considerable risk in attempting to keep the peace. That being so, he wanted to know what the position of magistrates was when they found those gatherings rather sanctioned than discouraged by the Government, and when railway companies were seen encouraging them from the base motive of gain?

Lord PALMERSTON—I distinctly stated that it was ruled by legal authorities that such prize fights were breaches of the peace, but I protest at the same time against the exaggerated terms in which the noble lord (Lord Lovaine) characterised the conduct of the spectators on those occasions.

Colonel DICKSON was surprised to hear his hon. friend (Mr. Scully) take the noble lord at the head of the Government to task for the remarks he had made on this occasion, for he (Colonel Dickson)

could not understand an Irishman objecting to fighting. (A laugh.) The noble viscount (Palmerston)
had not laid himself open to such taunts. He sat on
a different side of the House from the noble lord, and
did not often find himself in the same lobby with him
on a division, but he would say for the noble viscount
that if he had one attribute more than another which
endeared him to his countrymen, it was his thoroughly
English character and his love for every manly sport.
(Cheers.) He (Colonel Dickson) never saw a prize
fight in his life, but he would say that the two men
who fought on the recent occasion showed qualities
of which the whole English race had reason to be
proud, our own man in particular (laughter), who
evinced powers of endurance and an indomitable
pluck which entitled him to the admiration of his
countrymen. (Cheers.) Many men in this country
received honours who did not so well deserve them.
He did not think Parliament ought to legislate with
the view to put down manly sports; and, with regard
to the duties of magistrates, about which the hon.
baronet (Sir W. Jolliffe) professed to have doubts,
the law was clearly laid down. Magistrates themselves ought to know when to act and when to shut
their eyes. (A laugh.)

Mr. PAULL said, until the gallant gentleman (Col.
Dickson) had spoken he was not prepared to hear
that the noble lord at the head of the Government,
after fifty years of memorable public service, would
be known to posterity as the patron of prize-fighting.
(A laugh.) He thought it an unfortunate thing,
whether or not it was in the power of the Government to stop those exhibitions, that the First Minister
of the Crown and the Home Secretary should be
found palliating, if not sanctioning, them. (Hear,
hear.) After what the noble lord had said, he thought
the caricature in a certain facetious public print
which a few years ago represented the noble lord as
a bottle-holder was not altogether wrong. (A laugh.)

The motion was then agreed to.

THE FIGHT OF SAYERIUS AND HEENANUS.

A LAY OF ANCIENT LONDON.

supposed *to be recounted to his Great-Grand-children, April*
17th, *A.D.* 1920, *by an Ancient Gladiator.*)

(From *Punch*, April 28th, 1860.)

CLOSE round my chair, my children,
   And gather at my knee,
The while your mother poureth
   The Old Tom in my tea;
The while your father quaffeth
   His rot-gut Bordeaux wine,—
'Twas not on such potations
   Were reared these thews o' mine.
Such drinks came in the very year
   —Methinks I mind it well—
That the great fight of HEENANUS
   With SAYERIUS befell.
These knuckles then were iron;
   This biceps like a cord;
This fist shot from the shoulder
   A bullock would have floored.
Crawleius his Novice,
   They used to call me then,
In the Domus Savilliana,
   Among the sporting men.
There, on benefit occasions,
   The gloves I oft put on,
Walking round to show my muscles
   When the set-to was done;
While ringing in the arena
   The showered denarii fell,
That told Crawleius' Novice,
   Had used his mauleys well.
'Tis but some sixty years since
   The times whereof I speak,
And yet the words I'm using
   Will sound to you like Greek.
What know ye, race of milksops,
   Untaught of the P. R.

What stopping, lunging, countering,
  Fibbing, or rallying are ?
What boots to use the *lingo*,
  When you *hare* not the *thing* ?
How paint to *you* the glories
  Of BELCHER, CRIBB, or SPRING,—
To *you*, whose sire turns up his eyes
  At mention of the Ring ?

Yet, in despite of all the jaw
  And gammon of the time,
That brands the art of self-defence
  —Old England's art—as crime,
From off mine ancient memories
  The rust of time I'll shake,
Your youthful bloods to quicken,
  And your British pluck to wake.
I know it only slumbers ;
  Let cant do what it will,
The British bull-dog *will* be
  The British bull-dog still.
Then gather to your grand-sire's knee,
  The while his tale is told,
How SAYERIUS and HEENANUS
  Milled in the days of old.

The Beaks and Blues were watching,
  Agog to stop the Mill,
As we gathered to the station
  In the April morning chill.
By twos and threes, by fours and tens,
  To London Bridge we drew ;
For we had had the office,
  That were good men and true ;
And, saving such, the place of fight
  Was ne'er a man that knew.
From east and west, from north and south,
  The London Fancy poured,
Down to the sporting Cabman,
  Up to the sporting Lord.

From the Horse-Shoe in Titchborne Street,
  Sharp OWEN SWIFT was there ;
Old PETER left the Rising Sun,
  All in the street of Air ;
LANGHAM forsook his beer-taps,
  With nobby ALEC REED ;
And towering high above the crowd
  Shone BEN CAUNT's fragrant weed.
Nor only fighting covies,
  But sporting swells besides,—
Dukes, Lords, M.P.'s, and Guardsmen,
  With county beaks for guides ;
And tongues that sway our Senators,
  And hands the pen that wield,
Were cheering on the champions
  Upon that morning's field.

At last the bell is ringing,
  The engine puffs amain,
And through the dark towards Brighton
  On shrieks the tearing train ;
But turning off where Reigate
  Unites her clustering lines,
By poultry-haunted Dorking
  A devious course it twines ;
By Wotton, Shier, and Guildford,
  Across the winding Wey,
Till by heath-girded Farnborough
  Our doubling course we stay,
Where Aldershot lay snoring
  All in the morning grey,
Nor dreamed the Camp what combat
  Should be fought here to-day !

The stakes are pitched, the ropes are tied,
  The men have ta'en their stand ;
HEENANUS wins the toss for place,
  And takes the eastward hand.
CUSICCIUS and MACDONALDUS
  Upon the Boy attend ;

SAYERIUS AND HEENANUS.

SAYERIUS owns BRUNTONUS,
　And JIM WELSHIUS for friend.
And each upon the other now
　A curious eye may throw,
As from the seconds' final rub
　In buff at length they show,
And from their corners to the scratch
　Move stalwartly and slow.

Then each his hand stretched forth to grasp,
His foeman's fives in friendly clasp;
Each felt his balance trim and true,—
Each up to square his mauleys threw;
Each tried his best to draw his man—
The feint, the dodge, the opening plan,
Till left and right SAYERIUS tried;
HEENANUS' grin proclaimed him wide;
He shook his nut, a lead essayed,
Nor reached SAYERIUS' watchful head.
At length each left is sudden flung,
　We heard the ponderous thud,
And from each tongue the news was rung,
　SAYERIUS hath 'First blood;'
Adown HEENANUS' Roman nose
Freely the tell-tale claret flows,
While stern SAYERIUS' forehead shows
That in the interchange of blows
　HEENANUS' aim was good!
Again each iron mauley swung,
And loud the counter-hitting rung,
　Till breathless all, and wild with blows,
Fiercely they grappled for a close;
A moment in close hug they swing
Hither and thither, round the ring,
Then from HEENANUS' clinch of brass
SAYERIUS, smiling, slips to grass!

I trow mine ancient breath would fail
　To follow through the fight,
Each gallant round's still changing tale,
　Each feat of left and right.

How through two well-spent hours and more,
　Through bruise, and blow, and blood,
Like sturdy bulldogs, as they were,
　Those well-matched heroes stood.
How nine times in that desperate Mill
　HEENANUS, in his strength,
Knocked stout SAYERIUS off his pins,
　And laid him all at length;
But how in each succeeding round
　SAYERIUS smiling came,
With head as cool, and wind as sound,
As his first moment on the ground,
　Still confident, and game.

How from HEENANUS' sledge-like fist,
Striving a smasher to resist,
SAYERIUS' stout right arm gave way,
Yet the maim'd hero still made play,
And when in-fighting threatened ill,
Was nimble in out-fighting still,
　Did still his own maintain—
In mourning put HEENANUS' glims;
Till blinded eyes and helpless limbs,
　The chances squared again.
How blind HEENANUS in despite
Of bleeding mug and waning sight
So gallantly kept up the fight,
　That not a man could say
Which of the two 'twere wise to back,
Or on which side some random crack
　Might not decide the day:
And leave us—whoso won the prize,—
Victor and vanquished, in all eyes,
　An equal meed to pay.

Two hours and more the fight had sped,
　Near unto ten it drew,
But still opposed—one-armed to blind,—
　They stood, the dauntless two.
Ah, me, that I have lived to hear
　Such men as ruffians scorned,

Such deeds of valour brutal called,
   Canted, preached down, and mourned!
Ah, that these old eyes ne'er again
   A gallant Mill shall see!
No more behold the ropes and stakes,
   With colours flying free!
But I forget the combat—
   How shall I tell the close,
That left the Champion's Belt in doubt
   Between those well-matched foes?
Fain would I shroud the tale in night,—
The meddling Blues that thrust in sight,—
   The ring-keepers o'erthrown;
The broken ring,—the cumber'd fight,—
HEENANUS' sudden, blinded flight,—
SAYERIUS pausing, as he might,
Just when ten minutes used aright
   Had made the fight his own!

Alas! e'en in those brighter days
   We still had Beaks and Blues,—
Still, canting rogues, their mud to fling
On self-defence and on the Ring,
   And fistic arts abuse!
And 'twas such varmint had the power
   The Champion's fight to stay,
And leave unsettled to this hour
   The honours of the day!
But had those honours rested
   Divided as was due,
SAYERIUS and HEENANUS
   Had cut the Belt in two.
And now my fists are feeble,
   And my blood is thin and cold,
But 'tis better than Old Tom to me
   To recall those days of old.
And may you, my great-grandchildren,
   That gather round my knee,
Ne'er see worse men or iller times
   Than I and mine might be,
Though England then had prize-fighters—
   Even reprobates like me.

*The following pieces In Memoriam claim a place
in the Biography of the departed Champion.*

(From *The Daily Telegraph*, Nov. 10th, 1865.)

TOM SAYERS is dead; the last of the great gladiator's fights is lost and won. He has met with the
silent Victor who waits for us all, whom the swiftness of the runner cannot baffle, whom the brawny
arm of the boxer cannot smite, whom the agile
wrestler cannot throw—nay, who faces Virtue and
Wisdom themselves and makes them halt, though
only for a moment, and checks them, albeit he has
no power to kill. In the equality of the tomb the
poor fellow who has just departed may rest, undisturbed, with many better men and many worse; but
his fate suggests certain lessons, which may be enforced with advantage whilst his memory has not
yet faded away. The man's one claim to notice at
our hands was his connection with a practice which
we have never joined in denouncing; though we
would not be blind to the ugly accessories by which
it was surrounded. Yet even our censure must be
qualified by a certain pity for the hero of the scene
—nay, with even a certain amount of respect. If
Sayers lived a poor life, of hard combats and of doubtful triumphs, he had in him many of the instincts
that we should be sorry to miss amongst the rank
and file of English manhood. The Prize Ring, especially of late years, may be said to have more than
shared the proverbial ' degeneracy of the age.' It is
not an elevating trade; and positively its least offensive moments are those when a couple of bruisers,
stripped to the skin, pummel one another into in-
sensibility. Infinitely more revolting, from a moral
point of view, however, are the coarse orgies with
which the victor celebrates his triumphs, stupifying
his brain, and wasting away the grand physical
strength in which chiefly he surpassed his neigh-

bours. It is seldom that these athletes live to be
old.* With constitutions prematurely shattered by
'fast living,' they are left to starve by the 'patrons'
who once made money out of their prowess; they
have neither the desire nor even the capacity for
honest labour; and when vice and gin have done
their worst, they are carried to the hospital to die,
and thence carted away to a pauper's grave.

Nor will we, for our part, consent to take a 'sen-
timental' view of the man who is just dead. He
represented whatever was good in the vocation that
he chose; but he was not free from the faults of his
fellows. Had he led a prudent life, he might have
survived for many years, and been free from the
dread of want; but he yielded with only too much
readiness to the temptations that beset him, and died
at thirty-nine, a worn and wasted shadow of a man.
Nevertheless, it is not suprising to those who understand the English character that he was immensely
popular, and that many who are usually indifferent
to what is called 'sporting' will be sorry to hear of
his decease. There is nothing necessarily degrading
in the trade of a boxer, apart from the associations
of the ring. Quarrels will happen, even in these
most civilised days of ours, and it is a bad thing for
a man not to know the best use of his natural weapons. Always there is the chance of an ultimate
appeal to force, and he who has not learnt how to
manage his fists has neglected what many have accounted a part of the proper education for every
gentleman. A gentleman should always be able to
defend himself against attack, and he should always
be able to help a woman who is suffering ill-treat-

---

* This is a common error. Of our champions, whose ages are
ascertainable, we find Broughton, 85; Daniel Mendoza, 73;
John Jackson, 77; Tom Owen, 75; Paddington (Tom) Jones, 67;
Tom Belcher, 71; Tom Cribb, 67; John Gully, 78; Bill Rich-
mond, 67; Tom Spring, 55; Jack Martin (still living), 69; Tom
Oliver (still living), 76; and Jim Ward (still living), 64. We
have taken these as men who have fought some of the heaviest
battles, and they present a fair average. Men kill themselves by
excess in all professions.—ED. PUGILISTICA.

ment. The most peaceful personage who reads these lines may, as he passes through the streets to-day, see a brawny ruffian beating his wife; and unless he is a cripple, or suffering from dangerous illness, he is bound to interfere. 'Yes,' it may be answered, 'but he can call the police;' an excellent plan—if the police are at hand. Now it was the good fortune of Sayers to show, more convincingly than it had ever been proved before, how skill and courage can hold their own against vastly superior physical strength. No doubt, national feeling was the main cause which made Englishmen rejoice that the fight between their little 'Champion' and the young American giant was a drawn battle. But they were glad also to see how their old practice of skilled boxing was proved to be so effectual against mere brute force. As a matter of pure physical hardihood, that encounter at Farnborough five years ago was well worthy of all the attention it received. Knocked down again and again, the indomitable little man would never admit that he was beaten. When one of his arms was disabled, he quietly went on fighting with the other. As long as his features allowed him to smile, he smiled; when his mouth was beaten out of shape, he gave a cheerful wink of encouragement with his eye; when his eyes had likewise ceased to be available for the expression of emotion, he was still eloquent by the vivacity with which he used his two legs and his one fist. What was to be done with him? What was the use of knocking down a little fellow who bounded up again like an india-rubber ball? A dozen times and more he was levelled to the earth; a dozen times and more he rose, imperturbably good-tempered, as one who knew that it was 'all in the day's work.' The giant was almost blinded when at length he got the Champion in his grip, and proceeded to deal with him in a way that led to the interruption of the fight. After all, it was really the battle of Waterloo on a small scale. The accessories were sickening and repulsive; heroic, on the other

hand, was the spirit of Tom Sayers, as, time after
time, he renewed the unequal contest, and gallantly
mastered the sense of pain by the strength of his
will.

He was the lion of the day, and for once the public
enthusiasm in his favour took a sensible form. A
sum of money was raised, to which politicians,
clergymen, men of letters, artists, were not at all
ashamed to contribute; it was settled upon him as
an annuity; he was not allowed to touch the principal; and it was made a condition that he should
forfeit it if he ever fought again. Two years ago he
entered a ring for the last time, not as a combatant,
but as the second of his former antagonist; and the
accounts of the conflict tell us that he looked the
very picture of good-humour—a grotesque 'squire,'
with big boots, a yellow jacket, a fur cap, and a blue
and white shawl twisted round his neck—a merry,
active little man, who never lost his temper, but ever
and anon looked up at Heenan with a queer sort of
wondering expression, as though he marvelled at his
own temerity a couple of years earlier. It was poor
Tom's last public appearance of the kind. Even then
his health had begun to fail him. The prize-fighter,
when in training, has to obey a strict discipline. His
diet is regulated; his ablutions, his slumbers, his exercise, are all under control; in fact, he is allowed no
more freedom than a horse, and wonderfully like an
animal he appears when his seconds bring him to
the ring-side, wrapped and swathed in huge rugs
against the cold. When he stands up to fight, you
see a man brought to a wonderful pitch of physical
perfection, and the sight is thought to be so fine as
to overwhelm for a moment the objections of the
most philosophical spectator. Then, during the combat itself, it is not mere animal bravery that will
suffice. The pugilist has to keep his temper, even
when the blood is streaming down his face; for the
Ring has its rules, and the boxer who violates them
—who hits an unfair blow, or strikes his adversary

when he is down—becomes *ipso facto* the loser.
Through this stern ordeal, which does not try the
physical powers alone, no man ever went more gallantly than Sayers. The misfortune was, that he
could not make head against the subsequent reaction
and temptations. One portion of his nature had been
stimulated into excessive prominence; the rest had
been left without sufficient food or culture. The
bookworm who neglects his body, or the so-called
' saint' who despises what should really be cared for
as the living temple of God, pays the penalty appropriate to his fault; the merely animal type of man,
having no nobler employments, passes his time in
recklessness and riot, and *he* too has to pay for it.
Sooner or later the settling-day arrives, and in this
case it has come soon. For the rest, it is recorded of
the dead man that, living much amongst disreputable
associates, and often tempted to dishonesty, he was
true as steel to those who trusted him; that he was
a liberal giver, a kindly and genial companion. As
his illness grew worse, he was—as he deserved to be
—more fortunate than most of his comrades; warm-
hearted friends tended him to the last, and assuaged
his sufferings. That, and the fact that no braver man
ever wore a soldier's uniform, are the pleasantest
things to remember about poor Tom Sayers.

(From *The Sporting Life*, Nov. 11th, 1865.)

' POOR TOM'S a' cold!' Within a brief space, Lords
Lyndhurst and Palmerston, Leech and Herring, the
very cracks of their calling, have gone down, and now
Sayers, the hero of so many fights, has joined the
silent dead. It was a plain, homely name, but there
was not a corner of the world where it had not been
heard. His Championship had been won and held on
a harder tenure than riding a charger into Westmin-
ster Hall, throwing down a mailed glove, and then
backing out again. Three titled Thomases furnished

inspiration to the poet of the old 'Tommiad,' and
Cribb, Spring, and Sayers are heroes meet for the
new. With 'Little Tom,' as the world loved to call
him when he 'gave away five inches and nigh three
stone,' the choicest memories of the Ring die out.
They date back to the days when stars and garters
thronged the Newmarket cockpit—when the Fives
Court, with Tom Johnson or 'Big Ben' on its stage,
was as popular with the Corinthians as Vauxhall—and
when princes of the blood did not scruple to back their
man beneath the gibbet of Jerry Abershaw. Dean
Milner, in his zeal for universal knowledge, did not
scruple to cross-examine Mendoza as to his art when
they met on the deck of a packet-boat; and Dick
Christian assures us that the Rutlandshire magistrates
rushed off, when sessions were over, 'the whole kit
on 'em,' to the fight at Thistleton Gap. Midland rus-
tics were long wont to preserve 'Yon day, when Cribb
walloped Mollineux,' as a guiding date in family
matters, and in the witness-box as well. Modern
history will have its work cut out to decide between
rival beliefs whether the Spring and Langan tourney
or 'the crowning mercy' is the *bona fide* battle of
Worcester; and despite the cacklings of the clan
Hadfield, the Farnborough meadow where Sayers and
Heenan stripped to the buff for the Championship on
that bright April morning, has a solid significance
for millions. Tom's challenge, and its prompt acceptance in the New World, touched a 'truly British'
chord. Patriarchs burnished up their memories, and
boasted how the 'Gentleman Jackson' of their boy-
hood was wont to be Lord Panmure's guest at Brechin,
and told strange anecdotes of the bold Belchers and
Pearce, the Game Chicken.

A perfectly new body of fistic literature sprang up.
Stately papers, which had hitherto frowned on the
Fancy from a distance, were compelled to come into
the fashion, and even the more serious ones quoted
them, merely, as they said, for reproof and warning,
but really to get the leading facts on to *the record.*

'Essays in the intervals of business' were oral and highly pugilistic in their tone. Paterfamilias knew by close application to his sporting paper how Heenan had evaded the Buffalo bail bonds, and how the London legates had greeted him as he stepped from his Cunard cabin on to English soil. 'Bulls' and 'bears' paused amid their labours to discuss what diocese he would next choose for his training, when the Bishop of Salisbury had cursed him by candle, bell, and book. 'Pleaceman X' chuckled over the discomfiture of the Meddlesome Matties from Ely, who begged the Newmarket bench in vain to endorse their warrant against 'one Thomas Sayers;' and the spirit of the faithful Commons ran so high on the eve of the fight that, if 'the intelligent foreigner' had penetrated the smoking-room, he would have left it with the rooted conviction that Sam Rogers would be called to the bar of the House, and publicly thanked by the Speaker for smuggling Tom out of Newmarket in a horse-box. If ten thousand had been the bail, the Stock Exchange and Tattersall's would have found the money rather than mar such a meeting. As for Sir Richard Mayne and the Home Secretary, who could doubt that the Premier had made them 'safe,' or that Pam

Held the bottle and Europe the stakes

on that truly eventful day ? Even gentle women who would have shrunk from any sympathy in the events of a common Ring Tuesday, felt the soft infection, and did 'so hope our man will win.' And yet 'our man' was the most unconcerned of all. On Sunday, the only news of him was that he had taken his walks abroad, or rather mused, in the Highgate meadows with his children. On Monday he had only seen a few friends who were anxious to feel his muscle, and had 'gone to bed at an early hour.' The 'Southeys of the Ring' have told what came with his waking—how from the recesses of his carriage, just as the grey dawn struggled into day, he saw, for the first time, his tall rival, gliding like a ghost, in a long, loose

coat, and a false beard and moustache, along the platform—how he turned and took a nap, as if such an
immensely muscular Christian had been quite a
soothing vision—how, with his left arm disabled and
folded helplessly on his breast, he stood up to the
forty-first round, and all but reduced Heenan to
blindness ; and how, from that day forward, the right
arm of man received a name new to anatomists, to
wit, 'the auctioneer.'

Then came the second act of the Farnborough drama,
rich in strange incongruities and 'startling effects.'
Heenan rancorously persisted in living when one, if
not two, non-sporting journals, in their new-born zeal,
had killed him; and his American doctor was presented at Court. Tom bore himself modestly, and
only wore a ring, or two more, and a magnificent
diamond brooch, which he valued at thirty guineas.
A Blucher or a Wellington could not have been
received more rapturously on the Stock Exchange,
which felt in its breeches' pockets as well as its heart
for him ; and 3,000l. was invested for himself and
his children. Then the 'bottle-holder,' unshackled
by official reserve, came out in his true light, and gave
his 'fiver' when the Parliament purse went round.
Mr. Gully greeted Tom with all the warmth of an old
gladiator, when they met on the Heath, and added,
as he well might do, '*I don't know Tom how you did it.*'
After this we had dismal and diurnal 'reconciliations,'
and buckling on of borrowed belts at the Alhambra;
and when 'benefits' began to run dry, the man who
had been the genius of one ring essayed to be the
Widdicomb of another. The managerial business
was not Tom's *forte.*. He liked well enough the
triumphal-car entry as Champion into a town, drawn
by all the available horse strength of the establishment, and the mules, Pete and Barney, as his esquires;
but that didn't last long. A chat with his old Camden Town friends or driving his dun cob in a gig was
his mode of enjoyment. There was a sort of sublime
indifference or quiet stoicism about him. He believed

thoroughly in Heenan and Captain Barclay, very slightly in magistrates, and certainly not in the existence of an Oxford Vice-Chancellor, or the necessity of a license from 'such a stiff cove' before he pitched his circus. Hence his best friends found him a child of nature uncommonly bad to guide, when keeping in condition was all-essential, or whenever 'a difficulty,' domestic or otherwise, turned up. In short, save that he scorned to sponge on anyone, he was much of the same turn of mind as 'Mr. Toots's Chicken,' who reduced all his practical advice to 'go in and win,' and considered when consulted on an affair of the heart, that doubling-up the stern father of your lady-love was decidedly a move in the right direction. Such men may not do as counsellors, and such bull-dog valour may not have a general application, but still it carried our men with a steady tread up the heights of the Alma, and kept the square unbroken at Waterloo. Tom knew no pain himself, and hence he had no perception of the delicate duties of a second; and, clad in a fur cap, a yellow flannel vest, and jack-boots, he handled Heenan by his hair, or wherever he could first catch him, in the fight—the last he ever attended—when he seconded him against King. Although by no means pugnacious in his temper, he had no idea of being chaffed, and did not care much for being *fêted*. When he was once made the hero of a supper-party, he merely lay down on the sofa when he had finished his meal and went to sleep; and when, on another occasion, he fancied that he was asked merely to make sport for the Philistines, he growled out that he would presently walk round the table and '*punch all your heads*.' A bench of county magistrates also remember well his stony British stare, and his growl of '*Who are you?*' when the 'fastest' of their body claimed acquaintance with him, as a show off, in front of a county hotel. His features, however, wore their kindliest glow when Sir Tatton sought him out in the Doncaster enclosure, and congratulated him on his triumphs. The old Baronet was dainty in his fistic recognitions, and merely walked round 'the Staleybridge Infant;' but when Nat Langham took his stand next to him at the rails, and reminded him how he had beaten Tom in his day, he at once drew off his venerable beaver glove, and, suiting the word to the deed, said, in his gentle way, ' *Well, then, Sir, I can now say that I've shaken hands with two brave men.*'

A word on his early life. Tom was the youngest of eight, and his father, who is a *fac-simile* of the son —barring the broken nose-bridge—is a hale old fellow of seventy-three, and nursed him tenderly to the last. One brother, Charles, is a shoemaker in Crown Court, Haymarket, and another is a butcher in Pimlico, Brighton, where Tom was born. They do not remember much about his babyhood, except that it began at eleven on a moonlight night, at the time of Black Rock Fair. He was very ' masterful ' from the first, and soon got the better of his mother when he could do little more than toddle and clutch her by the gown. ' Do what we would, he was always fighting some boy or another;' and when he was only thirteen, and along with a Brighton coal-dealer, he had trained a mule to ' box ' out of business hours. He was like a young Bendigo with it—now cross-countering it, now slipping under its belly and then on its back, till the beast, half wild with rage and baffled science, would snap round at his legs. No persuasion could induce him to go to school, and he hardly knew his alphabet. He became too much for the coal-dealer, whom Tom, even at his tender years, never scrupled to bring home by the collar out of his bacchanalian haunts, and he was only in his fourteenth summer when he reached London on foot, or by lifts on the waggon as his half-pence held out, and presented himself at the house of his brother-in-law, Mr. Robert King, a builder in Camden Town.

Mr. King remembered the lad's saucy reply about his boots when he visited Brighton a year or two before with his wife (who was the eldest of the

family), and when he learnt that he had come for a
trade, he put him to 'serve the hod' to the plasterers.
Tom gave him a world of trouble, as he would get
off the scaffold and set himself to the best work when
the men's backs were turned, and, as a matter of
course, spoilt it. He had been playing off some of
these tricks during a job at a sea captain's, who took
the complaint second-hand to Mr. King. 'I'd like
to take you to sea, you confounded young Turk; I'd
have some of your lazy blood out of you,' said the
son of Neptune. 'I'd have some of *your* lazy blood
out of *you*, old fellow,' replied the undaunted little
Tom; 'if you dared tackle me, we'd roll overboard
together.' With that Tom brushed home to his sister,
but he was in no humour to listen to reason. 'I'll
pay the man off who told of me,' he snorted out;
' *and, what's more, I'll make my name rattle through
all London*;' and with this startling prophecy, which
he clenched with 'I'll be up in London soon; I'll
learn no other trade,' he sheered off without a good-
bye, and walked fair heel and toe to Brighton, round
by Portsmouth. He was true to his word, and his
brother-in-law found him a few months after at a
building he was completing in Holloway Road. He
had put himself to work without asking anyone, and
he would vouchsafe his relative no explanation except 'I won't stir from here till I'm a bricklayer.'
Mr. King had always a sneaking fancy for this little
King Absolute, and as it was no use to look at that
determined little face and be angry, he told him to
'Go home to your sister, and tell her to give you a
plumb-bob and trowel.' And so Tom did, and not
only flatly refused to say 'please' to her when he
delivered the order, but shortly commenced putting
other Brighton boys to work without referring them
to anybody. In fact, there never was a more daring
young dog. He would be at the top of the tree one
way or another, and by trying at arches, &c., long
before he learnt his trade, he set all the men laughing at him. A turn-up with one or two of them who

were too demonstrative decided his new profession. He conveyed his decision to his sister in his own terse way—'*I like to stand up; I've to stoop too many times to lay bricks.*' His mother (unlike the bold Bendy's, who showed the paps which he sucked, and only felt frightened lest her son should kill every man he met) fretted sorely over his choice, and in one of his milder moods he confessed to his sister when she pressed him, '*Of course, I was happiest laying bricks.*'

Life in a gig was what Tom loved best, and half London remember, when they were waiting for the Prince's bride, how, with a face as imperturbable as a door-knocker, he drove down the whole line, as if it was an hereditary Champion right, and no 'blue' bid him nay. This was about the last time that the general public saw their 'little man.' He had lived from the very first time he was matched as if he never thought that his legs were to carry a Champion, and when he had worn the belt, he was still prodigal of himself and the finest of constitutions; but Nature had her full revenge six months before he was forty. The late hours of the circus, and facing the sons of harmony, with their appetites as boundless as the Dragon of Wantley's for brandy and cigars, wore him out at last. In the early part of this year he had wasted to a shadow, but was skilfully patched up by the spring, and there he was seeing the Derby horses saddled, with a face which rather wore the Honduras mahogany hue of his fighting days than the hectic flush of disease. It was, however, only a Ventnor recovery, and even during the long warm summer he drooped, day by day. He longed to see Tonbridge once more before he died. It was the place he liked best in his days of health, when he lived at the Brown Jug and trained on the Hadlow Road. So he drove down in his gig, and made his headquarters at 'the Bull,' and once got as far as Hastings. His appetite was so feeble that he could hardly fancy a new-laid egg, and if he had a partridge he would scarcely swallow a couple of ounces. He would lie by day on the sofa in the smoking-room, and go to bed at eight only to face another long and restless night. All knew, as poor young Broome (Bill Evans) said of himself, that he was 'sent for,' and his face of deep settled pain showed what he suffered, but be met his doom in silence, with the stern calmness of a Mohawk chief. Day by day they watched him growing weaker and weaker, and when he could hardly crawl out into the sunshine he sold his gig, and came back by the train to London to die. This was on the Saturday of the Doncaster week, and there were still two weary months before the grand relief came to that brave and suffering soul.

On his return from Tonbridge, on September 16, he came to his sister's (Mrs. King) house, and stayed with her about three weeks. His cough was very bad, but he never spat blood, and his appetite and health improved so much that at one time they quite hoped he might come round. None of the family had ever been consumptive, and they thought that his death, and much of the pain he suffered, was owing to a severe blow on the left shoulder-blade, about six months ago. He was driving near St. Pancras Church, when some one on the pavement, who had inflicted on him a grievous wrong, insulted 'the sick lion' with a gesture as he passed. He pulled up instantly, and giving the reins to his father, jumped out to chastise the fellow, and fell heavily on the kerb-stone in his hurry. This accident, added to diabetes and a severe cold, which he caught at Brighton Races, sealed his fate. He left his sister's on the Saturday three weeks before his death, and removed all his things to an old friend's (Mr. Mensley), a large shoe manufacturer, of 257, High Street, Camden Town, who had always made his fighting-boots. On the next day he dined in the country with a friend, and then he took to his bed, and never left it again. His clergyman often came to see him, and when he stayed away for a day or

two under a misapprehension that Tom, in one of his
wayward moods, had turned against him, he chid him
for his absence. In the earlier part of his illness
he never alluded to the chances of death, and such
was his curious and reserved temperament, that
with almost savage energy, he charged his sister, who
had ever done a true sister's part by him—'*Never
say that you taught me a prayer and read the Bible,
and that I prayed after you.*' A fortnight before his
death he was more teachable, and, for the first time,
he was heard to confess that it was '*all up.*' At
times, he would call out bitterly in his agony; but
for forty-eight hours before the close he was almost
insensible, and for nearly half that time he was dying
hard. His doctor thought that he could hardly have
seen the morning of Wednesday, but it was six
o'clock that evening before he found rest.

He was lying in his coffin when we saw him on
Friday. The muscles of the face stood out boldly for
such a wasted skeleton, and there was still much of
the life expression left in his half-closed eyes. The
box, with the trophies and belts, was not there, but
his own photograph, with his medals on his breast,
and the print of the '*Farnborough Morning,*' took us
sadly back from that pale and still troubled face, to the
days of his lusty prime. On the wall above it, and
keeping, as it were, watch and ward to the last over
the coffin, whose brass plate bore no vaunting inscription, hung the photograph of Harry Brunton,
the faithful second in his great battles, and, as Tom
was wont to say of him, '*The kindest soul to me that
ever breathed,*' and faithful to the last. Tom leaves
two children, one of them, a very fine boy, called
after himself, and at present at school at Harlow.

Lightning Source UK Ltd.
Milton Keynes UK
UKOW051457121211

183640UK00001B/116/P